# The
# Fun-da-mentals
# of
# Baseball

## MICHAEL N. BLEWETT

ISBN: 1-4196-7911-2
ISBN-13: 9781419679117

Visit www.booksurge.com to order additional copies.

# Table of Contents

Preface      vii

Acknowledgments      xi

Thanks      xv

Special Tribute to William Lester "Billy" DeMars      xvii

Chapter 1
History of Baseball      1

Chapter 2
Specifications of a Major League Baseball Field      9

Chapter 3
How to Play the Game      13

Chapter 4
Analysis of Each Player Position and
General Responsibilities      17

Chapter 5
How to Think the Game of Baseball      29

Chapter 6
The Team: Offensive and Defensive Strategy      41

Chapter 7
Proper Stretching Exercises      49

Chapter 8
Bursitis and Its Effect on Joints      55

Chapter 9
The Baseball      67

Chapter 10
How to Hold and Throw a Baseball      69

Chapter 11
The Release Point and Why It Is So Important      77

Chapter 12
The Act of Catching a Baseball      83

Chapter 13
The Act of Fielding a Ground Ball      89

**Chapter 14**
**The Proper Way to Make the**
**Double Play Pivot at Second Base**                    95

**Chapter 15**
**How to Learn to Hit a Baseball**                       103

**Chapter 16**
**What Is a Strike Zone and Why**
**Is It Important to Know Yours?**                       119

**Chapter 17**
**Pitching and All That Is Involved**                    129

**Chapter 18**
**The Micro-mechanics of Holding**
**and Releasing Various Pitches**                        151

**Chapter 19**
**How to Learn to Pitch**                                173

**Chapter 20**
**The Art of Bunting**                                   181

**Chapter 21**
**Running the Bases, Lead-offs, Stealing Bases**         191

**Chapter 22**
**The Run Down or Pickle**                               203

**Chapter 23**
**The Outfielders**                                      207

**Chapter 24**
**Advantage / Disadvantage between Pitcher / Hitter**    215

**Chapter 25**
**Sliding into Bases**                                   221

**Chapter 26**
**Signs**                                                225

**Chapter 27**
**Handling the Fans and Parents**                        229

# ADDENDA

I.  **Addendum I –**
    **The FUN-DA-MENTALS by Chapter**                231

II. **Addendum II –**

    **The History of the Game of Baseball**          243
    *Early bat and ball games,*
    by Thomas R. Heitz and John Thorn.

⚾ ⚾ ⚾

# PREFACE

*"The FUN-DA-MENTALS of Baseball"* is a light-hearted, micro-mechanical explanation of the fundamentals of the game of baseball compiled for the purpose of teaching or guiding anyone interested in knowing how to play the game. Its contents span young to maturing players, coaches, parents, and fans alike, as it explains the most important details of the game.

A number of the **FUN-DA-MENTALS** are supported by detailed illustrations and specific drills to quicken the reader's learning curve without having to sit through hundreds of innings to experience each and every one of them. *The FUN-DA-MENTALS of Baseball* teaches everything a player, coach or fan should know about each and every position on the team with particular emphasis on the micro-details of pitching.

Learning directly from this book or teaching the **FUN-DA-MENTALS** contained within it will help prevent a young player from incurring unnecessary personal injury or developing bad habits that are so difficult to correct as the player matures. For the non-player, I am certain it will make each and every game more interesting. If you never learned it before, get ready to learn it now.

The intent of this book is to present and explain every facet of the game of baseball that one must understand, learn, and practice over and over to reach his or her highest level of competency. This book is only about the game and how it should be played. It is written without gender bias. As there are only two types of human beings on this earth, male and female, it doesn't make much sense to rule one or the other out of playing this great game. Boys and/or girls, men and/or women should all play the game the same way by learning the exact same **FUN-DA-MENTALS** as the other.

So where I have used the pronouns *he, his, him or himself* throughout this work, it is in no way intended to be interpreted by the reader as a gender specific action. It could be carried out by either a male or female player. It does however eliminate the need for me to write, and for you to read, hundreds of times, *he or she, his or hers, him or her, or himself or herself,* in every instance where one of the pronouns is used throughout this book. It's just a book about baseball and its **FUN-DA-MENTALS**.

## Why Get So Micro?

Before you begin reading *The FUN-DA-MENTALS of Baseball* you may be wondering why I thought it important enough to write such a micro-instructional type manual. The answer is quite simple. My baseball career began with sandlot pick-up games in my neighborhood as a young boy, matured through Junior American Legion, American Legion, High School, and College, and ultimately the professional level in the Baltimore Oriole's Minor League Organization.

I was taught the fundamentals of the game by four of the finest coaches of their times, Ben Lefebvre, Harry "Bud" Brubaker, Raoul "Rod" Dedeaux, and Billy DeMars. I reasoned that it might be possible to help young players or baseball enthusiasts willing to spend some time to read a clear explanation of the fundamentals they would have a much better understanding and appreciation for the game if they learned it from the inside out.

I have worked with young players off and on for almost forty years and I am acutely aware of the blatant weaknesses in their pre-season conditioning, practice habits, focus, and lack of knowledge of the fundamentals of the game contained in this book. My feeling is that a baseball player can't get by any longer on talent alone. A young player must learn how to play the game smarter and earlier to keep up with athletes from all over the world who play baseball year around.

I was a pitcher on my Dorsey High School Baseball Team in Los Angeles. We won the LA City Baseball Championship in 1954. I was honored to have made All Western League Honors in 1953 and 1954 with four of my teammates. At Dorsey I lettered in all four major sports; was selected as a member of the Los Angeles Daily News High School Hall of Fame; and chosen to participate in the Ninth Annual Hearst National Junior Baseball Championships.

At the end of my Freshman baseball season at the University of Southern California, Coach Rod Dedeaux invited me and two of my teammates to join the 1955 USC Varsity Baseball Team for a 35 day - 28 game, Department of Defense Entertainment Tour to Japan, Okinawa and Korea.

Our schedule included three Japanese Universities in Tokyo; US Marine and Air Force Bases throughout Japan; US Marine All-Star teams on Okinawa;

Korean civilian teams and US Army All-Star teams in Seoul and Inchon; and US Army All-Star teams at the 7th Division, 24th Division, and I Corp Divisions deployed along the 38th Parallel located half way between Seoul, South Korea and Pyongyang, North Korea.

I remember pitching the first game of a double header in Inchon in front of 55,000 people who were fanning themselves in the 100 degree 95 percent humidity weather. Not one person made a sound throughout the entire game until our first baseman hit a 440 foot home run. The only sound they uttered was "OOooooh! If you haven't heard 55,000 people say "OOoooOH" at the same time, you can't imagine the thrill!

We were 27-1 on this tour and honored by Coach Rod Dedeaux as the greatest "traveling team" in the history of the University of Southern California. He proclaimed us, "Champions of the Far East." Each of us received a Far East Air Force watch for that honor.

In the summer of 1957 I played the infield, outfield, and pitched as a member of Edmonton Eskimos (Alberta, Canada). We won the Western Canadian Baseball Championship. I was 3-0 with a 2.25 ERA. At the end of the summer we represented Canada in the Global World Series in Briggs (Detroit Tigers) Stadium losing to Japan in the finals. I gave up the game winning single in the 12th inning in relief and have never forgotten that pitch to this day.

At the University of Southern California I played third base on the 1958 NCAA College World Series Championship Team where in the bottom of the 9th inning I came to bat with two outs, a man on third, with the score tied 7-7 in the first extra inning NCAA Championship final in Omaha history. John O'Donoghue was pitching for the University of Missouri. He abruptly struck me out with the winning run on third base to send the game into extra innings. Big out for him, bad out for me.

I came to the plate again in the 12th inning, this time with runners on second and third with two outs and the score still tied 7-7. I worked O'Donoghue to a three and two count, and fouled off three or four pitches protecting the plate. I remember stepping out of the box to try to break his rhythm, collect my thoughts, and calm my adrenalin which was flowing wide open. I thought about the last time I was up here 30 minutes earlier and was struck out on four good pitches. I said to myself, "There is no way I am going to let this happen again, to me, to my team, or to my roomie, Bill Thom." Bill was pitching magnificently in his fourth inning of relief after throwing all nine innings and beating this same Missouri Team the night before. During this five second time out of the box I also noted that O'Donoghue was throwing the same sequence of fastballs OUT-IN-OUT-IN. So when I set up back in the batters box I was looking for his strikeout pitch to me to be on the outside half of the plate and wide open. A few seconds later, there it was, almost in slow motion, and with such perfect underspin. The shot went over the right fielder's head scoring Rex Johnston with the winning run from third base and my roomie was chosen as the College World Series Most Valuable Player. It doesn't get any better than that. To my USC teammates, congratulations to you one and all "Tigers."

Returning home to Los Angeles I signed a two year bonus contract with the Baltimore Orioles and reported to the Wilson Tobaccos (Tobs) Wilson, NC in the Carolina League. My rookie year was spent playing third and short with the Tobs and three weeks with the Bluefield Orioles in the Appalachian League.

Following a successful Spring Training in Thomasville, GA in 1959 I was assigned to the Stockton Ports in the California State League under the direction of Billy DeMars. I switched off playing third, shortstop and second, until one of our pitchers was released and another was lost due to a sore arm. DeMars asked me if I could convert to relief situations. I said yes and closed out the season winning 4 losing 0 with a 1.83 ERA. We finished third in the league.

In 1960 I missed Spring Training due to a late discharge from US Army Reserve Basic Training Center at Fort Ord, CA. I reported back to Stockton as a starting pitcher with a completely different group of teammates and without the preparation of spring training. Into the second half of the season it became apparent to me that it was going to take another year or two in the minors to make the transition back to pitching full time for any shot at the big leagues. Since I was planning to be married immediately following the 1960 season, I had no interest in having my new wife live the minor league experience, so I opted to retire and put the game behind me.

All in all, I won a few, lost a few, and some were rained out, but I have seen it all. That's about the last you'll hear about me from now on. Please appreciate that this book *is not* about me. *It is about* playing the game of baseball by the FUN-DA-MENTALS!

⚾ ⚾ ⚾

# ACKNOWLEDGMENTS

As we begin I would like to acknowledge a number of very special people who were influential in guiding me through my athletic career. Each had his individual wisdom. Each had a true passion for competition. Each was gifted with a deep knowledge of the fundamentals of sport, and all had their own special ways of teaching them. This book is about the fundamentals of the game of baseball, actually experienced and passed on to you for your own level of appreciation. I pay my deepest respect to the following people:

To my Dad: William F. (Bill) Blewett, Sr. (1903-1967) attended Manual Arts High School in Los Angeles and went on to The University of California at Berkeley to play on Andy Smith's Golden Bears Wonder Team. In 1955, at the age of 52, he was selected and honored as the "Best All Around Athlete" ever produced at Manual Arts High School in Los Angeles up to that time. I love you Dad, rest well, and thanks for your guidance and never-ending support.

To my brother Bill Jr., who was most instrumental in teaching me how to win. Without question, he was, and still is, one of the most competitive athletes I have ever known. Thanks Bill, for all the help.

To my son, Mike Jr., who endured my day-in and day-out coaching throughout his young life. I taught him all that I had learned and even some stuff I made up. What a terrific student! At eleven years old, he threw consistent strikes with fastballs, curveballs, sliders, screwballs, changeups and knuckleballs. He was able to throw all these pitches at his young age without damaging his arm because he threw every pitch properly without any stress on his elbow or shoulder. When he outgrew Little League and basketball, the golf bug took over his world. At 15 years old he decided that golf would be the sport in which he would concentrate his efforts. He had the best rotation on a curve ball I had ever seen. All this baseball talent wasted on a beautiful golf course in some exotic land across the ocean with warm tropical trade winds, beautiful people and marvelous food. No yelling! No hot dogs! Who needs that! What a waste! I love you Mike. Thanks for putting up with me.

To Ben Lefebvre, my Junior American Legion coach and father of ex-Dodger second baseman Jim Lefebvre. At the age of 14, Ben converted me from an outfielder to a pitcher. In just a few days, he taught me fundamentals of pitching that I still remember vividly to this day. He'd say, "In order to generate full body torque start with a full rotation of the left shoulder and show the hitter the number on your back." Obviously, somewhat exaggerated, but nevertheless, basically true. And "Drop in over your right knee as the body begins pushing off the rubber to generate more explosive lower body drive speed." Thank you Ben for your contributions to this book. Rest well.

To Harry F. "Bud" Brubaker, my high school football and baseball coach at Dorsey High School in Los Angeles, under whose direction we won the 1954 Los Angeles City Baseball Championship. In 1951-52 he coached Billy Consolo, Boston Red Sox Bonus Baby, and George "Sparkey" Anderson, on the same team. George, of course, went on to manage the Cincinnati Reds and the Detroit Tigers and was inducted into Major League Baseball's Hall of Fame in Cooperstown, NY. Coach Brubaker passed away a number of years ago in Del Mar, California, following a very successful career as a high school coach, an NFL referee, and a racing official at Del Mar Race Track in his retired years. He was tough minded but always had a twinkle in his eye as he worked with us, which made learning from him so easy at such a young and impressionable age. He taught me that courage and mental toughness grew from "focusing" on the task.

While attending the University of Southern California for my BS in Business Administration, I learned how to execute the fundamentals of baseball under the tutelage of Raoul "Rod" Dedeaux. Coach Rod, without question was one of the most successful baseball coaches in NCAA collegiate history. During his tenure at USC he won an unprecedented 11 NCAA Collegiate World Series Baseball Championships in Omaha, one of which I had the pleasure of being a member of in 1958. He was solely responsible for opening the international doors for competition in college baseball between the United States and Japan back in the mid 1950's. He was the ultimate perfectionist when it came to knowing precisely how the game of baseball should be played—and played to win. "Number 1," thanks for your knowledge of the greatest game and for sharing it with so many of us who had the pleasure of playing for you. Coach Dedeaux suffered a massive stroke on December 2, 2005 and passed away two weeks later at the age of 91 years young. Be easy on them in heaven coach.

Following spring training in 1959, I was assigned to Baltimore's California League Franchise, Stockton Ports and played under the direction of Manager Billy DeMars. Billy was an absolute winner, a hard-nosed, stick-to-the-fundamentals, play-the-percentages, "don't make any mental errors" type of manager, and one of the most dedicated coaches I have ever known.

Due to a late release from the US Army Basic Training Facility at Fort Ord, CA I missed spring training in 1960 and reported back to Stockton with Billy for a second year. Billy, remember this? "DaDa DitDit DaDitDa Dit, you've got'a lousy name in Morse Code Mike! Listen to mine, DaDitDitDit DitDit DitDaDitDit DitDaDitDit!" Skip, keep the ball in the fairway, and always stay on the top of your bike. Stay healthy!

# THANKS

To my daughter Diane (Mrs. Kurt Rogers Burger): I am so deeply grateful for the help and advice garnered from your marvelous wit and enormous capacities with the English language and the game of baseball. Thank you.

To my granddaughters, Katie and Christy Burger for your time and creativity spent doing "great things for me" with your cameras and computers. I am deeply grateful.

To Jacquie Maroun, a highly trained and experienced physical therapist in Monarch Beach CA, who provided a full routine of critical stretching exercises contained in Chapter 7.

To Jill M. Boorman and Dawson Cherry: co-owners of Premier Physical Therapy in North Charleston, SC, for providing "The Thrower's Ten Exercise Program" for pitchers and players to strengthen and/or rehabilitate their arms following an injury or surgery. Special friends.

To my wife Laura: My most ardent supporter and listener of my baseball stories over the last 47 years. She has heard every one no less than thirty or forty…or a hundred times! But I still like to think that she really enjoys hearing them. Every time I start telling one of my experiences, her eyes glaze over and she begins to stare up into the corner of the ceiling of the room. I know she's right there with me…**OR NOT!** Oh well, onward and upward!

⚾ ⚾ ⚾

# SPECIAL TRIBUTE

# TO

# WILLIAM LESTER "BILLY" DeMARS

### 1925 - Present

This Special Tribute is extended to "Billy" DeMars who in my modest estimation was the best minor league manager in professional baseball never to have been given the opportunity to manage a Major League Team.

Billy signed his first professional baseball contract with the Brooklyn Dodgers in 1943, and served the next three years in the Navy from 1944 to 1946. In 1947 he was assigned to the Asheville Tourists, and in 1948, drafted by the Philadelphia Athletics. In 1950 he was traded to the St Louis Browns and spent 1950 and 1951 in the big leagues. In 1954 the Browns were moved to Baltimore, Maryland to become the current day Baltimore Orioles. Billy remained as a player-manager in their minor league system through 1968.

In 1969 Billy was hired away from the Orioles by the Philadelphia Phillies to be the third base coach and hitting instructor during his twelve year tenure. He moved to the Montreal Expos from 1982 to 1984, and then to the Cincinnati Reds from 1985 until his retirement at the end of the 1987 season. Billy's reputation as an elite hitting instructor has since been recognized by many ball players throughout the major leagues, including the likes of Mike Schmidt, Eric Davis, and Larry Bowa.

Billy, this special tribute is meant as a thank you from all us who had the pleasure of knowing you, playing with you and for you throughout your marvelous career. A wonderful human being with a marvelous family, your positive attitude is still the best in the game. Congratulations!

⚾ ⚾ ⚾

# CHAPTER 1

## The History of Baseball

It's always fun to know the history of the game you are learning to play. So here is a capsule look at the how, when, where, and by whom, the game of baseball has evolved. As a reader, you must appreciate how long ago certain aspects of the game of baseball began in their most primitive form.

## Ancient Times

It may be difficult to imagine, but the game of baseball in its earliest form actually began in the time of William the Conqueror, a few years after the Battle of Hastings (1066 A.D) as noted in *Early bat and ball games* by Thomas R. Heitz and John Thorn. In the book, they write, "The game of baseball is a derivative of many games, from many cultures, and is the result of over 1000 years of human ingenuity. We know a game called 'Stool Ball' which utilized a stick and ball was known to have been played in England around 1085."

In the 1200's it was noted in a book written by William Fitzstephen called *Sports and Pastimes of Old Time Used in This City*, "That scholars of every school have their ball, or baton, in their hands; the ancient and wealthy men of the city come forth on horseback to see the sport of the young men."

On Christmas Day in 1621, Governor Bradford of Plymouth Plantation wrote, "that his men were frolicking in ye street, at play openly; some at Virginia pitching ye ball, some at stool-ball and shuch-like sport." About that same time in Eastern France it is said that bat and ball games were used in religious observances.

In 1744, *A Little Pretty Pocket Book* describes a woodcut drawing of boys playing baseball, and a poem of the game.

For a compilation of events covering the ancient era of the game, please refer to Addendum II located in the back of this book.

## The Modern Era

In more modern times, two men have been acknowledged, by two separate and independent commissions, to be the "creators" of the game of baseball as we know it today. The facts follow, and you may draw your own conclusions as to which one, or both, is, or are, the most deserving of such an accomplishment.

## Abner Doubleday

Abner Doubleday was the first person to be formally credited with inventing the modern game of baseball. Born June 26, 1819 in Ballston Spa, NY he was schooled at Auburn and Cooperstown, NY. He accepted an Appointment to the Military Academy at West Point in 1838 and graduated in 1842 as a Commissioned Officer (2nd Lt.) in Artillery. He then served in both the Mexican and Seminole Wars. His actual contributions to the game of baseball have always been in doubt, and his induction into the Hall of Fame still remains somewhat legendary at best.

In 1855 he was promoted to the rank of First Lieutenant and later to Captain. While stationed in Charleston Harbor in 1860-1861 he was credited with firing the first Union shot from Fort Sumter after the bombardment of the Confederate ironclad battery of that fort. While that revelation may or may not be true, my investigation of the Battle of Fort Sumter suggests that either a soldier from Virginia by the name of Edmund Ruffin, or a Captain James actually fired the first shot of the war. It is still being discussed 146 years later. We do know however that in 1861 he was promoted to Major in the 17th Infantry and served in the Shenandoah Valley defending Washington. He became a Brigadier General and saw action at Rappahannock, 2nd Bull Run, South Mountain, Fredericksburg and Antietam. It seems to me that not a lot of his time could have been spent structuring the game of baseball during this period.

In 1863 he was promoted to Major General. During his Command of Union troops in the Battle of Gettysburg he was credited with holding the Confederate army in place long enough for Union reinforcements to arrive. He then led the Union troops to their final victory over the Confederate soldiers on the third day of the battle. He retired from Military Service in 1873 and died on January 26, 1893 in New Jersey.

One can only conclude from limited documentation acquired during his time as a cadet at West Point, and the testimony of a childhood companion, Abner Graves, that Doubleday allegedly mapped out the first baseball diamond. Verification of Mr. Grave's story was substantiated upon the discovery of a rotten old baseball among his personal effects, following his death.

Long before Doubleday, the early rules for the game included such things as running to much shorter bases, playing on a field with no foul lines, teams consisting of many more players than nine (9) basic positions of today's game and the posting of an "out" accomplished by throwing a ball hit into the field, at the runner! Even though the ball was softer and larger, can you imagine the headaches and bruises you would have today if those were the rules? Wow! Only a few players would be able to finish a game!

The selection of General Abner Doubleday as the inventor of the game of baseball, and his induction into the Baseball Hall of Fame are more mythological legend than fact, as Doubleday himself never claimed to have invented the game in Cooperstown NY in 1839. However, a commission led by Al Spaulding in 1905 investigated all sides of the controversy and awarded official credit to him even though evidence to the contrary was overwhelming.

**Alexander Joy Cartwright, Jr.**

The other man credited with being the creator of baseball was Alexander Joy Cartwright Jr. In 1842, Cartwright, a bank teller from New York, suggested that he and his group of ball playing friends organize themselves into a baseball team. They called themselves the New York Knickerbockers. They started by making 20 changes to the basic rules, of which three changes to the field specifications still hold true today. The overall changes they were responsible for making are as follows: As quoted from the Mr. Baseball.

com web site, "Cartwright gave us the baseball diamond and specified the distance between the bases (a measurement that we still use now) ... he did away with the practice of hitting the runner with the ball to achieve an out and replaced this with either tagging the runner with the ball or getting it to the base ahead of him.. he specified the number of players on the field and invented the position of shortstop... he decided there would be three outs per side and the ball would be considered foul if knocked out of the ninety degree quadrant of the field... And these were just some of the things that Cartwright included when he wrote out baseball's first standardized set of rules." The photo below shows Cartwright in the middle of the back row.

Picture copied from the Internet

From New York and New Jersey, to Philadelphia, Detroit and Chicago, baseball gained in popularity and provided Cartwright with an easy task of promoting it across the United States to New Orleans and San Francisco as he traveled to find gold in California. He became ill and abandoned the search for gold for the beautiful climate of the Hawaiian Islands. He became one of Honolulu's most successful merchants and bankers, managing the finances for the King and Queen.  His controversial contribution to the game of baseball was judged after his passing on September 13, 1938, when a review of his journals brought about his election to the Baseball Hall of Fame in Cooperstown, NY.

On June 19, 1846 the first game of baseball following the new rules established by Cartwright was played at Elysian Field in Hoboken New Jersey, between the New York Knickerbockers, the team Cartwright founded, and the New York Nine. Cartwright did not play, as he was the umpire in the contest.

Sean Lahman, of the Baseball Archive (www.baseball1.com) writes, "Professional baseball was built on the foundation of the amateur leagues that preceded it. Interest in baseball as a spectator sport had been nourished for more than 25 years when the first professional league began operation. The National Association fielded nine teams in 1871, and grew to 13 teams by 1875.

Picture copied from the Internet

"The National Association was short-lived. The presence of gamblers undermined the public confidence in the games, and their presence at the games combined with the sale of liquor quickly drove most of their crowds away. Following the 1875 season, the National Association was replaced with the National League. Previously, players had owned the teams and run the games, but the National League was to be run by businessmen. They established standards and policies for ticket prices, schedules, and player contracts."

What do you think? Which of these two men was most instrumental in formulating the specifications and rules for the game of baseball? It's not an easy question to answer. If Alexander Cartwright Jr. hadn't had the foundation from the game initially designed by Abner Doubleday, he may not have ever thought of starting the Knickerbockers. On the other hand, Cartwright had come from England, where he played a game known as "rounders" as a boy. Rounders actually resembled the game of "town ball" or "base ball" initiated by Abner Doubleday in the United States. I'm so confused!!

The final result is that both men have been entered into the Baseball Hall of Fame in Cooperstown, having been recognized for their contributions on behalf of all of us who have played, or are preparing to play, the greatest game in the land.

## How long is a baseball season?

A Major League Baseball season is played over 162 games, not including postseason National and American League Championship Series, and the World Series. Tee Ball, Little League, Pony League, American Legion, high school and collegiate baseball seasons are much shorter, of course. But if you ask a young player's mom or dad how long their son or daughter's season has been, I'll bet they say it seems like at least 1,000 games or more! By the way, many thanks should go to all the moms and dads for their support and participation. Without them it would be pretty lonely out there for the beginner. A full season of baseball, proportionately speaking, is a lot of games no matter what level of play, and each game is most always approached with an emphasis on hitting, getting on base, scoring runs, and, above all, winning. But as you will find out, it's very difficult to play and win a game when you don't know what you are doing! It is correct to assume that the best-trained teams usually have better winning records than those that are not as well trained.

Major league teams play four, five, even six games a week, and travel on the off days, so fun and frivolity between the players becomes a psychological release from the constant and redundant pressures to win, which ultimately defines the game of baseball. Most of the pranks played on each other are superficial vents to maintain a positive attitude throughout the season, year in and year out. But you're not in the big leagues yet! And, you're not playing 162 games a year. So it's important to learn the **FUN-DA-MENTALS** of the game early in your career, so you will know what you're doing when the opportunity to play at a higher level presents itself.

Because *The FUN-DA-MENTALS of Baseball* is a micro analysis of the game and all that is included within its parameters, you will be exposed to the details of how to play the game from the standpoint of pure physical mechanics. It is purposely repetitive in a number of areas to stress the mandatory fundamentals in words and illustrations. It attempts to anticipate all that is necessary for a young player, male or female, to become a serious ball player. This book should be used as a guide for anyone willing to read and learn how to play the game. I hope you enjoy reading it to the end as much as I have enjoyed writing it from the beginning.

⊘ ⊘ ⊘

# CHAPTER 2

## The Specifications of a Baseball Field

To understand the configuration of a major league baseball field let's start with a review of the general specifications, so you will have a basis for comparison when you play on different baseball fields.

The game of baseball is played on a flat field. To gain full appreciation for the distances to the fences and around the bases, the following explanation might help.

There are four bases positioned 90 feet apart, forming a perfect square referred to as the "infield." Two foul lines are drawn on the surface of the field, both beginning at one of the bases called "**Home Plate**." From home plate, and at a 90 degree angle, the left and right foul lines are drawn to each of the extreme corners of the field. Normally there is a fence or boundary in place to hold the field within its maximum contours and keep spectators from entering into the field of play. See diagram, page 10.

The <u>average distance</u> from home plate to the left and right field corners on major league baseball fields built before 1958 ranges between 305 feet to 350 feet. The distance to the fence in straight away center field is usually the furthest point from home plate, somewhere between 400 feet and 450 feet, with the "power alleys" approximately 365 feet to 385 feet to left center and right center. The power alleys are the gaps on either side of the center fielder.

Newer stadiums built after June 1, 1958 must have minimum standard distances to the corners from home plate of not less than 325 feet down the lines to not less than 400 feet to straight away center field.

The playing field is complete when the raised area of the "**Pitcher's Mound**" is added to the field exactly 60'6" from home plate, and on a direct line between home plate and 2ⁿᵈ base.

"**Coaches' boxes**" are located outside the foul lines at 1ˢᵗ and 3ʳᵈ bases, and "**On-Deck Circles**" are placed between each team's bench and home plate, in which the "on deck or next hitter" waits to hit. "**Bull Pens**" are areas designated for relief pitchers to warm up. They are usually located in the far corners of the field, in foul territory. Today, many of the bullpens are enclosed with screens or fences to avoid the game being interrupted by errant balls coming onto the field of play, and for the protection of the players who have their backs to home plate. Players located in open bull pens down the lines must be careful not to interfere with any fair ball hit in their direction. Should a live ball hit them, even though they are in foul territory, all runners would be allowed to advance to the next base.

When you sit in the stands directly behind home plate and view the entire field down the left and right foul lines to the corners of the field, with the curving outfield fence arching in a half circle from the left field corner to the right field corner, the baseball "**Diamond**" becomes a reality.

First base is located down the right foul line 90' from home plate. It is the first base to which the batter runs after hitting the ball into fair territory, is walked by the pitcher, or is hit by pitch. Second base is located exactly 90 degrees to the left of first base and at a distance of 90 feet. Third base is located exactly 90 degrees to the left and 90 feet from second base. Home plate is located at a 90 degree left angle from third base, forming a perfect square. The following layout illustrates a normal baseball field. Some fields put the pitcher's bullpens behind the outfield fences, but it's all a matter of available space.

**The DIAMOND:**

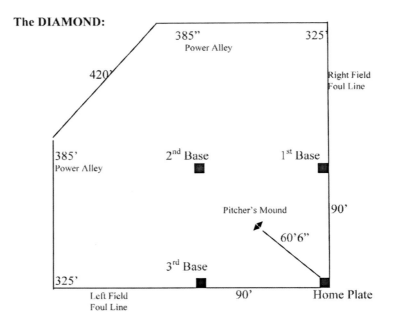

## Ground Rules

Each ball park has its own set of ground rules. Ground rules cover all the idiosyncrasies that are unique to that specific field, such as ground rule doubles, balls caught in the fences or vines around the field of play, and overthrown balls that enter the dugouts, etc. Such rules are always discussed at home plate between the two team managers and the umpires before the game begins. This resolves the need for a rhubarb later in the game by either team, suggesting that they were not aware of such a rule when called against them.

## Home Plate and the Bases

For the purpose of teaching the true beginner, maybe an explanation of each base will make your experience more successful. Home plate is the predominate base. It is the base that the catcher is positioned behind to receive throws from the pitcher standing on the mound 60'6" from home plate.

The pitcher's mound is on a direct line between home plate and 2nd base. The distance between home plate and second base is exactly 127 feet 3-3/8 inches. The pitcher throws from a 24 inch long x 6 inch wide rubber plate, known as the rubber, which is anchored into the top of the mound. The top of the mound is 10" higher than the playing field with a slope of 43 degrees toward home plate. A Major League Baseball Ruling in 1963 reduced the maximum height of the mound from 15 inches to 10 inches to reduce some of the pitcher's advantage over the hitter.

First, second and third bases all measure 15 inches by 15 inches. They are anchored to the ground inside the drawn foul lines. All the bases and the foul lines are "in the field of play." That means that any ball struck by the batter that hits home plate, first or third base, or either of the foul lines, all the way up the corner poles of the field is considered a fair ball and must be retrieved by the defensive player quickly to prevent the runners from advancing to additional bases. As previously stated, the distance to the outfield fences from home plate will vary from ballpark to ballpark. The distance between the bases, and between the pitcher's mound and home plate, never changes.

Over the years, league administrations have tinkered with the height of the mound and other variables in the game, in order to fine tune the delicate balance between pitching and batting. Thus in 1879, it took nine balls to draw a walk. Before 1887, the batter had the right to demand a high or low pitch. The distance from the pitcher's plate (rubber) to home plate was increased from 45 feet to 50 feet in 1881, and again to 60 feet 6 inches in 1893. It remains 60'6" from home plate today. The height of the mound was reduced from 15 inches to 10 inches in 1963 taking a distinct advantage away from the pitcher, making the battle between the pitcher and the hitter a little more equal. Remember, even the **great hitters** are only successful 3 to 3.5 times out of every ten appearances at the plate. If you were only successful 3 out of 10 times at school or work, how good would that be? Think about it!!! Ted Williams said he thought the hardest thing to do in sports is hit a baseball with consistency.

# CHAPTER 3

## How to Play the Game of Baseball

Today's game of baseball is played between two teams, each with nine starting players. There are extra players on each team who are substitutes or reserves. The reserve infielders and outfielders sit on the bench in the dugout until called upon to enter the game to pinch hit, pinch run, or warm up to enter the game. The relief pitchers to be used for this game sit in the bull pen waiting to relieve the starting pitcher. Until then they eat hot dogs and peanuts, drink cokes, crunch on candy bars, chew gum, eat pine nuts or split sunflower seeds. It's all part of the game. Just kidding ...no ...really! Well, some of it is true.

The game is played over nine innings. One complete inning is recorded when both teams have come to bat and made three outs. The **Home Team** starts the game by taking their positions (defensively) in the field. The **Visiting Team** sends its players to the plate first (offensively) to try to get on base and advance members of their team around the three bases and back to home plate to score runs.

A "run" is scored by the hitting team when batters advance from home plate and touch first base, around (touching) all three of the bases in a counterclockwise direction, reaching home plate before the defense can cause three of the offensive team players to make outs.

A batter may be safe at first base in a number of ways, including:
- Base hit
- Unintentional walk
- Intentional walk
- Fielder's choice
- Being hit by a pitch
- On an error by a defensive player
- Passed Ball, Wild Pitch or Catcher interference on a third strike

An "out" may be recorded in any of the following ways:
- When an infielder fields a ground ball and throws the ball to the first baseman before the batter can run from Home Plate and touch First Base

- o A defensive player may choose to throw the ball to one of the other bases before an advancing runner can get to that base, causing either a "Force out" where no tag on the runner is required by the rules, or a conventional tag where a runner tries to advance on a ground ball hit in front of him
- o A defensive player may tag out a runner in the base line when attempting to advance to the next base
- When the pitcher "Strikes Out" a batter on three strikes, either called by the umpire, or swung on and missed by the batter
- When the catcher throws to any one of the three bases where a tag is put on a base runner
- When a defensive player catches a fly ball hit into the air outside the foul lines (in "foul territory") before it hits the ground
- When a batter hits a pitched ball in the air into the field of play and one of the fielders catches it before it hits the ground
- When a batter attempts to bunt on the third strike and misses the ball or bunts it foul

**Let the game begin!**

The game actually begins when the pitcher throws any one of a selection of "pitches" to the catcher. The batter stands up to the plate inside a rectangular box called the **"batter's box,"** which positions the batter the appropriate distance back from home plate to receive the pitch. There is a batter's box on each side of home plate to accommodate both left and right-handed hitters. When the batter is ready to swing, the pitcher winds up and throws the selected pitch to the catcher. The batter either swings or lets the pitch go by, which may be **called** a strike or a ball by the umpire.

If you were the batter in this circumstance and hit the ball into fair territory for a single, you would run as fast as you could to first base before the defensive team player could throw you out at first base. If you were "safe" at first, the next batter up would attempt to advance you before making an out, and so on. When the defensive team registers three outs in that inning, the offensive team's side is out and the teams exchange places on the field. Over nine innings, the team that advances the most base runners around the bases, reaching home plate safely, wins the game. In case of a tie at the end of nine innings, extra innings are played until one of the teams wins the game.

**FUN-DA-MENTAL:** Upon hitting the ball into fair territory, you have two options to consider before touching first base. Option #1: If the play is going to be close, you can run straight down the line touching the base **before turning into foul territory** to come back to first base. Should the throw to first get by the first baseman, you may choose to turn **into the field of play** and try to advance to second. The fundamental here is that if you turn **into the field of play but do not continue on to second,** you can be tagged out at first base by the player covering first. Interesting, huh? Remember also that you must run outside the baseline, in foul territory, when approaching first base. If you run on the grass inside the foul line, you can be called out for obstruction if there is a close play on you at first base.

# CHAPTER 4

## Player Positions and General Responsibilities

Each of the nine position players on a baseball team has specific responsibilities when playing defense. It is very important for each player to know the skill levels and responsibilities of their teammates in their respective positions. It is also as important for each defensive player to know the capabilities of each of the opposing team's players, so they know where and how to position themselves to defend against the hitter's strengths and weaknesses. Baseball is a game of inches. The winning team usually takes advantage of its opponent through the use of its superior preparation defensively, speed, hitting ability, and aggressiveness on the bases.

So let's start by learning the names of each of the nine positions on a baseball team and understanding the responsibilities that each has on the field. In the descriptions that follow, each **player's position number** is shown after each position below. It is the number used to fill in the Official Lineup Card for the umpire before the game begins. These numbers are also used to mark each player's actions in the Official Scorebook as the game unfolds.

*For example, a double play ball that went from short to second to first would be described in the Scorebook as a DP 6-4-3 for that batter.*

## The Pitcher (#1)

The Pitcher is positioned on the pitcher's mound in the center of the infield. The job of a pitcher is to throw various "pitches" to the catcher at varying speeds and locations in an attempt to fool the hitter and cause the hitter to make an "out."

The pitcher throws fast straight pitches called fastballs, or makes the ball sail, curve, slide, or sink, as it comes over the plate. The pitcher's arm motion, grip on the ball, and release of each pitch in specific ways causes the seams of the ball to be affected by faster and slower air pressure over and under the spinning seams respectively. The ball will move in the direction of the rotating seams as it crosses the plate. Changing the speed and location of each pitch to each hitter is as important as the type of pitch being thrown. The combination of the selected pitch and the speed and location of each pitch thrown consistently for strikes is called Control. Those who possess this marvelous talent are the players who make the "big bucks" when it comes time to sign a professional contract.

**FUN-DA-MENTAL: When pitching, work smart, work quickly, and throw strikes!**

What is meant here is to get the ball over the plate. In the major leagues, a pitcher retires 80% of the hitters he faces if the first pitch is a strike. This information was provided by Billy DeMars, who spent his entire career in the game of baseball. Wow, what a statistic! Get that first pitch over the plate for a strike!

Defensively, the pitcher covers the immediate area around the mound for any ground balls or short pop ups that cannot be fielded by any other in-fielder, including the catcher. The pitcher must also field bunts laid down by batters trying to advance runners on base or attempting to reach first base on an infield hit. In the case of a high pop up in the infield over the mound the pitcher should get out of the way and call the appropriate infielder to make the catch. The reason for this is that the regular every day infielders have much greater experience catching pop flies than does the pitcher who only plays once or twice a week. There can be no argument here. Get out of the way! Please.

**FUN-DA-MENTAL: When pitching, field the position like an infielder, but get out of the way on a high pop fly around the mound.**

The pitcher must always back up plays at home plate or third base to catch errant throws that get by the catcher or third baseman. If a throw by an outfielder bounces into the dugout or out of the field of play, all runners may advance one base from the position they were in at the moment the ball left the playing field. The pitcher's job is to make sure the ball stays in play and the runners don't have a chance to advance on the overthrow.

The pitcher tries to keep the batter from making solid contact, or any con-tact for that matter. This is where the game begins. Nothing happens until the pitcher throws a pitch to the catcher behind home plate.

A young pitcher must learn to pitch at a reasonable pace, so the game isn't held up spending too much time getting back on the rubber after each pitch, or taking too long to get the sign from the catcher. You will bore your teammates to death if you take too much time between pitches. Note to the wise: Get your sign, wind up and throw the pitch. Remember what you threw and where you threw it. Get back on the rubber, get your sign, wind up and throw the next pitch, at a different speed, and to a different location, and do it again, and again, and again.

## The Catcher (#2)

The catcher is positioned behind home plate to receive (catch) pitches thrown by the pitcher. The catcher wears equipment known in the game as the "tools of ignorance." They include shin guards, a padded chest protector and cup, and a facemask over a protective plastic helmet. The catcher uses a specially configured glove, which is round in shape with no visible fingers like those of the infielders and outfielders. Some catcher's gloves are manufactured with slots in the heel of the glove to provide some flexibility. The catcher's glove is designed for very heavy-duty performance because it takes quite a beating during a game. Only the first baseman handles more throws in a game than the catcher.

The catcher gives signs to the pitcher with his fingers for the specific pitch he wants the pitcher to throw to the specific batter standing in the batter's box. Some of these signs are listed below. Almost every catcher studies the results his pitchers have had against opposing hitters in the past and should know what pitch to call to have the best results. Then it's up to the pitcher to throw the ball where the catcher wants it. On some teams, the manager calls the pitches from the dugout for the catcher to give to the pitcher.

Please understand that some pitchers are able to throw a lot of different pitches. Some young pitchers only have one or two pitches that they are confident enough to throw in game conditions. It doesn't make any difference what sign is given by the catcher for each specific pitch, as long as everyone in the infield knows what they are for that particular pitcher, in this specific game, and at this specific moment in time. There will be much more about this point later.

Going back to the basics, the following signs are learned early in a player's career and remain pretty standard throughout. In college and professional ball, to prevent experienced base coaches and base runners from picking up the signs from the catcher, the signs from the catcher to the pitcher need to be rotated with runners on base using an indicator sign followed by the pitch, where a catcher may want the second or third sign in the sequence. In any case, it doesn't matter what the signs are, except to the pitcher, catcher, and infielders, so they know how to set up for the next advantage or disadvantage reflected by the count on the hitter. The following signs are the normal beginning point for most young catchers and pitchers.

## FUN-DA-MENTAL:

| Fingers/Pitch | Finger / Direction |
|---|---|
| 1= Fastball | Right index finger / downward / hand to R/L thigh for in or out location |
| 2= Curveball | Right index and middle finger /downward / R/L thigh for location |
| 3= Slider | Circle right index finger / downward / Right thigh for location |
| 4= Changeup | Wiggle all four fingers / downward / R/L thigh for location<br>(May include circle change, screwball, sinker, or palmball) |
| Thumb Flip | High inside knockdown pitch / Location is automatically up and in |
| Fist | Pitch out    Chest high and out over opposite batters box away from hitter |

IMPORTANT NOTE: Any variation of these finger signs can be used for pitchers who throw different pitches, such as split finger fastballs, knuckleballs, bloopers, or whatever!

The location of each pitch to the batter can also be called for by the catcher. The catcher merely pats the left thigh or right thigh (for inside or outside) after giving the pitcher the sign for the pitch selection. The catcher also gives the pitcher a target for the location the pitch thrown. Some pitchers like to start certain pitches at the glove and allow them to break from that point over the plate. Some like to throw to the final point of the pitch. It's all a matter of pitcher preference and the depth in the **strike zone** where the pitch will end up.

After calling the pitch, a catcher must be ready to throw if a runner tries to "steal" a base without the ball being hit by the batter. Quick feet and a strong arm are academic for a catcher as they are required to throw out base runners attempting to steal second or third. It is a fact that a majority of successfully stolen bases are done so on the delivery motion of the pitcher rather than the arm of the catcher. The catcher is also responsible for backing up first base on throws from the infielders to first base, but only when there are no other runners on base to ensure that an overthrow doesn't go into the dugout. The catcher must be ready to catch pop ups in foul territory in back of home plate and to field bunts out in front of the plate.

"Fearless" describes a catcher when it comes to blocking pitches thrown in the dirt with men on base, or blocking the plate when tagging a runner trying to score. When blocking a wild pitch to the right or left, catchers must shift their feet and slide their bodies down in front of low incoming pitches with both knees on the ground and arms fully extended downward with the face of the glove filling the hole between their knees and bare hand behind the glove. From their knees, it is important to position their shoulders forward with their chest sucked in (concave) to soften the impact of the ball against their chest protector. Their heads and eyes must be focused downward at the ball to protect their neck and head. To prevent the ball from caroming off their bodies, it is important that they angle their shoulders back toward home plate to keep the ball in front of them.

The catcher is the real "work horse" of the team, and this position should only be played by someone who is tough and wants to be there. Getting foul balls off the arms and shoulders are common occurrences.

**The First Baseman (#3)**

As a general rule, first base is played by a relatively agile left-handed infielder, but it is not mandatory that he be left-handed. Two exceptions are Albert Pujols and Mark McGuire! The left-handed player is able to make a faster tag on a base runner returning to the base because the glove is on the same side as the runner. Secondly, lefties can make a more natural throw across their bodies to second base to start a double play. Right-handed fielders must shift their feet in order to throw the ball with enough speed to complete the double out sequence. But when you can hit 70+ home runs a year, believe me, they will find a place for you!

The first baseman is usually a better than average hitter capable of driving in a lot of "RBI's" (Runs Batted In). Most use a different glove than the other infielders because they need to scoop up errant throws from the other infielders throwing off balance, in the essence of time, to catch the runner. A first baseman's glove is tall and wide across the palm of the hand with no fingers showing, looking somewhat like half of a pancake with a long slender thumb on the other side of soft webbing.

A very important responsibility of the first baseman is being the **cutoff** man for all throws to home plate from the right and center fielders. It is their responsibility because they have nothing else to do during a base hit. They position themselves between the mound and the foul line to line up the throw from the outfielders to home plate then, either let the throw go though to the catcher, cut off the throw for a play at another base on an advancing runner, or cut off and hold a throw that is off line with no other play available. The first baseman is a key performer on a **bunt play** which is designed to get the lead runner at third base out, with no outs and runners on first and second. We will cover the bunt play later in the book.

## The Second Baseman (#4)

Those of us who have played second base know that you have a number of very important responsibilities that must be carried out when in the field. You must go after every short pop fly hit to short center, short right field, or into right field foul territory until called off by the outfielder that has the right of way. With a runner on first, you must cover first base on a bunt play to be ready to receive a throw from the first baseman or pitcher, both of whom are committed to fielding the bunt. At second, you must always be ready to start or complete a double play with either the third baseman or shortstop when there is a runner on first. You are the cut off man on balls hit deep to the right center alley and into right field. You are responsible to line up the throws from deep center and right field to the shortstop covering second base. Second basemen are generally quick and agile athletes that possess quick hands and are able to make instant physical adjustments based on the speed of the developing play. Both the shortstop and second baseman trade off covering second on steal attempts depending upon the game situation, the speed of the runner of first, whether the hitter is left- or right-handed, the hitter's capabilities with the bat, the particular pitch that is being thrown, etc. Most second basemen use gloves with a fairly shallow pocket broken in wide and flat so the ball can be extracted quickly and cleanly.

## The Third Baseman (#5)

Known as the "hot corner," some of the best baseball players in the history of the game have been third basemen. My favorite was Brooks Robinson of the Baltimore Orioles in the 60's and 70's. This is a tough position to play and I have the utmost respect for anyone who decides to take on the task.

Because hitters are stronger nowadays due to year long weight training programs, and hitting a juiced up baseball with metal bats (high school and college), the third baseman must have super quick reactions, a great set of hands and a strong arm to make the plays at this position. The increased strength of the hitters allows them to get out in front to pull pitches down both left or right field lines at speeds reaching 110 -120 mph from just 90 feet away. The ball shows up real fast! So you've got to be quick and fearless to play this position. The third baseman is the cutoff man for throws coming in from the left fielder for plays at home. Like the first baseman, the third baseman positions himself between the mound and the foul line to line up the direction of the throw from the left fielder to let it go through, relay it, or cut it off for a play at another base. The catcher will yell such instructions with the ball in flight so the third baseman must listen and react immediately, without any hesitation.

The third baseman uses a slightly longer fingered glove than the second baseman. It is usually broken in with a medium-deep pocket to provide a little better chance of snaring line shots and fielding ground balls hit down the line and in the hole at short.

We learned that a major league baseball weighs between 5.0 and 5.25 ounces and may neither be less than 9 inches nor more than 9.25 inches in circumference. Sort of like a round brick. When nasty hopping ground balls come screaming off the bat and carom off your arms, chest or shins leaving weeklong bruises, you begin to think that catching is a sissy position. In my mind, the third baseman on any team is "the man." God Bless all of you, dead or alive!

Speaking of being blessed, third basemen must have strong and accurate arms, because they have the longest throw across the infield to first base. When you play this position you must be able to field bunts down the line bare handed, catch pop flies hit between the mound and third base, and chase down pop ups in foul territory between home and left field until called off by the left fielder. The outfielder running in towards the infield has full visual control of who has the best chance of making the catch and should call out loudly who should make the play in plenty of time to avoid a collision with one of the other teammates. The toughest decision you must make is whether or not to field a bunt on a bunt play or get back to the base for a tag on the lead runner with two men on and no outs. This requires quick reactions, instincts, and enormous ability to make this play successfully. It ain't for the weak, slow and untalented Dude to carry out!

## The Shortstop (#6)

The shortstop is the field captain and usually the best athlete on the field. This position requires a high level of agility, speed, quick feet and a strong arm to get the job done. Most everyone of us has seen a shortstop go deep in the hole behind the third baseman to field a grounder and come up throwing a dart to first base for the out, and on the next play go behind second base to save a run from scoring. That's not luck. That's talent.

The style glove used by most shortstops is slightly longer fingered with a medium deep pocket because a great many chances to field balls hit to the shortstop can only be reached with one hand, rather than two, which is always recommended any time possible.

If you are interested in becoming a great shortstop you must possess quick reactions, be very instinctive, possess a powerful arm and, of course, be extremely coordinated. The size of the average shortstop varies from small to tall. In the last twenty years three of the best in the game happen to be of the taller, power-hitter variety, such as Derek Jeter, Alex Rodriguez, and the now retired, Cal Ripken, Jr. They are perfect examples of the best shortstops to ever play the game because they possess great range, great arms, great power at the plate, and great field management skills. This does not suggest in any way that shorter players cannot play this position just as well. And by the way, I am aware that ARod plays third base for the NY Yankees, but **when** he played short he was of the taller, more slender, power-hitter variety that I was referring to above. I love it when you pay attention! Now he's leaving the Yankees. Wow!

## The Left Fielder (#7)

The left fielder covers the outfield from the left field foul line to mid-center field and has two of the shorter throws of any of the three outfielders to second and third. When playing this position your longest throw is to home plate. So it goes without saying that your offensive capabilities as a hitter almost outweigh the defensive requirements of the position. A left fielder's predominant task is to score runs by hitting for a high average, including the long ball for home runs. Additionally, you always back up the center fielder on any ball hit to left center or dead center field.

All outfielders, at one time or another, have a problem with the sun when it passes over and behind the stands from first around to third base. At some moment in an outfielder's career, the sun will blot out the ball's flight in the air. Every baseball player should recognize that the sun has been up there for approximately 4.6 billion years, so each and every one of you must be equipped with appropriate sun glasses to deal with it, because it is not going to go away for at least another 5 billion years. That should be long enough to give Oakley time to come up with the perfect pair for you beginners. If sun glasses are not provided by the team, you must learn to shade the sun by holding your glove hand up to block it, with your eyes looking either over the fingers, around the fingers, underneath the thumb, or by cocking it to one side or the other. If you lose site of the ball while chasing it down you should immediately let your teammate know it and watch where the infielders are pointing to help track the ball as they come out to assist you.

It may be interesting for you to learn that the MLB Rules of Baseball, Section 1.04, requires that a baseball diamond be designed and constructed to face East/Northeast. It begins with a direct line East Northeast from Home Plate, through the Pitchers Mound, and over second base for the best physical position of the sun for all the players during a game.

## The Center Fielder (#8)

This position is usually filled by a very fast and fearless individual who has the natural instincts to get a jump on a ball as it comes off the bat. Should that individual be you, normal protocol suggests that you have the right of way to catch all balls hit in your direction, with the left and right fielders backing you up incase the ball gets by you. You have the complete right of way if you call for the catch. In return, you are responsible for backing up both the right and left fielder's attempts to catch balls that might get by them as well. The St. Louis Cardinal's center fielder Jim Edmonds is the epitome of center fielders who play this position as well as it has ever been played.

The Center Fielder has two long throws on the field, to home and third base. Either the shortstop or first baseman will line up as "the **cutoff** man" when throwing to either of those bases. If the throw is off line, the infielder will relay, or "cut off" the throw. So the center fielder must possess a strong arm and have great speed to run down fly balls hit deep in the power alleys, as shown on the following Positions Diagram. Another responsibility of the center fielder is to back up second base on a bunt play to prevent an errant throw from allowing a run, or even two, to score.

Like the left fielder, the center fielder should swing the bat with power and be one of the club's RBI leaders at the end of the season. Most likely, you would choose a very long fingered glove with a deep pocket to hold on to the ball while making running, diving, or climbing-the-wall-attempts to take away extra base hits. But the size of your glove is your choice.

**The Right Fielder (#9)**

Right Fielders must possess the strongest arms of the three outfielders because they have the two longest throws on the field from the alley in right and the deep right corner to both third and home plate. Like the other fielders, they too will use long fingered gloves with a deeply developed pocket to hang on to the ball as they run into the wall or dive for line drives. The right fielder is expected to be a leader on offense, hitting with power and driving in runs. When not directly involved in fielding a ball in the outfield he should be backing up plays at either first or second base.

**FUN-DA-MENTAL: If you are an outfielder and a ball is hit to you with runners on base, the most important thing for you to accomplish is to prevent the ball from getting by you for extra bases. The most common mistake outfielders make is to try to field the ball on the dead run with their entire body off to the side of the oncoming ball. You must become an "infielder" when attempting to catch a hot ground ball, by keeping the ball directly in front of you if at all possible. When fielding a ground ball base hit, you should attempt to catch the ball with your right leg forward if you are right-handed, or vice versa, if you are left-handed. It then only requires one step onto the opposite foot to release the throw back into the infield. Taking two or three steps to release the throw in this situation allows the base runner to cover too much ground between bases.**

# PLAYER POSITIONS AND GENERAL RESPONSIBILITIES

The following diagram will place all the players in their respective positions and show you all the markings on the field of play for your learning and understanding.

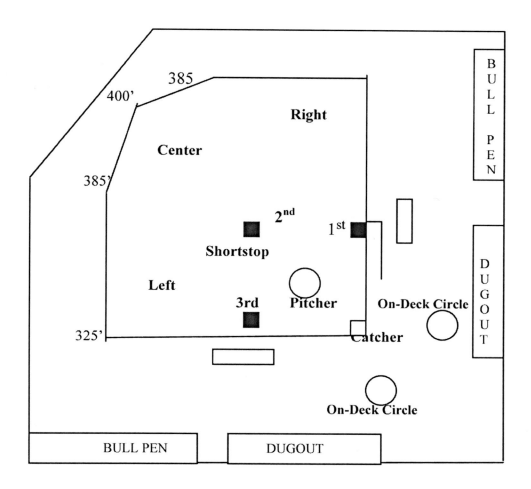

# CHAPTER 5

## How to Think the Game of Baseball

Now that we have some cursory knowledge about the field and the positions of the players, let's start thinking the game of baseball. In this chapter you will learn to sharpen your skills, which will enable you to advance to your highest levels of personal performance. **Remember, _THINKING the game_** differs greatly from **_thinking ABOUT the game_**.

Let's start with the home team's bench to learn the finer points of thinking this great game. The fundamental here is to appreciate what it is important as the game progresses, no matter what position you play on the team. If you are **on** the team, you are valuable **to** the team. If you don't know what is going on during the game, of what value could you possibly be? So based on this premise, let's take a trip from the bench to the on-deck circle, to the plate, and around the bases to give you some insight as to what you must be thinking about when you arrive at these various locations to be of value to your team. What you are about to learn is known as _thinking_ the game.

## The Bench

The "Bench" is located in the dugout. It is where all the players sit waiting to hit, waiting to play in the field on defense, sitting as back up replacements for a position player, such as a **pinch hitter, pinch runner**, or catcher. Relief pitchers usually sit in the bullpen area. Some next-day starting pitchers like to keep the record book on the number of pitches thrown and types of pitches thrown to the various hitters, as they prepare for their next start.

Every player who sits on the bench is there for a reason. You have to be warmed up and have your head in the game from start to finish. If you don't know the score, or how many outs there are, or who is on first, or how accurate and strong the fielder's arms are when throwing to third on a base hit to right, or any other scenario that might be happening, don't put the uniform on and take up space on the bench. If your head is not in the game, you don't belong in the uniform. If you're bored, go do something else. When a Manager needs you during the game, it is imperative that you be ready to play without having to be lectured to by him, explaining the current game situation, the number of strikes and balls on the hitter, and what your run means to the team. You should already know those things.

The bench is where you are able to rally your teammates when you are behind late in the game. The bench is where you give high fives to teammates that make smart plays to get your team out of trouble. It's not a place to fool around.

**FUN-DA-MENTAL: GET YOUR HEAD IN THE GAME! At all times, know the score, know how many outs there are, who is on base, what inning it is, what you would do if you were hitting at this very moment, what signs you might be given by the coach, and what pitches you might expect to see in this exact circumstance. Watch every pitch! You may be up next!!!**

**The On-Deck Circle**

When you come out of the dugout as the next hitter, you will wait in the On-Deck Circle. You are the **on-deck hitter**. This is a very important place on the field. This is where you prepare yourself mentally and physically for your at-bat by anticipating every possible game situation that might occur during your turn at the plate, but first things first. The first is to prepare your bat and adjust your gloves, if you use them, so your hands won't slip off the end of the bat when you swing at a pitch. Get into a routine so that all these points are covered without missing a step. Next, take a few practice swings to loosen up your back and arms.

Review what inning it is, the score of the game, and how many outs your team has made so far this inning. This is the time you anticipate what **signs** your third base coach might give you to advance existing runners or how many pitches he might have you take for strikes before letting you swing. This is where you think about the strength of the outfielder's arms if you hit a ball into either gap and try to extend the hit into a double or triple. This is where you decide which half of the plate you will "give" to the pitcher so that you can look for your specific pitch over only YOUR half of the plate.

As the on-deck hitter, you are responsible for clearing the plate area of the last hitter's bat if runners are attempting to score. You must be ready to give hand, arm or body signals to the runner coming down the third base line trying score. Show these signals by standing 5 feet behind the left-hand hitter's batter box, looking directly into the face of the oncoming runner and put both arms straight above your head to **stand up, or drop to your**

**knees and wave your arms to the right or left to slide to avoid the catcher's tag on a close play.** Remember not to get too close to the plate at home as you cannot interfere with the catcher's attempt to field the incoming throw or tagging the runner. If interference is called on you, your teammate is out even if safe! You got that? Ok.

*For example: It is late in a game, you are the home team, you are the hitter, your team is behind by one run, there are no outs in the inning, and your team has a runner on first base. The most obvious sign you will be given will be the bunt sign to sacrifice yourself, or "give yourself up," to move the runner on first base over to second, in position to score on a base hit by either of the next two hitters. You may also get a hit sign, for a hit and run, with the steal sign being given to the runner at the same time. You might get a "take sign" to see if you can get the pitcher behind in the count, and, to see if they might be anticipating a bunt. You must be looking for each and every one of these situations so that you and the base runner execute the signals successfully and without any hesitation.*

This situation exemplifies the need for the hitter to get ready in the on-deck circle **before going up to the plate**, not walking up to the plate and have to think about all these different situations in the box. Being mentally ready in the on-deck circle is the difference between a teammate who wants to win and a player who just came out to go through the motions of being on a team. It is not the place where you look up into the stands for your girlfriend, or your Mother and Dad, who may be in attendance. Keep your head out of the stands—always.

**FUN-DA-MENTAL: Anticipate all the situations that might present themselves before entering the batter's box. Be ready to execute any sign given by the third base coach. If you have the hit sign, choose the type of pitch and location of the pitch you are looking to hit until you get to a two-strike count.**

**The Batter's Box**

Before you step into the Batter's Box look at your third base coach, who is responsible for giving you the **hit, take, hit and run, run and hit, or bunt sign,** pitch by pitch, throughout the game. Get into the habit of watching the complete sequence of signs. If you look away immediately after seeing the sign early in the sequence and he continues to flash signs when you're not looking, you alert the other team that the signs are up front in the sequence, and they will begin to pick them off. If your opponent steals your signs, it gives them an absolute advantage from that moment on in the game because they know what you are going to do before you do it and can counteract your plan without you ever knowing it.

**FUN-DA-MENTAL: Never miss looking at your third base coach for a sign on every pitch as a matter of habit, especially when there are runners on base.**

After you receive your sign from the coach and before stepping into the box, take a look at where each of the infielders and outfielders are positioned. Assuming you are a right-handed hitter, notice if the third baseman and shortstop have moved to their right or left, and check the outfielders to see if they have shifted one way or the other. If so, they will most likely be telling you how they are going to be pitching to you.

*For example: if third, short and second all shift around toward first base, they will most likely be showing you your pitch out of the strike zone for balls, and the pitches they want you to hit will be thrown over the outside corner of the plate. By keeping the ball away from you, you will have to hit an away pitch into their defensive net. Patience is a great attribute at the plate. Look for your pitch where you like it, even if you have to take a couple of strikes on the outside half of the plate. When the count reaches two strikes, protect the plate at all costs. Most pitchers up through high school are unable to throw every pitch where they want them to go, so it is pretty likely you will see the exact pitch you are looking for almost every time you go to the plate. You just have to be patient to get it and ready to hit it.*

**FUN-DA-MENTAL: BE PATIENT AT THE PLATE!! Look for the exact pitch you want to hit until you get two strikes, then protect the plate. There are just as many base hits in right field as there are in left.**

After every pitch, remember to look at your third base coach for a new sign. If you're not sure of the sign, ask him to run through his sign routine again to make sure. You do this by rotating your hand in a circle. He will start the sign sequence again. And again, watch until the entire sequence is completed. Don't do this "ask again" thing more than once a season because it alerts the other team that something may be happening on this next pitch, especially if there are runners on base. We will get into actual signs later on.

## As a Base Runner at First Base

Let's assume that you reached first base. Did a run score? Did any of the games components change during your turn at bat? If not, when you reach first base there are a number of things you must do and know to be a viable base runner.

First and foremost, always look at your third base coach on every pitch for any signs given to the hitter and/or to you, the base runner. You must know the inning and the score of the game and just exactly what your run means at this moment in the game. Is this the appropriate time for you try to get to third on a base hit to left center with no outs and risk being thrown out, or should you hold up at second and allow the next hitter to score you from there?

During infield practice it is important that you observe the strength of the opposing team's outfielders arms, so that if and when a ball is hit to one of them during the game you will know whether you can advance or not. This is where you need to remember that if the outfielder is left-handed and fielding the ball with his glove hand moving to the right requiring him to shift his feet to throw to third, you have a step or two advantage on him. If you get a good jump from first base on a base hit through the hole between first and second, is the right fielder playing deep enough to allow you to make the turn and go to third without being thrown out? Is his arm strong enough and accurate enough to throw you out from his position on the field? This is where the game of baseball is unseen by many who play it and most who watch it. Keep your eyes on the third base coach as you round second and react accordingly. This is where you must be extremely careful not to hesitate rounding second, only to have the outfielder's throw come in behind you and cut off your return to the base.

The next thing you must be aware of as a base runner at first is how good the pitcher's "pick off" move is. If the pitcher is a left-hander, does he have two moves, normal and quick, or just one nasty one? If he throws a wild pitch past the catcher or by the first baseman on an attempted pick off, where and how far does the ball have to go **on this field** for you to make it to second base safely? Remember every field has different ground rules for wild pitches and overthrows to first. You must know them!

If you are given the steal sign, how big of a lead should you take without getting picked off? If the hitter is given the **Hit and Run** sign, how big of a lead should you take, since the hitter will be swinging at the next pitch to protect you? If you are given the **Run and Hit** sign, you must take a normal lead but make sure you get a good jump as the hitter is going to try to hit the ball behind you as you move toward second. A two ball one strike count is a perfect time to call either play. If the ball goes through the infield on the right side you must look at the third base coach for a wave to continue on to third or stop at second. He may hold you up at second based upon your jump and where the fielder is to the ball as you round the bag. If you look back to see where the fielder is, you will lose two or three tenths of a second of speed if you continue on to third. This can be critical in being called out or safe.

**FUN-DA-MENTAL: NEVER look back at a play behind you when running the bases! ALWAYS follow your third base coach's in-structions. TRUST YOUR COACHES. That's why they are there!**

When a ground ball is hit to one of the infielders to begin a double play at second, the speed of the ball hit will likely determine where the second baseman or shortstop is going to be around the bag when you get there. If you intend to break up the throw to first, you must make contact with the one turning the play to take him out. Practice **hook slides** into bases to the left and to the right, off both feet. You will be tougher to tag on a close play, and better prepared to hook a foot or roll your shoulder into the infielder as he makes the pivot to first base. Learn a **stand-up slide** also. If the throw is bobbled by the pivot man and rolls into the outfield, a stand up slide will put you back up on your feet quickly and on the way to third base, if appropriate.

**FUN-DA-MENTAL: Learn to hook slide to the left and to the right by beginning your slides off both feet. Caution: Always slide early enough so you don't get hit in the head with the throw to first by the shortstop or second baseman. The defensive player has just as many rights to protect himself as you do to prevent him from completing the double play.**

Note 1: Changes in the rules for high school and collegiate baseball teams over the last few years do not allow any physical contact between the runner and the infielder during a double play unless the defensive player is blocking the base. As a base runner you are obligated to slide straight into the base without extending your arms or legs to make contact with the defensive player. Any attempt to make contact with the defensive player is an automatic out unless the pivot dude is just standing on the bag with the ball. Then, and only then, can you make physical contact.

Note 2: I absolutely disagree with this rule for anyone's sake or safety. Baseball is a game of inches and should be played wide open to be able to take advantage of the other team's mistakes. If you can't stand the heat in the kitchen, don't go in there!

## As a Base Runner at Second Base

Now that you have reached second base, you are in a position to score on a base hit. In a game late in the 8th or 9th inning, no outs, with your team behind by one run, the opposing team may shorten up defensively. On a base hit, you will either make the full turn at third or be held up at the base solely at the discretion of the third base coach. When you are given the green light to go by the third base coach, you cannot hesitate in continuing on to the plate. If you stumble or miss the bag, you must stop. If you stop on your own, your decision must be based upon the speed and direction of the ball hit by the batter, the field to which it was hit, the position of the outfielders to the ball in motion, and the strength and accuracy of their arms from that point of the field against your raw speed. If you don't follow your third base coach's signal to hold up and get thrown out at the plate, you deserve a chewing out. When the game is on the line, you must follow your coach's instructions to the letter! It doesn't matter who you think you are. This is a team game.

When a line drive is hit off the bat, your first move as a base runner must be back toward the base, advancing only when you see it will hit the ground in the outfield. On a **deep fly ball** to the outfield with no outs, you must tag up and advance if possible. **Tagging up** means that you must return to second base and keep your foot on the base until the ball is either caught by the defensive player or it drops in for a base hit. You may then advance to the next base or stay where you are. On a deep fly ball to the outfield with one out, you must go half-way to third and wait to see if the ball drops into fair territory. If caught, you return to second. With two outs, you must run hard on anything hit and listen to your third base coach.

With no outs or one out and no runner behind you on first, and a ground ball is hit in front of you to third or short, remain as far from second base as the closest infielder is to that base, and do not try to advance unless the ball goes through the infield or is thrown across the diamond to first base. Try not to run into a tag out on a ground ball hit in front of you. This is a simple out for the defensive team to either tag you out between bases or throw the ball to the base ahead of you for the tag out.

### As a Base Runner at Third Base

When you arrive at third base, there are a number of options available to you to score a run for your team. Depending upon the inning, the number of outs, and the score, the following rules apply for a base runner at third base.

**On a line drive, move back to the base** until the ball has cleared the infield, then react accordingly. You don't want to get **doubled off**, meaning the line drive is caught and you are forced out at the base before you can get back safely.

**With no outs or one out and the infield in on the grass, make sure a ground ball goes through the infield before you attempt to score.** You would be thrown out easily by one of the infielders before you could make it to the plate. If the ball is hit to the second base side of the field and your run is vital, you must get a good jump and try to score. Again, whether or not you try to score from third on a ball hit to short or third is a situation play. It depends upon the inning, the score, how hard the ball was hit, its location, your speed, and what your run means to the game's result. In the Big Leagues a runner from third breaking to the plate on the hitter's contact with the ball will score 7 out of 10 times no matter where the ball is hit.

**With no outs, it is mandatory that you tag up on any fly ball hit to the outfield and try to score,** unless directed otherwise by the 3rd base coach.

**With one out, tag up on any fly ball hit to the outfield, and listen to your coach.** Listen also, to hear how hard the ball is hit off the bat. You will gain information about the carry of the ball toward a defender. When the ball is caught, you're ready to go, but you can't leave the base until the defensive player has made the catch. If you tag up and leave early, you are automatically out if the defender touches the base with the ball in his possession before the next pitch. By the way, in this situation, the pitcher must first put the ball back into play by stepping on to the rubber. He then steps off the rubber and tosses the ball to the third baseman who touches third base. The umpire must then rule whether or not the runner left early.

**With two outs, run hard across home plate and be ready to assist the runners trying to score behind you if the next hitter is not in place to do so.** For whatever reason, if there is any chance of a play being made on you at home, be sure to slide. Don't be lazy and cross the plate standing up on any close play because catchers will fake you into thinking the ball was thrown to some other base when it wasn't. Dirty guys!

As previously stated, on a throw from an outfielder to home plate, the on-deck hitter is responsible for clearing the bat away from the area around home plate before the runner arrives and should be in position to give the runner the sign to stand up, or slide right or slide left, to avoid a possible tag on a close play by the catcher at home plate.

## FUN-DA-MENTALS: GENERAL RULES FOR RUNNING BASES

**With no outs, tag up at second and third on any fly ball to the outfield and advance if the ball is hit deep enough to advance safely. The question to ask yourself: is the risk worth the reward? If you must risk being thrown out at home plate to win the game, go for it! The coach should be telling you exactly what to do. Listen and react accordingly!**

**Remember one fact: the speed of the fastest runner is going to be somewhere in the area of 22 miles per hour. An outfielder with a good arm can throw up to 85 or 90 miles per hour, or four times as fast as the runner can run.**

**With one out, a runner on second moves nearly half way** between second and third and waits to see the outcome of the play in the outfield.

Half way is a relative term. He must go to the furthest point between the bases that will allow him to get back to second safely if the ball is caught for an out. If the ball drops in or is bobbled, he can advance to third. When a runner goes nearly half way between bases, he may be a target for an outfielder with a great arm to try to throw behind him for a tag out. Be careful and vary your "half way distance" by the situation right in front of you.

**With no outs or one out, the runner on third automatically tags up and scores on deep fly ball to outfield. On a shallow fly ball hit into the outfield, the runner tags up and listens to coach for directions.** Remember, if there is a runner behind you on second base, he will be reacting to what you do, so don't confuse him by going back and forth between home and third. Stay calm and do what the situation allows you to do! More than one runner at the same base can be very embarrassing, and very OUT!

**With two outs, all base runners run wide open upon the batter's contact with the ball** and follow the directions of the third base coach whether or not to hold at third or make the turn and try to score. By saying this, that does not mean that you run straight into an out on a ball hit in front of you. You must protect your potential run by making the infielder throw the hitter out at first base. A base runner must also be careful not to overrun the base runner ahead of him. It's pretty busy at the base when there are two base runners standing there and a third baseman with the ball in hand. Woops!

Generally, a player with better-than-average speed can score from second base on a base hit through the infield. Secondly, younger outfielders will have less accurate arms, so scoring is relatively easy. But as players gain physical maturity, their arms get stronger and more accurate, increasing the chances of being thrown out if the base runner hesitates, slips, or has to change stride to touch a base when making the turn. Listen to your third base coach and follow his arm signals, no matter what you think!

With no outs or one out, if a runner slips or gets a bad jump from second trying score on a base hit, it's just as well to hold up at third, rather than try to score and be thrown out, with two more hitters coming to the plate. These decisions are inning and score dependent and include what hitter is coming up to the plate.

## Home Plate

Home plate is the last base on our trip around the infield. Behind home plate is where the catcher works his magic calling pitches and tries to throw out base runners who attempt to steal. He is the game general. Nothing happens until he gives the pitcher a sign for a pitch to throw.

Home plate is a rubber-topped plate that is anchored into the ground. It has five sides. The front side of the plate measures 17 inches wide. Two sides measure 8-1/2 inches each cut to a point of 12 inches each in the back. Remember, home plate and all the bases are in fair territory, so any ball hit by the batter that hits home plate or one of the bases and enters the field of play is a fair ball.

**The following illustration shows the dimensions.**

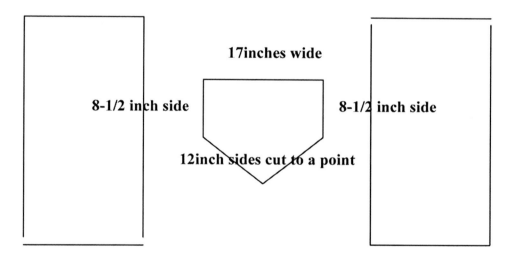

As a base runner, when you touch home plate, you either take a seat on the bench, or you take your position on the field to begin a new inning. In either case, you begin your preparation again just as you did last inning as every inning presents a new set of game parameters.

⌀ ⌀ ⌀

# CHAPTER 6

## The Teams

Half of the game of baseball is played on offense, and simultaneously half is played on defense. If properly coached, an opposing team will have done its homework in preparation for playing your team. It will have as many preconceived plans as to how they are going to play against you as you will have planned to use against them.

What pitching match up might they use to slow your scoring opportunities? What major or minor shifts in the offensive lineup might they make, no matter where you have seen them come to the plate in prior games? Remember again, baseball at any level is played one pitch at a time. This means that an advantage or disadvantage to both teams switches back and forth, simultaneously, on every pitch. There will be more about advantage and disadvantage later on. Your job on defense is to get the other team's players out without allowing them to score any runs.

## The Home Team versus the Visiting Team

The Home Team is the team that starts the game in the field, playing defense. The Visiting Team begins the game on offense by sending hitters to the plate. Let's focus our learning on the defensive team first.

## Defensive Team

The defensive team consists of nine team members with specific responsibilities playing their respective positions and backing up plays when necessary. As a defensive player, it is imperative that you learn each and every hitter's batting characteristics, on each and every team you play, so that you will know how and where to play against them when they come to the plate.

For purposes of this explanation, let's isolate on the lead off hitter for the Visitors. How big is he? How strong is he? Does he run, 1=Fast, 2= Fair, or 3=Slow. Does he take a lot of pitches because he is looking for one specific pitch? Does he usually hit the first pitch? Does he walk a lot? When he does swing, does he hit with power? When he hits the ball, where does the ball go most often? Does he **pull the ball** almost every time he goes to the plate? Is he one that you can look to drag bunt for a base hit? Is he a low-ball hitter or a high-ball hitter? Does he hit the breaking pitch, or does he look for the fastball?

*Let's make him a right-hand hitter, who most often hits the ball the opposite way to first, second, right center or straight away right field. A review of his success against your pitching will tell you all that you need to know.*

*Let's say he is hitting .325 against your team and .275 overall in the league against all other teams. It would seem that he likes your team's pitching! He has hit the ball poorly to short twice but has successfully bunted for base hits three times out of 40 at bats against your pitching. He has been safe on (or "legged") a number of slowly hit ground balls on the infield grass for base hits, but they have all been to the first base side of the infield. He has struck out 6 of his 40 appearances at the plate and has only hit the ball deep two times to straight center and right field out of the 40 at bats. He has no extra base hits. His 13 base hits have come on singles to right field over the second baseman and in the hole. Knowing all these facts, how do you plan to pitch against this hitter? How will you position your defense to take away his opportunities of getting on base? Before we settle on a new defensive strategy for this lead off hitter, let's review our previous experience with him from our record book.*

## Questions to Ask:

1. What has been our pitching strategy to this hitter in the past?
2. How can he hurt us offensively?
3. What can we do to take away his speed?
4. How can we change our defense to prevent the Drag Bunt for base hits?
5. How will we pitch him to prevent base hits to right with no power?

## Old Defensive Strategy:

Defense: Infield and outfield straight away.
Pitching: Fastballs in on hands for strikes to jam him
Breaking pitches outside and down to get him out
Results of Strategy: Hit .325 against us. Strategy not working!

## Analysis of Past Defensive Strategy:

1). Why throw fastballs inside **for strikes** when the hitter is a proficient drag bunter with no power? An inside fastball is a perfect location for a limited power hitter to attempt a drag bunt for a base hit, using speed down the line as the weapon of choice. We want to take the hitter's strengths away so we can't throw fastballs inside.

2). Hitter doesn't pull the ball, so throwing off speed breaking stuff away allows hitter to see the ball longer and make contact for base hits to right and right center. It also suggests that this hitter may be leaning out over the plate to make such contact on the away pitches.

## New Defensive Strategy:

- Bring outfielders in three or four steps
- Move left fielder toward center three or four steps
- Move center fielder four or five steps toward the right fielder
- Move right fielder five steps toward the right field line and in five steps
- Shorten up infielders from shortstop to first base by two or three steps to eliminate hitter's speed from the equation.
- Position third baseman three steps inside the bag (on the grass) and 5 feet from the line to prevent a freak double down the line and eliminate the possibility of an attempted drag bunt.

## New Pitching Strategy

With the new defensive strategy in place it will now be up to the pitcher to throw pitches that have a higher percentage of taking the hitter's advantage away. Hard sliders away out of the strike zone to get the hitter leaning over the plate, and hard fastballs in and up. All hard stuff! That means the pitcher will set the up for the strike out by moving the hitter back off the plate with a fastball in and up off the plate for a ball, throw hard breaking pitches outside for strikes to get him leaning, and then come back inside over the plate when we get to two strikes for the strike out. This takes away his bunting ability. **Nothing away or soft over the plate.** Jam the fastball K pitch in on the hands on the third strike.

The reasoning here is that the hitter has been thrown fastballs in but over the plate to bunt successfully for base hits. He has also seen off speed breaking pitches over the outside of the plate that he has hit away for singles. So since we have reset the defense, why shouldn't we continue to pitch him the same way? The answer to that question is that it's still a big field, and the defense has only been moved a few feet to try to stop this hitter from being successful. In the revised defensive scenario set out above, it might appear that we would continue to throw off speed pitches over the outside of the plate and fastballs inside to defend against this hitter as the defense is set up for balls hit to the right side of the infield. But this is precisely what has failed in the past against this hitter.

You must appreciate that if a hitter hits almost every pitch to the right side of the infield, he may be guilty of two or three things in his swing that causes him to hit the ball that way so consistently. Hitting the ball late is not a bad thing, especially when the pitches are thrown on the outside of the plate, which favors making contact early in the swing. But technically speaking, poor power and hitting everything late would suggest that the hitter is not seeing the pitch early enough to pull it, or he might not be strong enough to pull the ball, or the pitcher is pitching improperly with a defense set up straight away.

**Reasoning for the New Pitching Scheme**

By **showing this hitter** fastballs up inside **out of the strike zone**, we will try to straighten him up, then follow with hard breaking pitches outside and down in the strike zone. He will have more difficulty hitting the breaking pitch away when set up with **fastballs up and in.** He will also be more inclined to look at a hard fastball in for the strike out pitch. Should he make contact with the ball, your defense is set up to make the play for the out. The up and in fastball is tough to drag for a base hit because it straightens the hitter up and delays his exit from the batters box. It also sets up the hard fastball strikeout pitch scheduled for the low inside edge of the plate.

To reduce his attempts to drag bunt for base hits it becomes the pitcher's responsibility to throw hard fastballs up and in <u>at the chest, out of the strike zone for balls</u> as "set up" pitches, normally hard breaking curve balls, sliders or sinkers on the outside half of the plate. No off speed pitches should be thrown to this hitter because the data suggests that he can't get the bat around. So we will press him even more. The Strike Out pitch to him will be hard fastballs thrown down and in for strikes following either an up and in fastball or a hard breaking pitch outside off the plate. The pitcher should try to get the hitter leaning in and out and get him thinking about what pitches are coming. When he has done that, the hitter becomes less efficient at the plate. Right-handed hitters who are not natural pull-hitters have a tendency to wait a little longer before starting their swing on off-speed pitches. Their results will most often cause the ball to be hit straight away or more toward the second base side of the field. This changes when players get to the college and the professional level because most of them know their strike zones pretty well and are more difficult to set up. But almost everyone can be "worked" at the plate!

When a young pitcher is just learning the game, these are the types of confrontations with hitters that teach him, pitch by pitch, to think and use his brain, not just his arm. Successful outcomes separate the great prospects from the common everyday pitchers who just throw the ball with no aspirations of becoming a career baseball player. Now, back to the leadoff hitter.

Because of his speed this leadoff hitter will get some base hits on balls hit softly on the infield even if you properly defend against this opportunity. You have probably noticed that most plays at first base are very close. The runners are safe or out by only a half-step to a step and a half. So cheating forward one or two steps makes a great deal of difference when throwing across the infield to first base. Shortening the distance to first base tends to neutralize the speed of the runner. But there is a tradeoff here, as you have a split second less time to field the ball cleanly and get the throw off to first, especially if it's hit into the hole between third and short off a metal bat! Whew! There are always tradeoffs, because baseball is a game of inches.

Major league left-hand hitters with good speed, like the Ichiro Suzuki of the Seattle Mariners, can run to first from the left side between 3.4 and 3.5 seconds. Speedy right-hand hitters will go from the right side down the line from 3.7 to 3.8 seconds flat. So, as an infielder, if you shorten the distance to the plate a step or two, you take away one or two hundredths of a second speed advantage from him. All you have to do is field the ball cleanly and throw a strike to first base with something on it. When the infield shortens up, so should the outfield accordingly. It would depend on the inning and score of the game to place your team at such risk. You sort of dare them to hit the ball over your head, and sometimes they do. Then there is that "woops," where some opposing teams' player will have a great day and hit one in between the fielders or over their head for an extra base hit, or even go yard! The odds against that player doing it twice in the same game are pretty much in your favor, at least until you get to the high school level. Good hitters begin to take advantage of poorly thrown pitches in high school. When they are sixteen or seventeen years old, they begin to get physically stronger, grow in confidence at the plate, and have had many more trips to the plate against the same player personnel on the opposing teams. From Pony to Little League, American Legion and other types of summer ball, out through the end of their high school careers, most of the players within a given geographical area have usually played against each other for a number of years. The standout pitchers and hitters begin to separate themselves from the others due to raw talent, strength, personal desire to advance to higher levels of performance, and better execution of the fundamentals of the game.

As a middle infielder, second baseman or shortstop, your lateral movement toward the bag at second and into the holes at first and third must be a little quicker than normal because you are closer to the plate. But if you focus on the signs given by the catcher to the pitcher, you can anticipate where the ball may go off the bat from the pitch being thrown. Experienced infielders will angle back toward the outfield grass on hard hit balls in the holes rather than try to field that ball by angling straight across.

With full appreciation for the fact that the advanced review of the hitter above is a light year beyond where the beginning level player is able to think or respond, young and advanced coaches and players need to understand how to think the game. This keeps the great young prospects interested in playing the game and not leaving it for some other sport because they haven't learned to execute their position properly. Poor team results can be attributed to poor coaching, poor playing disciplines, improper player attitudes, poor parental support, limited talent, or a combination of all of them.

Bad habits acquired in a baseball player's early years are very difficult to break. Many bad habits are learned through improper coaching! This being said, there are different rules for different levels of baseball. The following list of bad habits is to give coaches things to look for when observing their young players actions on the field:

- Laziness – No self-discipline - no running or stretching before and after playing
- Catching with one hand instead of two
- Throwing sidearm (except for infielders)
- Incorporating a "hitch" in the swing as the ball is coming to the plate
- No communication with teammates during a play in the field
- Not sliding, sliding improperly, or ineffectively
- Throwing with arm only, not entire body
- Holding the ball incorrectly for the type of throw being made
- Not moving feet when catching every ball
- Throwing the ball inaccurately (without consistency)
- Not extending arms in front to catch a ball
- Poor attitude/Inattentiveness
- Throwing behind the runner

Most fledgling players need to learn the (very basic) fundamentals of the game before they get into playing the game itself. Such things as:

- How to wear a uniform
- How to hold the ball
- How to throw the ball
- How to catch the ball
- What to do with the ball when they get it
- Where the bases are located and why the bases are there
- How to get on base
- How to hold the bat
- How to hit a ball
- How to run the bases
- The importance of home plate
- What signs to look for in critical game situations
- What a strike zone is and how to learn to see pitches in it
- How to swing the bat properly
- How to "read" various pitches thrown by the pitcher

As you progress through the book you will begin to understand the need to learn and practice **THE FUN-DA-MENTALS** that will ultimately make the game fun to play. That's what it's all about.

⚾ ⚾ ⚾

# CHAPTER 7

## Proper Stretching Exercises

Coaches and players alike should learn the routines of mandatory before-and-after-game stretching exercises to lessen the chance of incurring an injury from a pulled or torn muscle, tendon, or ligament.

**FUN-DA-MENTAL: To lessen the chances of pulling muscles, tearing rotator cuffs or acquiring tendonitis in the knees, hips, shoulders or elbows, every player must stretch sufficiently before even thinking about throwing a baseball.**

So when you arrive at the baseball field, it is imperative to begin your warm up session by jogging no less than two complete laps around the entire playing field to warm up the body. When you have finished jogging, begin your standard regimentation of stretching exercises. Recommendations for a complete exercise program follow.

#1. **Neck and Shoulder Rotation:** From a standing position with feet spread at shoulder's width, hands on hips, gently begin a circular motion of the head in both a clockwise and counterclockwise direction for one minute in each direction. This action will unload tightness and stress in the neck and shoulders created during normal everyday activities.

#2. **Arm Rotation:** From a standing position with the feet spread at shoulder's width, reach your arms straight in front of your chest, rotate both arms slowly upwards to a position directly over your head, then slowly outward and downward to form a "T" and then move them back to the starting position. Do 10 repetitions of this motion. This is a gentle warm up motion that you can incorporate to loosen your shoulders and warm up the rotator cuff.

#3. **Circular Arm Rotation:** From a standing position with the feet spread at shoulder's width, reach your arms straight out from your shoulders to each side, forming a T with your body. With your chest held high, begin a circular motion (slowly) with large circles extending your hands from almost straight up to below your hips. Rotate your arms in a counterclockwise direction (backwards) for a minimum of 10 revolutions. At the end of the tenth revolution, begin to lessen the circumference (size)

of the circular motion for twenty more rotations, finally stopping with 4"
circles with your arms extended straight out to the side. Do not let your
arms drop as you carry out the rotations. Repeat this exercise in exactly
the same manner in reverse by circling in a clockwise rotation (forward)
with the large circles first, and finish out with very small, fast circles.

#4.    **Rotation at Waist:** From a standing position with the feet spread
at shoulder's width, place hands on hips and begin a circular motion of your
upper torso keeping your hips in a fixed position. Bend gently backwards at
the waist and half way down as you come forward in the rotation. Rotate
20 times clockwise and 20 times counterclockwise.

#5.    **Bending at Waist:** From a standing position with feet spread at
shoulder's width, place your hands on your hips and bend forward slowly
until you reach any point of stress or tension in your lower back. Do Not
Bounce your head down at this point! With slightly bent legs, bring your
hands to your knees and gently raise your head and body back up to a
straight standing position. Now bend down to the left and to the right.
This completes one revolution. Complete 20 revolutions of this routine.

#6.    **Hamstring Stretch:** Lying flat on your back, raise your right leg
straight up in the air to a point back over your head without bending it, as
far as it will go, without pain. Have one of your teammates hold your left
leg flat on the ground, as he <u>ever so gently</u> pushes your straight right leg
to a more upright position, then releases it, back to the ground. No pain
should be felt, just a firing of the muscles, then a full relaxation. Reverse the
procedure with the left leg up and carry out 20 stretches with each leg.

#7.    **Groin Stretch:** With legs apart beyond shoulder width and hands
placed on the top of the knees, bend sideways at the waist. Keeping the
right leg perfectly straight, lean your upper body out over your left leg and
bend it to begin a gentle stretch of your RIGHT inner thigh muscle. CAU-
TION: DO NOT BOUNCE THESE INNER THIGH MUSCLES! Reverse the
position in the opposite direction, stretching the upper LEFT inner thigh
area.

#8.    **Ankle and Knee Rotation:** Lying flat on the ground with arms
spread out wide at the shoulders, both legs perfectly straight with heels on
the ground, raise and bend right knee so that you can rotate right ankle

and knee in gentle circular motions. Carry out 10 to 20 rotations of both ankles and both knees.

#9.     **Hip Flexors:** Beginning from the same position on the ground with your arms extended outwards, bend your right knee to allow your right heel to be positioned as close to your right hip as possible in a modified hurdle position. Try to keep your right knee and all of your upper body as flat on the ground as possible. Hold this hip flexor stretch position for a maximum of 10 seconds before releasing the tension, then change over to the left leg.

#10.     **Back Stretch:** From a sitting position on the ground, spread your legs straight out in front of you forming a "V" Gently, bend straight forward, then out over each thigh, relaxing your lower back and breathing very fully. DO NOT BOUNCE! Lie back flat on the ground, and raise both knees up to your chest, aided by your hands if you wish, and then place them back flat on the ground. Carry out 20 repetitions of this exercise.

#11.     **Sciatic Nerve Stretch:** In exercise #6 above you stretched the large muscles in the back of your thighs, which are known as the hamstrings. These powerful muscles control the bending motion at the knee and are responsible for push off when you are on your feet. Because they are a long lever muscles and attach to the pelvis, the hamstrings must be well stretched every day to reduce the chance of straining or tearing them.

The hamstring muscles are controlled by the sciatic nerve. The top of the sciatic nerve is attached to the lower back at L4 and L5. It then penetrates the buttock and posterior hip muscles then continues down the outside of the thigh, knee, calf and ankle, to the bottom of the foot. It is helpful to visualize the anatomy in order to appreciate the various moves required to stretch the sciatic nerve. Nerves are meant to glide easily through muscles, however sometimes they are restricted by injury from swelling or scar tissue. While it is helpful to stretch the muscles, we do so in a static man-ner. This does not always assure good mobilization of the nerve within the muscles. In order to achieve this, we need to stretch dynamically or with movement. Following is an exercise to stretch the sciatic nerve. Please start this exercise by sitting on the edge of a firm surface with one leg straight out on a chair. Then move into position, placing the sciatic nerve on maximal stretch, as follows:

- 1st      bend forward at the waist / dropping the chin to the chest
- 2nd    rotate the hip inward slightly
- 3rd    keep the knee straight
- 4th    pull foot back / then point down and in

Then, because the nerve crosses the hip, knee and ankle joints, it is necessary to maintain a maximal stretch across all the joints except the one component you are working on. From a maximal stretch position, oscillate as follows:

- 1st    Raise and lower the chin to the chest
- 2nd    Slightly straighten and relax lower back
- 3rd    Rotate hip in and out (eg. slow log rolling)
- 4th    Slightly release and straighten the knee
- 5th    Pull foot back / then point down and in

Initially move each joint 5 to 10 repetitions in a *very small range of motion*.

**#12.   Abdominal, Oblique Crunches:** Lying flat on the ground, pull both knees up with your heels pulled back toward your seat. Cross your arms across your chest and begin a straight 10 inch roll-up motion with only your head and shoulders. This is known as a straight sit up. To maximize your efforts, come straight up off the ground about 4 inches and then gently force the left shoulder toward the right knee about 8 inches and return, then gently force the right shoulder toward the left knee about 8 inches and return to flat. Begin with 10 reps of this exercise on each side and increase to a maximum of 20 reps over a seven day period. The better shape your abdominals are in, the more aggressive the oblique movement can be carried out. **<u>Twisting at the top of the sit-up movement to strengthen these muscle groups can cause tremendous rotational stress on the lower back, which can lead to injury. Please exercise all major muscle groups with a large degree of caution.</u>**

Note: A powerful batting stroke begins with a tightening of the rectus abdominus muscles, better known as the stomach muscles, including the external abdominal oblique muscles, sometimes referred to as the internal and external intercostals. They take a lot of abuse and must be maintained throughout the season with a concentrated exercise program. If either muscle set is strained or torn, you will be out for a considerable time because they tend to heal very slowly.

#13.   **Shakeout:** Finally, assume the standing position and shake out your entire body from head to toe for twenty seconds.

You should now be ready to begin running 10 x 40 yard sprints. In the first three sprints, pick up the pace from jog to run and walk back to the start. By the fourth sprint, run wide open from start to finish. Remember, you're playing baseball, so start each sprint as if you were on first base getting a jump to steal second crossing the left leg over the right and driving off the outside edge of your right foot to complete the first step.

## Medical Explanation of Rotator Cuff Cause and Injury

You may have heard someone speak of having a sore arm. In extreme cases such soreness can be caused by straining or tearing the tendons that hold the arm bone into the (scapula) back of the shoulder. The following medical explanation will explain the injury that occurs to the shoulder muscles and tendons when they are hyper-extended, over used as in too many pitches when tired, stressed from throwing improperly, or throwing too hard without sufficient warm up. The injury is known as a torn rotator cuff.

> **<u>Rotator Cuff Injury Also Known as</u>**:
> Pitcher's Shoulder, Shoulder Impingement Syndrome, Swimmer's Shoulder, or Tennis Shoulder
>
> **<u>Definition</u> :**
> Rotator cuff tendonitis is an inflammation (irritation and swelling) of the tendons of the shoulder.
>
> **<u>Causes, Incidences, and Risk Factors:</u>**
> The shoulder joint is a ball and socket type joint wherein the top part of the arm bone (humerus) forms a joint with the shoulder blade (scapula). The rotator cuff holds the head of the humerus into the scapula.
>
> Inflammation of the tendons of the shoulder muscles can occur in sports, requiring the arm to be moved over the head repeatedly as in baseball, particularly pitching, swimming, tennis, and lifting weights

over the head. Chronic inflammation or injury can cause the tendons of the rotator cuff to tear. This type of injury can be career limiting.

**Risk of Injury:** The high risk factors are being over age 40 and the participation in sports or exercises that involve repetitive arm motion over the head, referred to above.

**FUN-DA-MENTAL:** The better the condition of a player's legs, the longer and stronger his arm will perform throughout a full season. Running and stretching are the secrets to a strong and injury free arm. Don't ever forget this as long as you play. It is more important to exercise and stretch repetitively than it is to throw repetitively during the season.

# CHAPTER 8

## Bursitis and Its Effect on Joints

An improper throwing motion is equally as dangerous to the body as aging and lack of conditioning. It is a direct cause for inflammation affecting the hips, back, and shoulders. Bursitis is a common problem that occurs when increased levels of stress are applied to the shoulder region. This additional stress can be generated from an improper throwing motion, or a tired arm trying to compensate for inadequate lower body support.

A physical impact, an improper joint motion, or out-of-sync rhythm with the rest of the body can cause enormous stress on the tendons in the elbows and shoulders, including the rotator cuff. Let's understand what bursitis is, what causes it, how it can be managed, and how to prevent it from ever happening to your arm.

## Anatomy of the Elbow and Shoulder

Bone chips, inflammation of the medial and lateral epicondyle tendons in the elbow, and stressing or tearing of the rotator cuff can be caused by any one of the following reasons: insufficient warming up and stretching, throwing too hard with a cold arm, snapping the wrist and elbow at the release point, improper throwing motion of the arm or body, and pushing a tired arm beyond its capacity to recover. A technical explanation of how such an injury affects the output of the arm for a tennis player is as follows. Injuries to baseball players, tennis players, and swimmers are caused by the same over use.

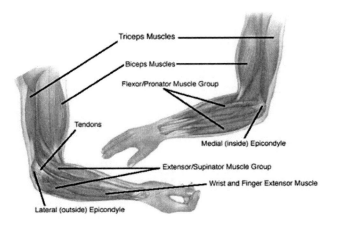

"Basically, tennis elbow is an overuse injury caused by repeated contractions of muscles connected to the elbow joint of the arm used to hit the ball. Stress on the elbow is inevitable, because some of the force created when the ball hits the racket automatically passes from the racket into the forearm and then to the elbow. This repeated impact produces trauma to the tissues surrounding the elbow, leading to inflammation and soreness. Unfortunately, continued play usually worsens the condition, heightens pain, and makes the elbow 'stiff,' the result of a thickening of the synovium, the lubricating membrane which surrounds the elbow joint. Routine activities such as turning a door knob, holding an umbrella, or shaking hands can become insufferable nightmares."

Now we know that there are a number of factors that can stress the elbow beyond its maximum output causing an inflammation of the epicondyle tendons. It is known as epicondylitis.

### What is bursitis?
(Copied exactly from MedicineNet.com) Bursitis is inflammation of a bursa. A bursa is a tiny fluid-filled sac that functions as a gliding surface to reduce friction between tissues of the body. There are 160 bursae (plural for bursa) in the body. The major bursae are located adjacent to the tendons near the large joints, such as the shoulders, elbows, hips, and knees.

### How does a bursa become inflamed?
A bursa can become inflamed from injury, infection (rare in the shoulder), or underlying rheumatic condition. Examples include injury as subtle as lifting a bag of groceries into the car to inflame the shoulder bursa (shoulder bursitis), infection of the bursa in front of the knee from a knee scraping on asphalt (septic prepatellar bursitis), and inflammation of the elbow bursa from gout crystals (gouty olecranon bursitis).

### How is bursitis diagnosed?
Bursitis is typically identified by localized pain or swelling, tenderness, and pain with motion of the tissues in the affected area. X-ray testing can sometime detect calcifications in the bursa when bursitis has been chronic or recurrent.

### How is bursitis treated?
The treatment of any form of bursitis depends on whether or not it involves infection. Bursitis that is not infected (from injury or underlying rheumatic disease) can be treated with ice compresses, rest, and anti-in-

flammatory and pain medications. Occasionally, it requires aspiration of the bursa fluid. This procedure involves removal of the fluid with a needle and syringe under sterile conditions. It can be performed in the doctor's office. Sometimes the fluid is sent to the laboratory for further analysis. Noninfectious shoulder bursitis can also be treated with an injection of cortisone medication into the swollen bursa. This is sometimes done at the same time as the aspiration procedure.

Infectious (septic) bursitis requires even further evaluation and aggressive treatment. The bursal fluid can be examined in the laboratory for the microbes causing the infection. Septic bursitis requires antibiotic therapy, sometimes intravenously. Repeated aspiration of the inflamed fluid may be required. Surgical drainage and removal of the infected bursa sac (bursectomy) may also be necessary. Generally, the adjacent joint functions normally after the surgical wound heals.

## GIRD

Injury to the throwing arm or shoulder may also be diagnosed as glenohumeral internal rotation deficit, or **GIRD**. Described as a possible link between the "tightness in the posterior inferior shoulder capsule, and shoulder/elbow problems, Gird disrupts the normal biomechanics of the shoulder, placing additional strain on supporting structures."

An explanation of the research can be found in the article "The Comeback Pitch" June 23, 2003 issue of ADVANCE for Physical Therapists & PT Assistants. In short, the higher the degree of flexibility in the shoulder capsule's connective tissue, the lower the strain on the supporting shoulder and elbow ligaments and tendons. So if the front of your shoulder or your elbow is sore from throwing, it is most likely caused by tightness in the back of your shoulder. Stop throwing immediately and start a rehabilitation program of stretching the back of your shoulder to regain needed flexibility. Usually, improper weightlifting techniques are the cause of this tightness. If you are doing free weight curls to build up your biceps, please stop throwing a baseball. Young arms cannot survive this stress. The following exercise program is designed to assist in recovering your arm's flexibility.

## Throwers TEN Exercise Program

The Throwers TEN Exercise Program is designed to strengthen and reha-bilitate the major muscles necessary for throwing and differs greatly from the warm up exercises 1-13 above. Its goal is to be an organized and con-cise exercise program. In addition, all exercises included are specific to the thrower and are designed to improve strength, power and endurance of the shoulder's complex musculature.

The following set of exercises was provided by Jill M. Boorman, Physical Therapist and Clinical Director of PREMIER Physical Therapy, located in North Charleston, South Carolina. Please note that most of the exercises below are held for a maximum of two seconds.

**CAUTION: This is not a program where you try to run up 100 sets of 100 reps! Please follow the instructions to the letter to avoid injury. Thanks, the management!**

1A.   **Diagonal Pattern D2 Extension:**
Involved hand will grip tubing or handle overhead and out to the side. Pull tubing across your body to the opposite side of your leg. During the motion, lead with your thumb.

**1B.  Diagonal Pattern D2 Flexion:**
Gripping tubing handle in hand of involved arm, begin with arm out from side 45 degrees and palm facing backward. After turning palm forward, proceed to flex elbow, and bring arm up and over uninvolved shoulder. Turn palm down, reverse to take arm to starting position. Exercise should be performed in controlled manner.

**2A.  External Rotation at 0 degrees Abduction:**
Stand with involved elbow fixed at side, elbow at 90 degrees, involved arm across front of body. Grip tubing handle, while the other end of tubing is fixed. Pull out with arm, keeping elbow at side. Return tubing slowly and controlled.

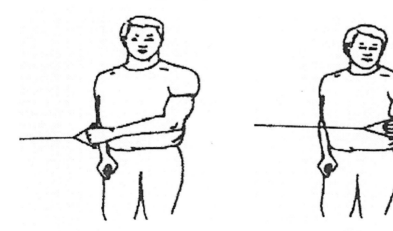

**2 B.** **Internal Rotation at 0 degrees Abduction:**
Stand with elbow at side, fixed at 90 degrees and shoulder rotated out. Grip tubing handle while other end of tubing is fixed. Pull arm across body keeping elbow at side. Return tubing slowly and controlled.

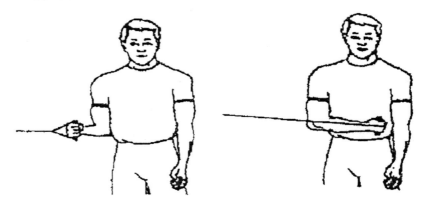

**2 C.** **External Rotation at 90 degrees Abduction:**
Stand with shoulder abducted 90 degrees and elbow flexed 90 degrees. Grip tubing handle while the other end is fixed straight ahead, slightly lower than the shoulder. Keeping shoulder abducted, rotate shoulder back keeping elbow at 90 degrees. Return tubing and hand to start position.

**2 D.  Internal Rotation at 90 degrees Abduction:**
Stand with shoulder abducted to 90 degrees, externally rotated and elbow bent to 90 degrees. Keeping shoulder abducted, rotate shoulder forward, keeping elbow bent at 90 degrees. Return tubing and hand to start position.

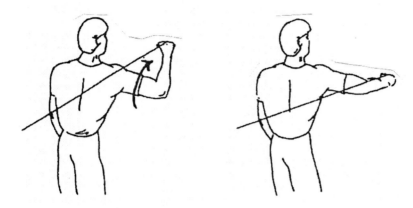

**3.  Shoulder Abduction to 90 degrees:**
Stand with arm at side, elbow straight, and palm against side. Raise arm to the side, palm down, until arm reaches 90 degrees, shoulder lever. Hold two seconds and lower slowly.

**4.**   **Scaption, Internal Rotation:**
Stand with elbow straight and thumb up.  Raise arm to shoulder level at 30 degree angle in front of body.  Do not go above shoulder height.  Hold two seconds and lower slowly.

**5A.**   **Prone Horizontal Abduction (Neutral):**
Lie on table face down with involved arm hanging straight to the floor, and palm facing downward.  Raise arm out to the side, parallel to the floor.  Hold two seconds and lower slowly.

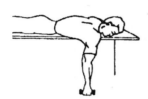 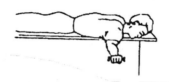 

**5B.**   **Prone Horizontal Abduction**
**Full ER, 100 degree ABD:**
Lie on table, face down, with involved arm hanging straight to floor and thumb rotated up like a hitch hiker.  Raise arm out to the side with arm slightly in front of shoulder, parallel to the floor.  Hold two seconds and lower slowly.

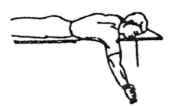 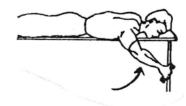

**6.**     **Press ups:**
Seated on a chair or a table, place both hands of the sides of the seat, palms down and fingers pointed outward. Hands should be placed equal to shoulders. Slowly push downward through the hands to elevate your body. Hold the elevated position for two seconds and lower body slowly.

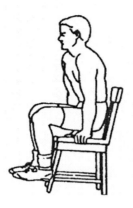

**7.**     **Prone Rowing:**
Lying on your stomach with your involved arm hanging over the side of the table, dumbbell in hand and elbow straight. Slowly raise arm, bending elbow, and bring dumbbell as high as possible. Hold at top for two seconds, then slowly lower.

8. **Push-Ups:**
Start in the down position with arms in a comfortable position. Place hands no more than shoulder-width apart. Push up as high as possible, rolling shoulders forward after elbows straighten. Start with a push-up into a wall, then gradually progress to a table top and finally to floor as tolerable.

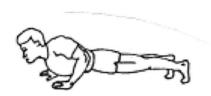 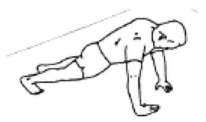

9A. **Elbow Flexion:**
Standing with arm against side and palm facing inward, bend elbow upward turning palm up as you progress. Hold two seconds and lower slowly.

**9B.** **Elbow Extension – Abduction:**
Raise involved arm overhead. Provide support at elbow from uninvolved hand.
Straighten arm overhead. Hold for two seconds.

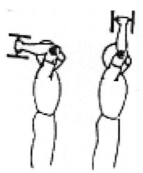

**10A.** **Wrist Extension:**
Supporting the forearm and with palm facing downward, raise weight in hand as far as possible, hold for two seconds, and lower slowly.

**10B.** **Wrist Flexion:**
Supporting the forearm and with palm facing upward, lower a weight in hand as far as possible and then curl it up as high as possible. Hold for two seconds and lower slowly.

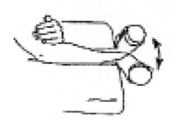

**10C.  Supination:**

Forearm supported on table with wrist in neutral position.  Using a weight or hammer, roll wrist taking palm up.  Hold for two seconds and return to starting position.

**10D.  Pronation:**

Forearm should be supported on a table with wrist in neutral position.  Using weight or hammer, roll wrist taking palm down.  Hold for two seconds and return to starting point.

Upon completion of this set of exercises for a period of two weeks of daily workouts you should begin to see some real results from your efforts.

# CHAPTER 9

## The Baseball

Now that we have made it through our warm up session, cracked a light sweat without pulling anything, let's learn some facts about the baseball itself.

**The Baseball:** As described in the Major League Baseball Official Rule Book

**9.09** **The ball** shall be a sphere formed by yarn wound around a small core of cork, rubber or similar material, covered with two strips of white horsehide or cowhide, tightly stitched together. It shall weigh not less than five nor more than 5-1/4 ounces avoirdupois and measure not less than nine nor more than 9 1/4 inches in circumference. That's all there is to it.

# CHAPTER 10

### How to Hold and Throw a Baseball

This section is very important for a young player or coach to study and learn for a number of reasons. First of all, the ball is sewn together with two strips of white horsehide. Both pieces of leather are shaped like the number eight (**8**). When you fit these two pieces together and stitch them up around a center of tightly wound yarn and a fluid center core, you end up with two sets of seams close together, and four open circular areas. When working with each other about how to hold and throw a particular pitch, it is vitally important to be talking about the same thing. Otherwise it would be apples and oranges, right?

So for the purpose of learning how to hold a baseball, we will call either set of two seams that are close together, the "TOP" of the ball, as shown in A. below. The open areas on either side of these two seams will be referred to as the "LOOPS," and the four (4) long seams between the TOP of the ball and the bottom of the LOOPS will be known as the cross seams, or long seams, as shown in B.

**Top of Ball**    **Four Seam or Cross Seam**

A                              B

If you are right-handed, take the ball in your hands and place your right in-dex or first finger on the left seam of the two on the **TOP** of the ball. Now place your middle or second finger on the right seam next to it. Place your thumb straight under the bottom of the ball in the open spot between the two close seams. This is known as a **Two Seam Fastball grip.**

## Two Seam Grip

A                                    B

You may wish to slide your fingers a ½ inch or so forward, over the top of the ball and hold it with a slightly wider fingertip grip, as shown in B. This places the fingers over the seams a little wider apart but right under the fingertips. The further out toward your fingertips you are able to hold the ball, the faster it will go. The further back in your hand you hold the ball, the more speed you will scrub off. So hand and finger strength is a very important factor when learning to throw. Finger strength also plays an important part in preventing soreness up into the elbow. When the fingers are stronger, you are able to grip the ball firmly but not so tight as to flex the muscles, tendons and ligaments up into the elbow structure during your delivery.

Now rotate the ball in your hand to the right so the two close-together seams on the TOP of the ball are seen coming out to the left from between your thumb and forefinger as if you were about to eat the name right off the ball. This hand position places your fingers across two of the four long seams that continue under and beyond your index and middle finger into the loop. Place the first joint of the index and middle finger over the seam. Your thumb should be located comfortably under the ball directly below your fingers, with the crease in your thumb on the seam about half way into the bottom of the loop. Be careful not to position it too far off to one side or the other. The third (ring finger) should be positioned as far down the right side of the ball as is comfortable, depending upon the size of your hands. Actually, the only part of the finger touching the ball is the knuckle of the third finger against the seam. When thrown properly, this grip will create under rotation of the four long seams that will keep the ball more on line to its target. It will also provide increased lift, enabling the ball to carry a greater distance. Holding the ball across the long seams is known as a *Four Seam* or *Cross Seam Fastball Grip*.

### Four Seam or Cross Seam Fastball Grip

A                                                                              B

If you are a beginner, or just happen to have small hands, the position of the fingers IN LINE WITH the TOP TWO SEAMS may be a little uncomfortable for you to hold. You may wish to turn the ball in your hands so that your index and middle fingers grip the ball across the TOP TWO SEAMS, as shown below.

### Two Seam Cross Seam Grip

 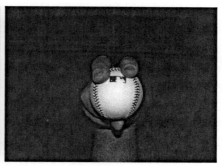

A                                                                              B

This will position your thumb between the close seams at the bottom of the loop on the underside of the ball. It may help in gripping the ball a little more firmly until your fingers and hands get a little longer and stronger. A ball thrown with this grip will remain relatively straight in flight. Movement can be generated by changing the angle of the wrist at the moment of release from the fingers. But, as this chapter proposes, when you are learning to throw, movement of the ball is of little or no importance.

## Proper Body Position to Throw a Baseball

The following section is one of the most important areas of this book as it establishes all the basic body movements to throw a ball properly from any arm position. This is all Fun-da-mentals.

## Lower Body Mechanics:

These instructions are meant for infielders and outfielders only. Pitchers and catchers have to deal with an entirely different set of circumstances that we will get into later on. So throwing a ball properly begins with both legs bent at the knees, from slight to extreme, depending on the type of throw being made.

For the beginner, when playing easy catch, the left foot (right-hand thrower) should be picked up and swung slightly around in front of the right leg and then back toward the target with toes of the left foot ending up pointing **almost** directly to the target. Simultaneously, as the left leg begins this counter rotation, the hips, upper body, and shoulders coil over the right leg and then uncoil back to the target all in the same continuous motion. In perfect synchronization with the hips and shoulders leading the upper torso unloading toward the target, the throwing arm comes forward in the delivery phase with the right foot pushing off to support the full rotation of the upper body. The loading and unloading of the right side takes the stress off the arm and shoulders during the execution of a throw from almost any position.

## Hands and Feet

In a real game situation, an infielder's hands should never drop when catching and throwing a wide open shoulder high throw during the double play "pivot" phase. Both hands should remain "shoulder high" and "quick" in their "rhythmic catch and release" relay of the ball to its intended target. Dropping the hands only takes time to return upwards in the delivery motion giving the runner a step advantage. The speed of the infielder's feet through this transition generates faster hand speed. The better the balance, the better the throw!

If the throw to the bag is low or off to one side or the other, a quick re-setting of the pivot man's feet will help adjust the player's lower body into the correct position to make the relay throw to first. A low incoming throw should be caught and relayed from that low position. Whether it is from sidearm or underhanded is of no consequence. There is no time to straighten up to throw the ball over the top. Possessing the capability to complete the double play with this type throw is what makes a shortstop or second baseman a great double play partner.

There will be many occasions where an infielder will have to throw the ball to first base on the dead run off either foot, from underneath or sidearm. The instructions above are not meant for those instances. They are meant strictly for the infielder turning a normal double play. Remember every inch and every split second in the game of baseball is important. In many cases, during game conditions, neither infielders nor outfielders will have the time to throw the ball properly because TIME IS of the essence.

## Upper Body Mechanics

In a normal right-handed (opposite for left-hand throwers) throwing motion, the upper body should be bent forward 4" to 6" at the waist, and it should rotate clockwise over and around the right hip with a comfortable majority of the player's weight loading the right leg. This position allows the left foot to be picked up and planted forward toward the target, followed by the unloading of the hips, upper torso, shoulders and arms, for the ultimate release of the ball supported by the drive of the right side.

With the ball held in the right-hand, the infielder's arm comes forward in sync with the dynamic opening of the upper body to deliver the throw. As an integral part of the catch and throw pivot at second base, the player's glove hand should move up to a position just below the right shoulder. This places the bent left elbow suspended across the front of the chest, about 6" under the chin. After catching the ball, the player's chin should be turned directly into the left shoulder with both eyes on the intended target, if possible. The quick opening of the left elbow aids in a complete shoulder rotation to the release point of the throw.

Remember that throwing a baseball is a continuous loading and unloading of the back leg to generate arm speed from the legs up and out through the arm. So as the hips open, they are aided by the glove-hand elbow, pulling laterally to the left to assist in squaring the shoulders back to the target. The throwing arm should be in sync with the opening of the left side of the body, as the right elbow leads a comfortably extended right arm on its path to the target. The player then lets go of the ball at the appropriate "release point" for it to travel the desired speed, line and trajectory to the target. An entire chapter on the release point follows.

## Controlling the Direction of a Thrown Ball

Why are all these mechanics so important to know and understand? Because, if you don't know where the ball is going, either something is wrong with your throwing mechanics, your grip on the ball is incorrect, or your feet are not setting the proper base from which to throw. If your throws never, ever, get to their intended target, there is a reason. And the reason may be one or many. You may just be physically lazy. If so, you need to work on quickening all of your physical actions. If you are able to throw hard, meaning fast, and you are throwing a reasonable distance, but the ball slides away from your target it may be the way you are holding the seams. For example, if you hold the TOP two seams with your index and middle fingers, with your thumb naturally hooked underneath, the ball will spin off your fingertips. There is very little carry on a two-seam grip. If you want the ball to track longer in a straight-line trajectory, switch to the cross seam grip and throw it with a three-quarter to overhand arm angle. The four long seams will rotate under to over, giving it lift and carry to its target. When the ball gets to its target you will be a much happier camper, right?

The direction of the spin on the ball is controlled not only by the manner in which you grip the ball but also by the angle of your arm, wrist, and hand when the ball comes off the ends of your fingertips. The arm, wrist and hand angle can vary from straight overhead, to three-quarters, to sidearm, to an underarm or submarine delivery, where the ball is actually released toward its target from a release point somewhere between the hip and knee.

**CAUTION: The consistent use of an underarm motion is not recommended for young players because it is extremely stressful to the lower back, the elbow and the shoulder muscles. Utilizing this motion will develop an entirely different shoulder motion by throwing underarm style. To transition from an underarm motion to a normal throwing motion will be a very difficult task and will not come without an enormous amount of stretching and retraining of the back, arm and elbow structures.**

As the arm and wrist angles move downward from straight up at the moment of release, the release from the fingertips will cause the ball to spin with increasing degrees of vertical spin or rotation. The amount of spin and the direction of the spinning seams will cause the ball to move or curve in the direction of that spin.

So in all good logic, it is obvious that a ball thrown over greater distance will have a tendency to move further in the direction of the spin put on it by the way in which the fielder holds and releases the ball toward his target. The player to whom the ball is being thrown must make an immediate adjustment with his feet and glove position to catch off-line throws as soon as he recognizes the throw is off line. The player receiving the throw will know whether or not the flight of the ball is on-line before the ball is even half way there, because it will continue to move in the direction the seams are spinning. So if it is offline to begin with, it will be even more offline as it continues its flight. This paragraph is very important to understand.

Outfielders try to keep the ball on line to the target, so they attempt to hold the ball across the four long seams and release it with their fingers almost straight up in an overhand arm motion. In situations where an in-fielder or outfielder doesn't have time to find the seams or throw correctly, he must rely on his experience to know how far off the target line (to the left or right) he has to throw the ball for it to end up at its target. By knowing the distance he is from the target, he releases the ball accordingly to compensate for its movement in flight. As an example, if a right-handed right fielder throws a ball to third base with four or five feet of movement of the ball in flight, the ball will end up at the base if the throw was started four or five feet to the left of third base. However, if the ball is started **AT third base**, the ball will be four to five feet to the right of its target when it arrives at third. That's what I'm talkin' about!! That's why both the third baseman and the catcher need the pitcher to back them up in the event a throw gets by either of them.

# CHAPTER 11

## The Release Point and Why It Is so Important

You've probably heard a lot about the release point. Here is an explanation of what it is and why it is so very important that you learn it early in your playing career.

**FUN-DA-MENTAL:** The **release point of any throw** is the precise moment in the throwing motion when the ball comes off the fingertips of the hand toward its intended target. The release point governs the trajectory of the ball to a specific target. As shown in the previous chapter, the flight of the ball is directly affected by three factors: the speed of the throw, the direction of the rotation of the seams on the ball at release, and the distance the ball must carry to the target. We are now going to learn how the release point affects the trajectory of the throw.

### Learning Your Release Point

Always try to throw the ball to a specific spot every time you throw it. For example, when you are playing catch with a friend or warming up for a game, remember to warm up your body first before even touching a ball. Then warm up your arm at a distance of no less than 60 feet if you are a Little Leaguer, or at 90 feet if you play on a full sized diamond.

Warming up at a distance less than 60 feet does not effectively stretch out the muscles as you begin your throwing motion. There aren't many plays in the game of baseball that require a **consistent** throw of less than 90 feet, except between the pitcher, catcher and first baseman, and the shortstop and second baseman on a double play—the word consistent being the operative word here. So warm up your body with the exercises, and warm up your arm by throwing a distance that will truly stretch out your arm and shoulder muscles. As you mature, your arm will warm up faster using this routine, and you will, by your own individual consistency, be training your mind to release the ball at a precise point in your throwing motion to make the ball go where you want it to go. This exact moment of letting go of the ball (as in C. next page) at a specific point is the **RELEASE POINT**. Pitchers in particular must learn their release point for each and every pitch they throw because it is slightly different for each one.

Sequence shows release point at C.

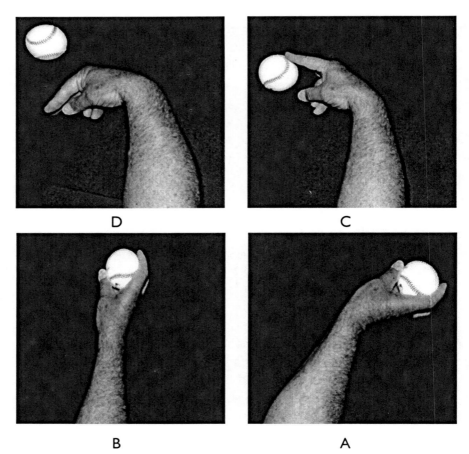

D

C

B

A

When you are warming up, try to throw every ball at your teammate's throwing arm shoulder. Why the throwing arm shoulder you ask? Because this is where you should throw the ball in a game situation, it will be automatic. A ball thrown up and at the **throwing arm shoulder** is the easiest spot for the receiving player to see the ball, the best spot for the receiving player to catch the ball with both hands, and the fastest location for the receiving player to get his throwing hand on the ball to relay it on to **his** target. That's why!

The confidence gained in throwing the ball wide open in game conditions to the player's throwing shoulder every time without missing is accomplished by practicing and learning your own release point for the type throw you are making. A good exercise is to stand 40 feet apart from your partner and throw the ball back and forth twenty times as quickly as you are able.

On each and every throw you should move your feet to set up your body every time you catch a throw, until someone throws wildly or drops the ball. Then start all over. It won't take long before you learn what I am talking about. The speed of the incoming ball, the quick catch, grab, and release back to the other player develops fast hands and greater confidence between the two of you, especially when all the throws are controlled to the other's throwing shoulder. Try it, you'll like it!

The release point will vary by only a few inches for most throws you make in a game and will be determined by the speed of the runner and the type of throw you are making at that moment. The type of throw necessary will depend upon how hard the ball was hit, where the ball was hit, and how fast the runner can get down the line.

For example, if you are playing shortstop, you may field a hard hit ground ball right at you and have time to step up and throw it over-handed to get the best rotation on the ball to carry the distance to first in the shortest amount of time. This type of throw requires one release point. In the same game, you may get a chance to complete a double play started by the second baseman, by throwing the ball from second to first in a side arm or even underarm motion, making the runner slide to protect yourself from being knocked down.

You may be the start of a play at second by making a short, off balance, underhanded shuffle toss to the second baseman on a ground ball hit near the bag for a force out.

And finally, you may have to be the relay man for a deep drive to the wall. You would then position yourself about 30-40 feet out from the base you are lining up for the outfielder, and, depending upon the accuracy of the throw, let it go, relay it, or cut it off for a throw to an alternate base. A relay requires a **blind turn and fire** type throw. You must be aware of exactly where you are on the field, because each of these throws requires a slightly different point of release to get the ball to its target.

## A Little Side Story

When my arm was really starting to develop at about 9 or 10 years old, I asked my Dad if he would play catch with me in the back yard of our home. After retrieving several of my wild throws from the geraniums behind him, he handed his glove to me laughingly and suggested that when I could throw more accurately he would be more inclined to work with me. In other words, if you're going to throw like that, do it with your buddies, NOT WITH ME! Not wanting to lose him as a throwing partner, I began to throw rocks by the thousands in the hills behind our home. In a short time I learned to control my release point for each of the different weighted rocks that I was throwing, and in doing so developed a very strong and accurate arm. Needless to say, my Dad was quite happy.

About this same time in my development, my best neighborhood friend and I would head down to the local park and throw every day, all summer long, for hours, back and forth, from street to street. We used one ball so much the cover came off. I remember we wrapped it with masking tape to get a few more days out of it before school started up again.

In order to keep these throws "in play," without bouncing the ball into in someone's front yard or getting it caught up in the tree branches, we had to throw it about 250 feet, and right on target. This is where I perfected my release point and it never left me.

**FUN-DA-MENTAL: To develop a strong and accurate throwing arm you must throw long distances at a high velocity (rate of speed) to learn your release point.**

Your eyes are your visual compass for the accuracy of your arm. If you don't look where you are throwing the ball, you can't possibly know when to release the ball from your fingers. There is one exception to this thought, and that is that most shortstops and second baseman turning a double play don't really have to see the first baseman to get the ball close enough for the out. It is by rote physical memory that the ball's flight during a double play ends up pretty close to first base. But, only after thousands of throws, can you expect to develop that degree of accuracy. The purpose of throwing the ball at a specific target every time is to develop visual memories in your brain from your eyes, and muscle memories from your back and legs out through your arm and fingers. Once all these components are sufficiently trained and in sync with each other they will respond accurately for as long as you are able to keep them tuned up.

**FUN-DA-MENTAL: Never take your eyes off your target when catching or throwing a baseball. Your eyes are your arms GPS system.**

Once you have gained control of your release point, you can throw balls to any location accurately and without hesitation. Practice throwing 90' from different body positions, bent over, moving to your left, off the wrong foot, and backing up, as you will probably have to do one or all of them at some moment in your playing career. Notice how each change in arm position and release point makes the ball move differently (looping or fading) as it carries toward the target. These directional changes are caused by the varying angles of your wrist, hand, and fingertips, at the point of release. The trajectory of the throw is also affected by how you grip the ball, with or across the seams, the distance to the target, and even the direction of the wind. You don't ever want these types of situations to be a surprise. Be Ready! Practice throwing into a box from 90 feet!

The harder (faster) you throw a baseball, the more exact your release point must be because of your increased arm speed. To be absurd and over em-phasize the importance of the proper release point, if you hang on to the ball too long when throwing it hard, it might end up hitting the ground a few feet in front of you. If you release the ball too early, in the top of your throwing motion, the trajectory of the ball might be over the roof of your house! Certainly, it won't be anywhere close to the person to whom you are intending it to go.

Throwing a baseball is a perfectly coordinated and sequential motion start-ing with your feet, moving up through your legs, your hips and upper torso, your shoulders, arms, hands, and ultimately your fingertips. To throw prop-erly, each of these elements must coordinate perfectly to achieve maximum output from your delivery. Body rhythm, body rhythm, body rhythm!

When a pitcher throws a fastball in the dirt in front of home plate it was ei-ther intentional, trying to get the hitter to chase a bad pitch, or more often, he hung on to the ball a split second too long before releasing it. Hanging on to the ball too long is a mechanical error and can be corrected by mak-ing incremental adjustments in the delivery side of the pitcher's physical motion to the plate.

So it is necessary to appreciate that the longer you hang on to the ball before releasing it towards your target, the lower and flatter its trajectory will be depending upon how far and how hard you are throwing. To throw a ball a long distance, you would need to release the ball earlier in your motion to get the proper upward angle to reach your intended target further away.

⚾ ⚾ ⚾

# CHAPTER 12

## The Act of Catching a Baseball

Now that you have become relatively proficient in the proper positioning of your fingers on the ball, throwing the ball a reasonable distance, and almost always to the intended throwing shoulder of a teammate, you must be ready to catch it when it is thrown back to you.

When beginners start to play catch with a hard ball for the first time, the normal tendency is to close their eyes, turn their head away from the incoming monster, hold the glove "palm up" and out somewhere in the space around them, hoping the ball will land in the pocket. When I see that, I cringe. All I want to do is to dress them in a steel helmet with an attached facemask, a set of football shoulder pads, a chest protector and a full set of ice hockey pants with all the padding, so they won't get hurt.

## Gravity

Actually, catching a baseball is quite simple if you understand physics. What goes up must come down. Sir Isaac Newton discovered the force of gravity when an apple that had fallen from a tree he was sitting under hit him on the head. Why did it fall downward to the ground, he contemplated. He discovered that the gravitational force of the earth caused objects in flight within its atmosphere to be pulled down by it at a rate of 32 feet/sec/sec. This he proved to be the force of gravity caused by the rotation of the earth. It equates to about 120+ mph at terminal velocity. Gravity is the reason that a ball thrown from one player to another drops in its flight path when thrown over a considerable distance. If we were playing on the moon where the gravitational force is ten times less than that of the earth, the ball would continue in its flight path 10 times the distance before angling downward.

So knowing this, in order to catch a ball, all you need to do is open the palm of your glove and insert it into the exact flight path of the incoming ball. With your eyes fixed on the flight of the ball your hands will go automatically to the path of the ball. With a relaxed glove hand, you merely allow the pocket of the glove to absorb the ball by allowing the glove to recoil backwards three or four inches at impact. Practicing this method of catching will develop naturally "soft hands." Based upon the speed of the incoming ball, the ball may drop short of you if it is not thrown far enough or hard enough. If it hasn't been thrown directly into the ground on purpose, gravity has most likely taken over and pulled it downward. In other words, the ball was not thrown hard enough to carry the intended distance, or the release point of your teammate was too late. You always want to play catch by throwing the ball on a line, or flat trajectory, to the other player, so the flight of the ball is less affected by the pull of gravity, and it's a lot easier to catch with something on it. Crank it!! No "Annie, Annie Over" throws, OK? Make it "pop" in the pocket of the glove.

The opposite of soft hands would be for a player to stick a stiff glove-hand out to catch an incoming throw and have it strike the hard pocket surface without allowing a little recoil of the glove hand. In a majority of cases the ball will bounce out before the natural action of the glove can close over it. This stiff style of catching is called "board hands." One solution to a player with stiff hands is to concentrate on positioning the palm of his throwing hand directly on the back of the left thumb of the glove at impact. The right-hand will close the thumb over the ball in the pocket and allow his throwing fingers to creep around the glove thumb to grip the ball and return it.

One drill that infielders practice is catching and throwing a ball back and forth to each other as fast as they can without dropping it or throwing wildly. This exercise develops what is known as "fast hands." In these practice sessions, the incoming ball hardly touches the pocket of the glove before the free hand grabs it and throws it back.

*In Baltimore's Minor League Spring Training of 1959 I witnessed an ex-New York Yankee catcher receive pitches from one of our rookie pitchers with a one-foot long 2"x4" board. The purpose of the demonstration was to teach all of us that a thrown ball need not be caught in the deepest part of the pocket of any glove, but should only make momentary contact with the center of the pocket to slow the ball down. As the ball struck the 2x4, his throwing hand was right underneath it to catch the ricochet off the board. After he had caught 10 or 15 throws around 85 miles per hour I was convinced he knew his stuff.*

Second basemen work hard on catching the ball in a very shallow manner by pushing the palm of the hand at the ball to widen and flatten the pocket. This "flattening out" of the pocket allows them to get their throwing hands on the ball for a very quick catch and release pivot, which becomes their double play rhythm.

**FUN-DA-MENTAL: For the maturing player, you will develop faster hands by catching, gripping, and releasing all of the throws that come to you by pushing out the center of the pocket of your glove to almost flat at the moment the ball strikes the leather, catching the ricochet in your throwing hand.**

First of all, if you are a beginner, you will have all the tendencies of looking away, as I stated above. The secret to catching the ball is to keep your eyes on it all the way into the glove. Never close your eyes on an incoming throw of any kind! Secondly, when playing catch or fielding a throw in a game, you will not be catching curve balls, sliders, sinkers or screwballs. The throws will be relatively straight, so the line on which they are thrown will remain constant until the ball hits your glove. The only variation in this thought process, as I explained above, is if the ball has been thrown from some odd arm position causing the seams to pick up some of the air currents. It will move gently in a constant direction. If the throw starts out moving toward your glove hand early in its flight, it will continue to move in that direction until it gets to you.

What you must learn to do as the receiver of this throw is move your feet quickly and accurately to position your upper body at the point where you can catch it in your glove in front of your throwing shoulder, if possible.

**FUN-DA-MENTAL: Quickly resetting your feet to position your body in front of the ball is the first component in catching a ball efficiently and effectively. The second is to extend your arms out in front of you so you can *see the ball* into the glove. It is difficult to see the ball into your glove when the glove is held too close to your body.**

**Glove Positions to Catch Incoming Throws**

Now, put your glove on your hand and stand in front of a mirror. Relaxing both your arms down at your side, let the palm of the glove hang fingers downward. Assuming you are right-handed, the glove is on your left-hand. Now, turn the glove counterclockwise, thumb to the left, until you can see the fully opened pocket in the mirror. Hold it right there. From this position, raise your arm away from your hip to begin an arc up and over your head with the open glove pocket still facing the mirror, to a position directly over your head. When you continue the arc downward on your right side, your left elbow will pass in front of your face. At this point, in order to keep the pocket of the glove open to the mirror, you have automatically turned the glove to a **"backhand"** position to continue seeing the open pocket in the mirror down to your right hip. This is the proper position to catch any ball that is coming to you in any area of that arc, with your face being the center of the arc. Now add the right-hand behind the thumb of the glove for a perfect two handed catch anywhere in this arc. However, the ability to catch a ball in the backhand position does not necessarily mean that you could not have taken one or two steps to the right to catch the ball directly in front of you. This would be the better of the two options. **<u>Always move your feet</u>** on every incoming throw to get into the best position to receive the ball.

Your feet should be shoulder width apart with your knees slightly flexed or bent. To catch a throw coming to you from your belt buckle down to your feet on the glove side, keep the palm facing "open to the mirror," from fully extended to the side, inward to the middle of your spread stance (half way between your feet). At a point where you cannot lay your palm open any further to the right, a point somewhere from mid-way between your feet and toward your right foot and beyond, you must rotate the glove over into the backhand position to catch balls arriving in that area. You will be looking at the back of the fingers of the glove in this backhand position.

You should try to catch any ball thrown at your belly button with the fingertips of the glove facing downward with the palm of the hand facing upwards and open to the ball. The throwing hand should be almost touching the little finger of the glove to close the pocket as the ball is caught.

On an incoming throw to your right side, at or above the waist where you cannot catch it comfortably with the fingers pointed downward is the point where you rotate the glove hand to a "fingers pointed to the right" and catch everything, from there to high above your head, with your eyes looking under, over, or around the back of the glove.

Previously, I suggested that your feet are the most important factor in catching a baseball. Anytime it is possible to do so, you must move your feet in front of every incoming throw to catch it in the most efficient manner. Whether the ball is thrown to you high left or low right, from close in or from a distance, you must learn to shift your feet during the flight of the ball to field the throw in front of you, rather than reaching with one hand to make the catch. However, if you are playing first base and catching a throw from across the diamond you must keep one of your feet on the base for the runner to be called out. This is the exception to the rule above. And there may be others, but whose counting!

One of the best games that any baseball player can use to prepare to catch odd bouncing balls is to engage in the game of "pepper." Pepper is played with three or four players fielding grounders hit back to them by a single hitter. The players stand about fifteen feet from the batter and catch every ball the batter hits back to them. It's a quick game that allows each fielder an opportunity to quickly catch many grounders and throw strikes to the hitter who, in turn, sharpens his eye on the ball by hitting controlled shots back to each fielder. Pepper has been played for a hundred years or more as a means of sharpening both the hitter's bat control and the infielder's fielding and throwing abilities.

**FUN-DA-MENTAL: Move your feet in front of every incoming throw to position your body and hands in the best location to catch the ball. Lazy feet cause a lazy and inaccurate arm.**

**Catching a throw with two hands versus one is the secret to fewer errors, and always taking the ball out of your glove upwards toward your throwing shoulder is mandatory. Never drop your throwing hand with the ball in it.**

Catching a ball with one hand amounts to pure laziness and is not something that will get you high marks from coaches or scouts. However, there are exceptions to all statements like that because there will be catches attempted and made by players where it is absolutely impossible to even consider getting two hands on the ball. Infielders who reach to their physical limits for ground balls hit through the infield, or outfielders who chase down fly balls high up the wall or dive for line shots hit into the alleys are obvious exceptions to this rule.

But we are not talking about those situations. We are talking about learning the proper techniques for catching a baseball, having never done so before or, having never done it correctly before. If you catch straight away fly balls with one hand on the glove side when you have plenty of time to position your feet to make the catch in front of you, you are lazy. For this infraction of the FUN-DA-MENTALS you should recognize that your lazy actions are eventually going to cost the team. This type of player will kill your chances in critical game situations. It's much easier to boot a ball when catching it with one hand. Catching a ball with one hand also requires extra time to get your glove, and the ball, over to your other hand, grip it properly, and throw it back into the infield. The time it takes you to do that gives the base runner a full step or two advantage. This action says nothing about having to move your feet into the proper throwing position to throw the ball accurately to the appropriate base or cutoff man.

**Fast Feet Set Up the Catch and the Throw**

Please allow me to say again, the first fundamental for catching and throwing a normal fly ball hit to the outfield is to run to the point where the ball will be caught. The second fundamental is for the player to position his body to catch the fly ball, when time allows, over his throwing shoulder with both hands. Once the ball is in the glove, the player should immediately grip the ball across the seams for the best carry, take the appropriate step toward the target, and throw the ball in one continuous motion. His overall catch and throw efficiency is created by his footwork prior to his two handed catch, and not allowing his arm to drop after catching the ball speeds up the return of the ball to the appropriate base or cutoff man.

**FUN-DA-MENTAL: The faster your feet move to set up your body position for the on-going throw, the faster your hands will be able to catch, grip, and release the ball to its intended target. Never allow your arm to drop down upon catching the ball. Keep your arms up and the ball moving back into the infield as fast as humanly possible.**

⊘ ⊘ ⊘

# CHAPTER 13

## The Act of Fielding a Ground Ball

As an infielder you are required to field (catch) ground balls and throw them to the appropriate base for outs. These ground balls may be hit straight at you, or to your left or right, and they will be hit at varying speeds. Some of these balls will bounce up making them easy to handle, while others will take bad hops off the grass or the infield dirt making the play more difficult. A good infielder must field both good and bad hops then throw the ball from various body positions to one of the bases depending on the situation. If you are unable to catch it in your glove, knock it down and throw'em out! If your chest holds out, you'll have a great season! Yada, yada, yada! It is easy to catch a grounder that takes a big hop upwards into your waiting glove. The test is to catch the bad hoppers with the same ease and success. It takes hours and hours of practice, and fielding hundreds and hundreds of ground balls to develop quick, soft hands. If you stay back on a normal ground ball it will "play you." It will literally freeze you in place, which dramatically increases the chance of booting the ball.

**FUN-DA-MENTAL: Expect the UNexpected! Anticipate that the ground ball coming at you will take a weird hop and train your eyes and hands to be quick to react. Remember, charging a ground ball will set up a better hop than staying back and letting the ball play you. As you field the ball, bend your knees, spread your feet apart, keep your seat down, your back straight, your arms extended out in front of you at ground level, and your eyes on the ball all the way into your glove. Your hands should be out in front so you can see the ball enter your glove. When your hands are positioned between your feet you can't see the ball into the glove.**

Fielding hard hit ground balls straight at you, in the hole, or over the bag at second, requires quick reactions to get to the ball. The ability to cover a lot of ground is called "range." If you have to move more than two steps in either direction to field a ground ball, you need to learn to cross over your opposite foot to get the best jump on the ball. Crossing one foot over the other makes the first step a full step, rather than picking up the right foot first to move to the right, which is actually only an eighth of a step in length. The ultimate in fielding a ground ball is to crossover on any ball hit to the right or left and make a same-foot hop before spreading out to field the ball. These two FUN-DA-MENTALS are very positive physical moves which will enable you to be in position to field the ball without getting handcuffed.

**FUN-DA-MENTAL: Charge every ground ball that you can and carry out a same-foot hop prior to planting your feet, bending your knees, and extending your arms out in front of you as the ball arrives. Relax your hands and absorb the ball into your glove.**

**Practice placing the finger tips of the glove on the ground with the pocket open to the plate as the pitch is delivered to the plate. Your bare hand should be along side your glove with your palm open to the plate as well. The reason for this pre-set position is that it is much easier to raise up to catch a quick bounce than it is to push your hands down for a grounder that doesn't bounce at all.**

Often when a ball is hit deep into the hole or over the second base bag, you won't have the luxury of time to spread your feet out when fielding the ball. You must get to it quickly and come up throwing off-balance and on the run. As I mentioned above, there is a fielding method for "setting up the bounce" as you are charging in on normal ground balls. The method is carried out by hopping on the same foot of the last step immediately before you begin to drop down to spread your feet and extend your arms in front of you to actually catch the ball in your glove. A quick, short hop on the same leg allows you to play the bounce of the ball and maintain your balance as you come up throwing. A great drill to practice to learn this hop is to have someone roll a ball to your left and to your right, three or four steps in either direction, from about 20 feet away. If you do this drill fifty times every day you will become an accomplished infielder, assuming you have all the other skills necessary, including a charming personality, good looks and are very smart. Just so you know that I know, a ball hit well off a metal bat gets to you very quickly and sometimes does not allow for any type of set up, more like self-defense! I understand. Balls hit off wooden bats come slightly slower, but only slightly.

The act of fielding a ground ball is one of the most rhythmically coordinated physical actions that you will see in a game. The actions include the fluid motion of the infielder getting to the ball, hopping to set up the bounce, spreading his feet with bent knees, head down with eyes on the ball, butt down, back flat, both arms relaxed with hands dragging on the ground as the ball is absorbed in his glove, then shifting the feet to throw across the diamond for the out. Poetry in motion!

## Fielding a Soft Hit Ground Ball Bare-Handed

There will be occasions where you won't have time to set up, or hop, or anything. This happens usually on a slow hit ball that travels by the pitcher's mound, where the actual fielding and throwing of the ball to first base must be completed by using only the bare throwing hand.

The play is made without ever raising up from a fully bent over position, on the dead run, and off either foot, which ever is out in front at that instant. All infielders should be adept at fielding on the run and throwing off either foot from underneath. To learn how to field this type ground ball bare-handed takes time and a lot of ground balls to be consistent. It is the most difficult throw for an infielder to make.

**FUN-DA-MENTAL: On a slow hit ground ball in the infield never take your eyes off of the ball. Field the ball bare-handed and throw it immediately from whatever body position you are in. Do not catch the ball in your glove and then try to make the throw. You just don't have that much time to make the out.**

The manner in which the pitched ball makes contact with the bat will govern if and how the ball might be spinning when it gets to you. The rest is pure speed and coordination. Remember, the hitter is going to be running down the line to first base in times between 3.5 seconds and 4.5 seconds, which is a range from very fast to slow average times. So you only have about three and a half seconds to charge this grounder, pick it cleanly with your bare hand and make a good throw from underneath to get the runner. Easy Deal, no sweat!

## Throwing the Ball Around the Infield After and Out

One routine learned over time is to throw the ball around the infield after an out in the following manner. When an out is made at first base, the first baseman should throw the ball across the infield to the shortstop, who in turn throws to the second baseman, who throws to the third baseman, who tosses the ball to the pitcher.

By throwing the ball in this sequence, each infielder will keep his arm warmed up and will be throwing across his body in a very natural way. Any other sequence looks bad!

Here is a diagram of how the ball should be thrown around the infield after an out at first base and, of course, with no runners on any of the bases. With runners on base, the first baseman should throw the ball directly back to the pitcher. It lessens the risk of throwing the ball wildly into the outfield, and it will speed up the game.

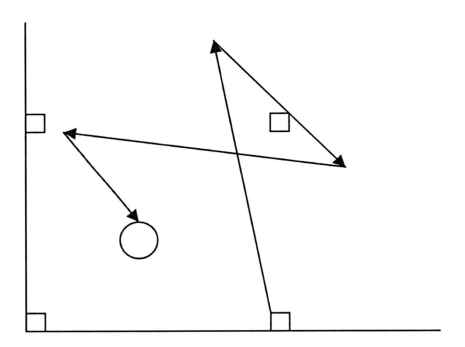

### Taking Infield before a game

**Infield** is a snappy fifteen minute sequence of fly balls hit to the outfielders, and grounders hit to the infielders of each team before every game. From the College level on down, when infield is performed with quick and accurate throws, it is a thing of beauty. Your opponent sees how strong and accurate your outfielders throw the ball to the various bases, how well you make the double play, how strong your catcher's arm is, and they see a fully capable opponent that has come to put it on the line. Even before the game begins, the better the infield is carried out, the more intimidating your team becomes to the opposing team. In the big leagues they all look good.

It also works in reverse. If they see your outfielders throwing the ball weakly and offline, they will know they can run on that player any time they need to. If they see you boot normal ground balls and throw inaccurately around the infield, they will know they can take advantage of you when the situation calls for it. If they see that you are unable to field bunts cleanly, they may set up to score critical runs that way.

**FUN-DA-MENTAL: Infielders must throw the ball hard and accurately every time they take infield. Try to hit your teammate in the chest with the ball on every throw. Be quick and be accurate. Outfielders must throw hard and hit their respective cutoff men.**

The infield routine starts with balls hit by the coach to each outfielder, starting with the left fielder. Each outfielder will make one throw to second, third and home. On the shortest of the throws, the ball can carry in the air all the way to the base. On the longer throws, each should hit the cutoff man about head high. In order to accomplish this head high accuracy, it is the cutoff man's responsibility to be positioned in line with the outfielder's targeted base, and no more than 30 feet out from the target base.

**Position and Purpose of the Cutoff Man**

First of all, let's recognize that an outfielder who has chased down a base hit into the left field corner is going to come up throwing to third with no runners on base. When the left fielder comes up with the ball, he will be looking for the shortstop (who is the cutoff man in this case) positioned on the left field foul line about 30 to 40 feet out from third base. The cutoff man listens for any one of following four options from the third baseman and reacts accordingly:

1. **Let the throw go through to third** for the tag if the throw is on line
2. **Relay the throw to third** for a play on the runner if it was thrown off line
3. **Cut off the throw to make a play at another base**, or
4. **Cut off the throw and run it into the infield** if no other play.

**FUN-DA-MENTAL: The infielder waiting for the throw at the base makes these calls loudly to the cutoff man. LET IT GO, RE-LAY, CUT/BASE, or CUT are the calls.**

If the left fielder were throwing home, the cutoff man would be the third baseman with the shortstop covering third. The third baseman would be positioned inside third on the infield grass, between the mound and the third base line, awaiting the call from the catcher to let it go, relay, or cut the throw off. If the ball were thrown off line with no play at the plate, the catcher would call CUT / THIRD, and the ball would be cutoff and thrown to the shortstop covering third to tag the runner trying to stretch a double into a triple.

In the same game situation, but with a base hit to right field, the right fielder would come up looking for the shortstop to be the cutoff man for a throw to third, with the second baseman covering second. Depending upon the speed of the base runner, the right fielder would throw on line to the second baseman covering second if the runner tried to stretch a single into a double. The shortstop would be in the cutoff position on the infield grass between second and third, in case the runner tried to stretch a double into a triple.

With runners on first and second, and a base hit to right field, the first baseman would become the cutoff man for the right fielder throwing to home plate with the second baseman covering second. On a throw in flight from right field, the first baseman would listen for **RELAY (home)** or, if too late for a play at home, **CUT/SECOND** to hold the runner at first to set up a possible double play.

Accurate throwing by the outfielders and proper positioning by the cutoff man are **FUN-DA-MENTAL** to the success of keeping the other teams runners from taking advantage of you when they are on the bases. Loud and decisive communications by the infielder at the base are imperative.

# CHAPTER 14

## The Proper Way to Make the Double Play Pivot at Second Base

The completion of a double play is one of the best examples of physical timing and player coordination that occurs in professional sports. When you consider all of the actions that are going on simultaneously, it's a wonder that one is ever completed.

## The Pivot Man and His Responsibilities

The pivot man on a double play at second base will be either the shortstop or the second baseman, depending upon where the ball is hit with a runner on first base. The pivot man is the one taking the throw from the infielder to start the double play. Advanced level shortstops and second basemen will have signs between them on almost every pitch with a man on first base, as to which one will cover the bag if the runner attempts to steal on the next pitch. Which one covers the base is dependent upon whether the hitter at the plate is a right or left-hand batter, what pitch is being thrown, and whether the game situation calls for a hit and run. Which one covers the throw at second also depends upon the score of the game, the speed of the runner at first, the specific batter at the plate, and how many outs there are in the inning. The primary responsibility of the pivot man is to get to the bag on time to catch the throw from first, third or short, and relay the throw to first to complete the double play. How shortstops and second basemen adjust their feet to make the play will be covered below.

First of all, on an attempted steal, or a ball hit by the batter, the base runner will be coming full bore from first. The runner's primary job is to get to second base safely. His secondary job is to physically break up the double play if he can get there in time to do so. If he has been forced out by the throw in front of him, he will try to hook the pivot man's foot to knock him off balance so he can't complete the throw to first, or he will try to roll up underneath him and knock him down.

Physical contact between players in the 2005 high school and college baseball rules require the incoming runner to slide directly into the base, without making any effort to go outside a direct line to the base to contact the pivot man's body. If the pivot man is standing right over the base to complete the throw to first, then, and only then, can the runner try to break up his throw.

To defend against this effort to get taken out of the play, a second baseman taking the throw to start the double play has a number of options available to him as he prepares to catch and relay the ball to first. Most of these options depend upon the line and location of the incoming throw, outside the base, inside the base, low or high. Please remember, the actual steps shown below are for the beginner to learn and practice. As a young infielder's feet and hands become faster, the relay throw to first base will happen so fast that these steps will become a single pivot motion of catch and release. When you get to the point of actually talking with your infield teammates during the play, your physical actions will become academic.

Here are some options available when the **second baseman** is the pivot man.

1). **If the incoming throw _is right over the bag, the infielder can straddle the base_, catch the ball, and relay it from right over the top of the bag.** This is the fastest relay position. If the play is going to be close, he must rotate his shoulders and push off his right foot to throw to first base. As he concludes such upper body rotation he merely drives upward off his left foot and flattens out in the air two or three feet above the base, landing on top of the sliding runner. This move is a very natural body motion following the completion of the throw. No big!

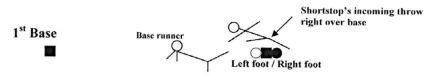

2). **If the incoming throw is to the outfield side of the base, the second baseman should set up touching the outfield side of the bag with the side of his left foot as he catches the incoming throw.** As part of the entire pivot motion, he simultaneously steps onto his right foot (toward left field) and pushes back off the right foot to complete the pivot throw to first. This entire movement is done in one motion.

3). **If the incoming throw to the second baseman is right over the base,** but this time the base runner is **very close,** the pivot man should come across the base in full stride, catch the ball and touch the bag simultaneously with his left foot, continue onto his right foot one full stride toward the mound and complete the pivot onto the left foot to throw to first. If the right foot is on the bag when the out is made, the pivot throw will come off the left foot. If the left foot is on the bag, the pivot man can back up to throw off the right foot. It makes no difference, as the second baseman times his pace to be in full stride across the bag, catching and releasing the ball in one motion off either leg.

**4).** **If the incoming throw is to the infield grass side of the base, the shortstop must catch the ball and brush the base at (1) to ensure one out.** Your forward motion continues toward right field onto your left foot **(2)** as you replant your right foot **(3)** to make the pivot to first onto your left leg at **(4)**. The infield side of the bag is the "sui-side" of the base, because the oncoming runner has an unobstructed shot at you and will be right in your line of sight as you release your throw to first base.

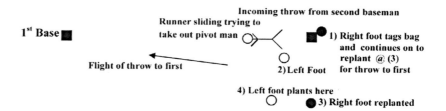

**FUN-DA-MENTAL:** Practice making every double play **IN ONE CON-TINUOUS MOTION,** catching the ball, touching the base, pivoting and throwing to first base.

In reality, where the pivot man touches the base and with which foot is inconsequential. In an extreme circumstance, he might even touch the bag with his glove if he happens to end up on the ground fielding a throw, but it must have the ball in it for the out to be legitimate. This brings up the question of how to tag a runner, and we'll cover that in the next segment.

## For the More Advanced Infielder

For the more advanced infielders, you already know how important it is for your feet to set up the speed of your hands for your relay throw. The physical location of the ball thrown to you will automatically determine how you relay the ball to first. If the throw is low, you must stay low, throwing sidearm or underarm. If the ball is high you must make the pivot from a straight up position, keeping your hands high all the way through the relay transition. On a hard hit ball, if you have time to clear out of the immediate area of the base after catching the incoming throw, do so without hesitation. If you don't have time to get out of the way, make the pivot and get up in the air as high as you can off either foot to avoid contact with the oncoming runner.

**FUN-DA-MENTAL:** **When making the pivot on a double play, always relay the throw to first from the position you caught the ball. For example, if you catch the ball low and outside the base, you must relay the ball to first from that same low position. Normally, you just don't have time to straighten up to throw the ball to first base in time to catch the runner.**

One very important point to learn is to make the runner slide by throwing your relay throw right at him if he refuses to slide early enough. If you hit him, I guarantee, he will never make that mistake again. Be ready to throw over, under, around, or through the base runner. In other words, complete your throw to first as if the runner were not even there. This is the only protection an infielder has to avoid getting absolutely wiped out by the oncoming runner. When the opposing team knows that both the shortstop and second baseman will not hesitate to throw low to protect themselves from being run over, the base runners will be sliding 20 feet out from the bag to avoid getting the relay throw between their ears! This is not dirty baseball, by the way. It is how the game is played. If a base runner stands up coming into second base on a possible double play, he deserves to get decked!

When a **shortstop** takes the throw at second from either the first or second baseman, he has the entire play in front of him, so he knows how much time he has and where he needs to go to make the throw. His body is in continuous motion toward first base. The second baseman, as shown above, is blind to the runner, as he is standing sideways to him and is much more vulnerable. Depending upon the direction of the throw from the first baseman, the shortstop must move to the outfield or infield side of second base to catch the incoming throw. He will then complete the double play from that same side of the base.

## How to Tag a Runner

The act of tagging a runner sliding into a base is quite simple. First of all, for the runner to be called out, you actually have to make the tag with the ball in the glove or hand, somewhere on his body. But as a young infielder, you need to learn the most fundamental tag of all, which is to catch the ball in your glove and slam it down on the runner and right back up in the air in one motion. It just speaks of "OUT." Another type of tag is to place the ball against the base and let the base runner slide into it. This type of tag is usually taught in the early years of playing the game and is fundamental in your learning. It's pretty simple to understand that the runner has to touch the bag to be safe. So there is no reason for the infielder to go out after the runner to make a tag. The runner has to come to the bag. Best teaching suggests waiting until some part of his body is close enough to tag and place the glove (with ball) between the bag and the body and let him run into it.

This type of tag is all well and good if you have the time to wait for him. The base runner may try to kick the glove hand with his free foot to dislodge the ball. Should the ball be knocked loose, he would be safe. So as you all mature as ball players, you must tag the runner and raise the ball up to show it's all over. You don't want to leave the glove there long enough for him to make any contact with it.

A "sweep tag" is made by catching the ball and "sweeping" your glove across the area between the runner and the bag, from the ground to high above your shoulder, simultaneously tagging some part of the runner's body near the base. You must make physical contact with some part of his body for him to be called out. Because of the sweeping motion through the tagging area, the glove and ball are sometimes not there long enough to see the actual contact with the runner. Just make sure you tag the guy!!!

Additional thoughts about making a tag on a runner includes the infielder's actual position straddling the base or setting up in back of the base. This is always predicated upon the location of the incoming throw. When the catcher makes a perfect throw to second on a steal, you will normally see the infielder straddle the base, catch the throw, and tag the runner with the ball in front of the base in one continuous motion, down and up, as the runner slides in. This is textbook perfect. When receiving a throw from a teammate, be sure to keep your feet moving before catching the ball and making the tag. If your feet are fixed in place, you reduce your range of motion to handle a ball that may be thrown off line to you.

Not all throws from the catcher are perfect either. If a throw to the first base side of the bag requires you to move off the base (between first and second) to catch it, it puts you right in line with the oncoming runner. Assuming the runner does not slide into you and take you out, you must: 1) hang tough, catch the throw and tag the runner, if possible; 2) catch the ball at all costs to prevent the runner from advancing on a loose ball; and 3) attempt to tag the runner with a punch tag motion. If the ball is thrown high and the runner is down low sliding to the outfield side of the bag, it will be very difficult to get the glove on him anywhere, coming from front to back and high to low.

If the catcher's throw bounces in the grass in front of second base, you must, as well as possible, block the ball from going by you even though you will probably be backed up by the shortstop, and/or catch the ball on one hop positioned in front of the base and shove the glove in against the first base side of the bag if possible. Because you are late getting the tag on the runner, any other position of the glove except against the base will give the runner a safe call.

The last word of wisdom for the infielder tagging a runner is to make the tag and get out of the way! On a close play the runner will always try to make contact with the pivot man in some manner. It keeps everyone honest!!! Be nimble and be quick with your hands and your feet.

⚾ ⚾ ⚾

# CHAPTER 15

## How to Learn to Hit a Baseball

Throughout the history of the game of baseball only 28 major league players have hit over .400 in any single season. For your information, Hugh Duffy holds the highest <u>single season</u> hitting average of .4397 in the year 1894. There has never been a hitter in major league history who has a **life-time** average over .3664 and that was Ty Cobb of the Detroit Tigers. That means, year in and year out, the very best hitter EVER was only able to hit safely 3.66 times out of every ten times at bat. So please don't be discouraged if you don't get on base every time you go to the plate. No one in history ever has!

What makes it so difficult you ask? Well, first, there's a strike zone, and there's an opposing swing plane. There is a round ball thrown at a high velocity that may be changing speed and direction in flight. Then, you are supposed to hit the ball on the sweet spot of the bat which is round. And you are supposed to hit it squarely! And after all this, you have to hit it between some foul lines for it to be in play, and between a bunch of defensive guys trying to prevent you from doing that. What could be any more difficult than that?

For most players, hitting a pitched ball for a high average is the toughest thing to accomplish in the game of baseball. The reason is that it requires super physical, mental, and reactionary skills that need to come together simultaneously to be successful. They include mental and visual focus, timing, quick reactions, mental agility, precise hand/eye coordination, good physical balance, strong legs, well-developed hand and arm strength, strong abdominal muscles, and most importantly, a properly executed swing of the bat, and some luck. That's about it. Shucks.

Many young players between the ages of 7 and 11 years old may have developed reasonably adequate hand/eye coordination. They may also possess better than average physical balance. But at this early stage in their growth, they have not yet developed adequate strength in their legs, hands, forearms, shoulders and abdominal muscles necessary to swing a bat with any degree of consistency or power. However, this is the best age to learn the proper mechanics of how to swing the bat, so they don't develop bad habits early-on that they have to correct later to advance to higher levels of play.

In the early years of physical development, most young pitchers lack speed and control. Similarly, young infielder's and outfielder's arms lack strength and accuracy. You can be sure of one thing: base hits will happen, and runners will reach first, second, and third, and ultimately score, just as in any level game. So this early stage of learning the fundamentals of **how to hit a baseball** will be the most important stage of all, because, usually, if you can hit, the coach will find a position for you to play.

Proper fundamentals of hitting learned between the ages of 7 and 13 years old will form the foundation for more sophisticated hitting strategies later. I believe it is more important to develop a mechanically sound swing and understand the strike zone to avoid swinging at bad pitches than it is to be getting base hits swinging improperly against limited competition at this age.

Improper swing habits learned at an early age are very, very difficult to correct as you mature. This is because you were so successful against others who were also only learning their position that you may have generated a false confidence, and because of this early fame, you think you can keep doing it as before. Not so. Poor hitting mechanics and lack of plate strategies will absolutely kill your ability to play at higher levels without correcting these bad habits. Why not learn them properly in the beginning, so that when the physical maturity kicks in, all of the fundamentals are in place to advance easily to these higher levels of competition?

**When you are learning how to play this wonderful game your actual game results** are not nearly as important as the proper **repetitive motions** you carry out each time you go to the plate. The repetition raises your confidence through the successes achieved so that you will want to do it again, and again. A little success at this level is a terrific catalyst. Things like establishing a comfortable stance at the plate from which you can learn to swing the bat with power. The proper placement of your hands on the handle of the bat and the final **SET POSITION** of your body and bat as the pitcher begins to deliver a pitch are extremely important things to learn early on.

The more times a hitter goes to the plate, the more relaxed he becomes. The more relaxed he becomes the better he will see the ball. The earlier he sees the ball, the better he will begin to pick up the actual rotation of the seams. The earlier he sees the rotation of the seams, the longer he will be able to wait on the pitch because he won't be fooled by it. The longer he can wait on the pitch, the more consistent his swing will be into the various planes of pitch trajectories.

By the time young players reach early high school ages of 14 to 15 years old, they will have practiced the proper fundamentals of hitting for four or five years. They will be bigger and stronger, and they will understand their respective strike zones better than the beginner. They will have learned some degree of patience at the plate, looking at more pitches before committing their swing on their pitch of choice. Each of these actions will bring about new levels of achievement.

Without question, the act of hitting a baseball is the most important component of the game. As I said before, if you can hit, the coach will find a place for you. So let's get to the fundamentals of setting up in the batter's box to swing at a pitched ball. This set up is called the hitter's stance.

## Normal Hitting Stance

First of all, there is no single hitting stance. A normal and comfortable stance for an individual hitter will vary all over the board. This is due to their differences in height and weight, hand/arm strength, leg length, length of arms and type of swing the player has developed for himself. No single hitting stance is used universally since everyone's body is unique compared to all others.

So let's begin with what can be safely referred to as the most basic position of the feet in the batters box and move up the body from the feet to the head. When we get to the top of your head, you should be able to step into the batter's box and set up to swing at the ball with some confidence that you will be in a reasonably sound hitting stance. For you left-hand hitters, merely reverse sides. Stand in front of a mirror and practice these fundamentals of setting up to swing the bat.

## Positioning the Feet in the Batter's Box

First of all, batter's boxes are positioned on each side of home plate, one for left-hand hitters and one for right-hand hitters. The boxes are each 4 feet wide by 6 feet long and set 4 inches back from the inside edges of the plate. These dimensions give all batters plenty of room to set up in their individual stances to hit. Little League batter's boxes are 3 feet wide by 6 feet long and 4 inches back from the edges of the plate.

The back foot, or right foot for a right-handed hitter, is normally positioned parallel to the back line of the box and anchored approximately 6" to 8" inside the back line. The front foot is positioned comfortably beyond shoulder width with the toes of both feet in line to the mound. This basic stance locates the center of the hitter's body just off the back half of the plate. Some hitters position their back foot up against, or on, the back line of the box. This gives them the longest time to see the ball before start-ing to swing. Even though it may be only a hundredth of a second, it's a long time when you are trying to make contact on a ball coming in at 90 plus mph.

If a hitter sets up too deep in the box (too far back) for his own swing characteristics, a talented pitcher can throw breaking pitches short, over the front and outside corners of the plate, which are very difficult to hit for a high average. They also cause the hitter to reach out over the plate to make contact, diffusing any power in the swing. Some hitters set up more in the middle of box, so they can swing at pitches before they move too far off the plate. Additionally, your location in the box depends on your specific bat/plate coverage and how quickly you are able to pick up the pitch and begin your swing. If you can lean over and touch the outside edge of the plate from the set position of your feet in the batter's box, you most likely have what is known as plate coverage.

Incidentally, in Ted William's book, *The Science of Hitting*, he says of his pitch preferences over the years that, "...the most I could hope to bat was .230 on pitches thrown away and down to me." Now remember, this is a state-ment of fact made by one of the greatest hitters baseball has ever known, and these are the types of pitches that Tom Glavin of the Atlanta Braves and NY Mets fame has been so remarkably capable of throwing year after year. Down and away, down and away, down and away. So, plate coverage is your key to success when you are setting up in the box.

Once your feet are comfortably positioned, your weight should be equally balanced over both feet, knees bent slightly, with a very slight lean forward onto the balls of the feet. Weight should be distributed from 50-50 to as much as 40-60 from front to back foot. Most hitters feel better with more weight on the back leg, and the back foot set firmly in the dirt so it can't move <u>during the loading and unloading of the swing sequence</u>.

As the pitch is released from the pitcher's hand, the hitter must begin his loading sequence by turning his front hip and shoulder back toward the catcher. He starts by dropping his left knee inward a few inches, and rotates his left shoulder in and slightly downward to transfer his full weight onto his back leg. This action cocks his hips and allows him to lift his left foot to stride into the pitch. This "turn," as it is referred to, is the most important component in starting the swing because it "loads" the entire right side of the hitter's body, including his right leg, hips, shoulders, arms and hands for a quick bat response. It initiates the hitter's natural rhythm as he prepares to swing. Without any motion to start his swing the hitter would be like a dead guy. No rhythm, no power, no nada! Remember, at this moment we are only learning how to pick up the left foot to stride into the pitch.

## Position of the Knees through the Swing

Both knees should be bent from slight to moderate to allow a smooth lateral body motion back to the right side as the hitter loads for the swing. As the hips cock laterally, the left knee turns slightly inward enough to allow the left foot to be raised to stride into the pitch. The left knee only needs to travel a few inches to enable the transfer of weight back onto the right leg, so don't be making a big deal out of this movement. It's very subtle.

In the same motion, the left foot strides into the pitch anywhere from 4 inches to 8 inches, as the hips open fiercely, leading the upper torso into and through the swing. As you stride into the pitch your left knee remains slightly bent at impact and your arms fully extended as the bat continues into the follow thru segment of the swing. Upon contacting the pitch with the arms fully extended, the front leg begins to straighten, becoming a lever against which the center of the upper body rotates around as the follow thru continues. The left leg remains straight to the finishing point of the swing arc. The hitter's right knee remains bent throughout the entire swing, ultimately pivoting as the bat makes contact with the pitch. The right knee remains bent through the contact zone, with the hitter's upper body ultimately coming off the back foot at the end of the swing arc to take the first step towards first base.

Power and bat speed are both generated by the rapid opening of the hips as they rotate to the left side. The hitter's upper body should be relatively upright from head to knees through the entire swing, bending slightly forward at the waist as the bat moves through the contact zone. Try to keep the swing arc compact and quick.

## Action of the Legs through the Swing

Not to be redundant, but once the front foot is planted in its forward position, the lead leg remains bent through the contact of the ball and then straightens to become the "lever" against which all of the force (power) being generated through the lateral motion of the hips will transfer upward through the torso, out through the shoulders, out through the arms, and finally out to the hands on the bat. The already bent right leg drives the entire right side of the body through the swing plane, and the right foot ends up pivoting onto the ball of the foot acting as the rear support for the finished swing position. When you can do this without loosing your balance, you have achieved your first major step in becoming a good hitter.

**FUN-DA-MENTAL: Get in front of a mirror and practice swinging your bat for as long as you can hold up your arms. Make the above motion a perfect and simple transfer of weight from over both feet, back to the right side, and immediately back to the left side, unloading the built up torque out through your hands and around the straight left leg.**

## Action of the Hips through the Swing

To start the loading segment of the swing, the left knee, left hip and left shoulder must turn slightly down and in to the right to load the right side. This turn cocks the hips and allows the left foot to be raised to stride into the pitch. As the unloading segment of the swing begins, the stride of the front foot starts the hips moving toward the incoming pitch, opening laterally around to the left, as the shoulders, forearms, and hands whip the bat through the contact area. As the swing goes through the contact area, the hitter's belly button should be straight away to the mound, with his left hip rotating horizontally, but a few inches higher than his right hip. The left or front shoulder should begin to move through the contact area slightly higher (two or three inches) than the right shoulder.

## Position of the Elbows in the Set Stance

A comfortable position for the elbows is critical in the execution of a compact swing. Some teach that the back elbow should be down and in a little closer to the body. Some hitting coaches teach beginners that the back elbow should be up in back, parallel to the ground, with the hands positioned high above the back shoulder. Most beginners will find it difficult to get comfortable trying to get the bat started with their hands and elbows extended so high above their shoulder in the back. Quite frankly, from this position they just don't have the strength in their arms to hit anything below their waist.

Billy DeMars taught his players to keep their left elbow slightly bent and comfortably across in front of the chest, in a very relaxed position. With the back elbow raised only a few inches away from the body, it feels like you have more bat control and power in a little tighter swing arc. The arms must be fully extended at the moment of impact on the ball. This compact swing will ultimately unload more of the force generated by the opening of the hips and shoulders, out through your forearms and hands, as the bat makes contact with the ball. Remember to keep the palm of the top hand up at the moment of contact into the back of the ball. This position exerts the most energy possible onto the surface of the ball at the point of contact. The position of the arms will be covered below.

## Motion of the Shoulders during the Swing

During a slightly upward swing plane on a low pitch, it is perfectly natural for your right (back) shoulder to drop from 4 to 5 inches below the left shoulder as the bat travels through the contact zone. However, if the back shoulder drops too far down through the contact zone, the swing plane becomes too steep, which takes the bat through the contact zone at too steep an angle for solid compression of the ball. You don't want to do that. Swing the bat slightly upwards, or slightly downwards, but just above or below dead flat. On a pitch at the knees, it will be necessary to swing at a slightly steeper angle to keep the bat in the plane of the ball as it passes through the contact zone. This would be considered a normal swing plane for the type of pitch thrown.

To be a long ball power hitter your swing plane through the contact zone must be slightly upwards and always in the plane of the ball as long as pos-

THE FUNDAMENTALS OF BASEBALL

sible. It's a fact that a majority of pitches in flight from the pitcher to the plate move downward through the contact zone. So, depending upon the type pitch thrown, the hitter's swing plane must be at an equal and opposite angle upward through the contact zone **to keep the bat in the plane of the ball for the longest period of time.**

The angle of your shoulders through the hitting zone will determine how steep your entry into the pitch will be. Ted Williams points out in his book that fastballs require about a 5 degree entrance angle upwards, where a down breaking splitter or curveball requires about 12 degrees, a slightly steeper upward stroke. Check out the following diagram if you are confused. It reflects the position of a fastball and curveball being thrown by a right-handed pitcher to either a right- or left-handed hitter.

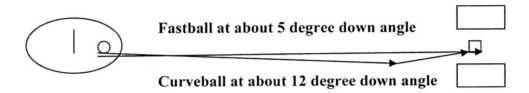

If you don't happen to possess long ball power, you may wish to groove your swing in a flatter plane to hit more line drives for base hits, rather than fly balls and ground balls for outs, depending upon whether you are early or late through the hitting zone. With the flatter swing plane, the bat enters and exits the hitting zone at a slightly downward angle all the way through the stroke. As the bat contacts the ball, the downward angle puts an under spin on the ball as it leaves the bat, providing it with lift and carry. The physical mechanics of this flatter swing, from start to finish, vary only slightly from the upward power stroke mentioned in the previous paragraph. But the objective with the flatter swing plane is to intersect the ball's flight at the point of contact with the bat moving in a flat to slightly downward angle, making contact with the bottom half of the ball.

You must remember that you are trying to make contact with a round ball thrown at high speeds, and possibly changing directions, and you are supposed to hit it square with a round bat! How you get the bat to that contact point is up to you. But you must get there consistently to become a good hitter. Either of the two methods described here are perfectly acceptable. In the real world of baseball there are two kinds of hitters, power hitters and the rest of us. Work on making solid contact with every pitch thrown. If you develop a power stroke and it works, stick with it. If you are not getting the results you are looking for with the power stroke, try flattening out your swing plane to hit more line drives.

**FUN-DA-MENTAL: The secret to hitting is to swing the bat at the same angle upwards as the ball is coming to the plate downwards, keeping the bat in the plane of the pitch as long as you can through the contact zone. When you accomplish this, you will have increased your chances of making contact more often.**

## Rotation of the Shoulders and Arms

The shoulders and arms automatically load or cock themselves for the actual swing as they follow the rotation of the hips onto the back leg. With the upper body turning onto the right side, the shoulders, arms and hands move back a few inches to fully set themselves in the **GO / NO GO** position. This is the "moment of truth" position, where the entire body is cocked and ready to move into the pitch. All systems are loaded and ready for a **GO** to swing. If the pitch remains in the strike zone, then have a rip at it. If the pitch moves out of the strike zone and becomes a bad pitch to hit, your mental agility and reaction time computes that the pitch is a **NO GO** and you take it! At this instant, the shoulders, arms and hands are all loaded and ready to fire. The trigger is whether the eyes tell the brain to swing or take the pitch. If you take the pitch, relax, and rethink the pitching strategy taking place, and reset yourself in the box for the next pitch. Isn't this hitting thing easy?

## Gripping the Bat

The bat should be held firmly with both hands but not tight. The handle of the bat should be laid into the base of the fingers and then rolled into the palm of the hand. If you don't hold it firmly, a pitcher throwing a heavy fastball will knock the bat right out of your hands. Hold the bat in the first and second joint of the fingers of the middle, ring, and little finger, and then roll them up against the calluses that will form across the top of your palm. These calluses will build up as you hit more. The right index finger should be loose and almost off the bat. It can touch the thumb but only lightly. The reason for keeping the index finger off the bat is that when it is held tightly with the thumb it slows down the speed of the bat through the contact zone. The little finger of the bottom hand should be placed against the knob on the bottom of the handle. The little finger of the top hand is positioned down and against the big knuckle of the index finger of the left-hand. All eight knuckles on both hands should be lined up flat from top to bottom, as if you were lining up the front of both fists flat across the top. The reason for this alignment is to preset your wrists to move through the hitting zone with the palm of the top hand facing upwards at contact. You should be looking at the fingernails on your top hand. A hitter looses all his power when the top hand turns over before making contact with ball. So keep the palm of the top hand underneath the handle as you swing the bat through the contact zone.

For the beginner, if you are a right-hand hitter, place your left-hand at the bottom of the handle with your right-hand resting on top of your left index finger. If you are a left-hand hitter, place your right-hand at the bottom of the handle with your left-hand on top. Never swing a bat cross-handed.

If you don't feel you are strong enough to swing the bat from down at the knob end, you have a couple of options available to you. Slide both hands up the handle two or three inches toward the label. This will allow you to swing the heavier bat quicker through the contact zone. If this is not comfortable, try to find a lighter bat to swing. Sliding both hands up the bat a couple of inches is known as "choking up." You might also spread your hands apart from one to two inches. Younger hitters will gain more bat control by spreading their hands apart as it helps to strengthen the top hand's control of the bat through the contact zone. Ty Cobb hit this way. He actually hit with his hands split apart and choked up a couple of inches. It's just not for everybody.

## Position of the Bat in the Set Stance

To get the bat in the ready position your hands should be set comfortably in front of the right shoulder, with the right-hand about shoulder high. The barrel of the bat may be positioned from a point almost straight up in the air, to as much as flat back over the right shoulder, a la Cal Ripken, Jr. Wait, wait, we're not done yet.

## Distance from the Plate in the Batter's Box

When you take your position in the box, get into the habit of leaning over and touching the outside corner of the plate to see if you have plate coverage. Every batter's box is different, so you need to be aware if the lines in the dirt are a proper distance from the plate before you settle in to hit. To cover the plate means that during your natural swing you can reach a pitch thrown on the outside corner of the plate. When you have plate coverage, you are the right distance from the plate. In the normal stance we are developing for you to begin hitting, you should place your toes back 6 to 8 inches from the inside line of the box. Remember, you can be so close to the plate that you can be jammed with inside fastballs on the hands, unless you are an absolute "dead pull hitter!" Also, when you set up too close to the plate, the chances are better than not, that you will get hit more often by pitches thrown inside. If you're tough, go for it! Please be aware that you never want to be so close to the plate in your set position that your head hangs out over the plate, ever. If you do that, the pitcher has every right to stick one right in the ear hole in your helmet!

## Position of the Head and Eyes during the Swing

Your head should be turned comfortably to the left, looking at the pitcher, over, and just in front of your left shoulder with **both eyes on the pitcher at all times**. Get into the habit of watching the ball all the way into the catcher's glove on every pitch. See where the catcher is catching the pitches. It's a great way to learn how they are pitching you...in/out, up/down, fastball/breaking, hard/slow, and so on. Keep track of the pitches mentally, so you can write them down when you get home, and look back on them when you play the same team again. Based upon what you see should enable you to make instant adjustments at the plate in your hitting strategy.

In order to become a long ball power hitter you must possess strength, quickness and power, and your swing plane must be slightly upwards through the zone of contact. To give the bat the longest time in the plane of the ball through the contact zone, the bat should be traveling somewhere between 5 and 12 degrees upwards, depending upon the type of pitch thrown.

When a 6 foot tall pitcher releases a fastball on level ground from a three-quarter overhand motion, the ball travels to the plate on a line between 4 and 5 feet above the ground and at a slight downward angle. When that same pitch is thrown off a pitcher's mound that is 10 inches higher, the hitter would be looking for a knee-high strike crossing the plate at an approximate down angle of 5 degrees. To have the greatest chance of making solid contact with this pitch, the hitter must swing the bat slightly, and I emphasize "slightly," upward to be in the same plane as the ball for the longest period of time. That is the contact zone, and that's where hitting happens.

**FUN-DA-MENTAL: The Equal and Opposing Angle Theory of hitting requires the bat to be in the same trajectory as the pitched ball through the contact zone. Remember that the hands are always in front of the head of the bat through the contact zone. To hit a pitch early enough to pull it, your hands must travel further around in front of your body before making contact with the ball <u>early</u> in the contact zone. On a pitch thrown <u>over</u> the center of the plate, your hands should again lead the barrel of the bat to make contact with the ball over the center of the plate. On a pitch over the outside edge of the plate, the hands again lead the handle of the bat, but the barrel of the bat makes contact <u>later</u> in the contact zone to drive the ball to the opposite field. Hitting is all about bat speed, bat trajectory and timing through the contact zone. The hitter must have his bat moving through the contact zone at the same time the ball is passing through the contact zone. Being late or early through the hitting zone is the difference between missing the pitch entirely or not waiting long enough and hitting it with much less power. When you understand this paragraph, you will be on you way to becoming a great hitter. Until you do, you won't!**

If a hitter swings the bat at a **downward angle** through the contact zone, the length of time the bat is in the same plane as the ball, is only that moment in time (X) when the two vectors of the bat and the ball cross. That means that the full width of the sweet spot of the bat and the center of the ball must be at the same point at exactly the same time to compress the ball to its maximum. Limiting the length of time the bat moves through the contact zone dramatically reduces the odds of hitting the ball consistently.

## Finally, How to Swing the Bat through the Contact Zone

Now that we have learned how to set up to swing the bat to get the best results, let's move on to the fundamentals of how to get the bat on the ball with consistency.

As the pitcher is getting the sign from the catcher, your weight should be evenly distributed over both feet in a pre-ready position. As the pitcher begins to deliver the pitch to the plate, your knees should be slightly bent to allow for a counter turn of the left knee, left hip and left shoulder smoothly onto the right side to load the hips, arms and hands. Simultaneously, your hands push back a few inches from your body to cock your wrists and hands. This action of the hands is absolutely essential to get the bat moving.

The hitter's left side should reach its maximum counter turn, or maximum load point, an instant before the pitcher releases the pitch from his hand. As the hitter identifies the pitch and its location, he should already be in motion striding into the pitch. As the left foot steps into the pitch, the left leg straightens, and the hips open violently against the left side, leading the upper body, shoulders and arms through the swing. The hitter's head must always remain behind the point of contact of bat and ball. This places the maximum force of the bat against the balls surface at the moment of contact. If the hitter's head slides in front of the contact point of the bat and ball, a majority of the counter-rotational torque would be lost, and he would only be able to exert force against the balls surface with his hands and arms. It's called getting fooled, and it will happen many times when you are learning!

From the cocked position of the arms, wrists and hands, in the fully loaded position, the hitter's arms begin to unload back into the contact zone with the hips (leading the shoulders) turning laterally. Be careful here not to let the hips get too far ahead of the speed of the hands. The hips need to rotate open, leading the shoulders, arms and hands through the full swing. But if they open too soon, the arms won't have any lower body support, and the hitter's power will be totally defused. Opening the hips too early makes it very difficult to hit a pitch that moves away over the outside of the plate. If the hips open too late, they will prevent the full rotation of the upper body, allowing only an arm swing with no power. As the bat moves through the contact zone, the left-hand pulls the knob end of the bat through the zone with a quick, compact and powerful arc, maintaining the underhanded grip of the top or right-hand into and through the back of the ball.

The ultimate finish of a great swing is to be balanced over both feet, with a straight front leg, a fully flexed back knee, and the upper body finishing completely open to, and facing, the pitcher. The toes of the left foot should finish slightly closed to the mound, and the left foot should be rolled slightly onto the outside edge of the shoe. The right foot should have turned onto the ball of the foot and should be in line to the mound at the finishing point of the swing. The arms should have continued through the contact zone around to a maximum point, and the upper body should be pulled back against the front leg.

The hitter's hands must be quick and strong as they control the alignment of the bat and ball through the contact zone. During the swing the arms must be kept in close to the body throughout the contact zone to achieve the optimum power transferred from the legs, out through the shoulders, arms and hands. As a general rule, the more compact the swing, the better the bat control.

During the arc of the swing that we are learning here, the hands lead the end of the bat all the way through the contact zone to impact. The rolling of the wrists takes place naturally, and full extension of both arms happens after the ball has left the bat, not before.

**When to Start the Swing**

The counter-loading to swing the bat starts as the pitcher gets to the delivery side of his motion. As the pitch is released toward the plate, the hitter's body must be in its optimum ready position, or the pitch will be by him before he can get it all going. During this optimum ready position, the hitter has two-tenths of a second to determine what pitch has been thrown, and another two-tenths of a second to determine if it is the pitch he is looking for, if it is where he wants it to be in his strike zone, whether or not it is going to be in his strike zone, and then get the bat to the ball in the contact zone. There just isn't a whole bunch of time to wait around before starting to swing the bat, as you well might reason. But it is not impossible to do either.

Normally, a hitter will "load" his front knee, hips and shoulders on every pitch to ready himself, whether he is going to swing the bat, or not. The action of moving in on each incoming pitch establishes the pitcher's motion and release characteristics in the hitter's mind. From these visual memories, the hitter will begin to get into the pitcher's throwing rhythm that will help him establish exactly when to start swinging the bat. This will become very clear to you after you have gone to the plate a hundred or so times and hit against a number of different pitchers.

⚾ ⚾ ⚾

# CHAPTER 16

## What Is a Strike Zone? Why is it Important to Know Yours?

**FUN-DA-MENTAL: The vertical strike zone runs from the bottom of your kneecaps to the bottom of the letters on your chest, or just above your belt buckle when you are in your normal stance at the plate. The horizontal area of the strike zone is the exact perimeter of home plate, plus one additional ball width each for the inside and outside edges. To the average six-foot baseball player in a normal hitting stance, the strike zone is a little over 4 square feet.**

If you swing at pitches that are just a couple of inches inside or outside those parameters, the area of the strike zone can expand to over 5 square feet. All the pitcher has to do is find where you have the most difficulty making contact with a ball in that zone, and that's most likely where you will be seeing most of the pitches when you come to bat.

The lower limit of the strike zone can be defined as an area extending from the inside front corner of the plate across to the outside front corner of the plate at a height of your knees. The lower limit extends back to the inside rear corner of the plate, and across to the outside rear corner of the plate. By raising the walls of that square to the bottom of the letters on the hitter's uniform, completes the upper limits of the strike zone.

Every hitter's strike zone is different due to one's natural height, and batting stance. So for the average 6 foot tall player with a normal hitting stance, the total area of his strike zone would be approximately 4 square feet. For the beginner standing 4 feet 8 inches, the strike zone would be considerably smaller. For a pitcher at a young age to throw three strikes to a smaller player of this stature would be quite an accomplishment. That is why you must learn to be patient at the plate taking a pitch or two until you get a strike and putting the pitcher in a hole before you start to swing the bat. Don't be too anxious. Look at a couple of his pitches before you go to work. You'll be surprised how often you will get walked, and a walk is as good as a base hit!

The upper limits of the strike zone are defined in the Official Rules of Baseball, but are seldom allowed by umpires who have lowered the upper limits to an area just above the belt. Many umpires have their own definition of what the strike zone should be. Some will call a slightly "wider plate" giving the pitcher the benefit of the doubt on pitches that may have just missed the outside or inside edges of the plate. Some call pitches for strikes that just nick the bottom of the kneecap, a full ball lower than the kneecap itself. Overall, umpires need to be consistent in calling the limits they are going to allow throughout an entire game. Then it's fair for both teams.

When a beginner is learning his individual strike zone, it is important to understand that any part of the ball touching any part of the plate area is a strike. So when a ball thrown over the outside edge of the plate looks like a ball, it may be a perfect strike with only a portion of the ball hitting the edge of the plate.

The following illustration will give you more of a visual understanding of what is stated above. Each of these pitches is a strike, but entering from different directions. It will show you what can be called a strike. Any pitch location outside these limits should be called a ball, but we're talking about a 90+mph pitch that may have some movement in, out, up or down. So it's very difficult to say whether a pitch truly caught the corner of the plate or not. That's where consistency in umpiring comes into play.

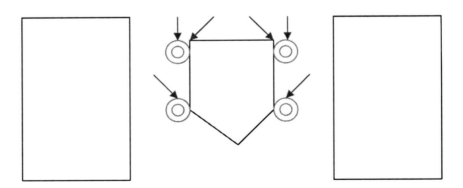

## Does the Pitcher Have an Advantage?

Once the pitcher receives his sign from the catcher, he winds up and throws that pitch to the plate. As the ball leaves the pitcher's hand at the release point of his delivery motion, the stride of his front leg toward home plate shortens the distance of the flight of the ball to the plate between 4 and 5 feet. So at the moment of the release, the ball is going to travel only 55 or 56 feet to the plate, instead of the full distance of 60 feet 6 inches.

When the ball in flight has traveled approximately twenty feet from the pitcher's hand, now only 40 feet from the plate, the hitter begins to recognize the rotation of the seams of the ball. The rotation of the seams identifies the type of pitch that has been thrown. The direction of those rotating seams identifies what the approximate trajectory of that pitch will be when it passes over the plate. The earlier a hitter is able to identify what the pitch is and where it is going be when it passes over the plate, the more accurate the hitter's swing path adjustments can be to hit the ball in the "sweet spot" of the bat.

By the time the ball has traveled about 40 feet from the pitcher, you will know what the pitch is, and if it is the pitch you're looking for. When it gets 20 feet from home plate, you will know if it is in your "strike zone." If this pitch were a 90 mph fastball, you would have already loaded your right side as the pitcher released the ball, and started your swing the instant you recognized the ball was going to be a strike. You must pre-load your body before you recognize that the pitch is a strike or ball. That's the **GO / NO GO** decision you must make before actually commiting your hands, and swing through the contact zone. Every good hitter tends to cock his hips and shoulders at every pitch that is close. The single caution here is not to commit your upper body without full intention of swinging through the pitch. On occasion the pitcher will fool you, and you will commit your hands without swinging through the ball. If the end of the bat passes over the plate, whether or not you intended to swing at the pitch, the pitch will be called a strike.

Good hitters swing at pitches in their strike zone, and "take" pitches that are out of their strike zone. Every hitter should know his strike zone well enough to take pitches that are not good pitches to hit, unless forced to swing at a pitch out of the strike zone to protect a runner. When a batter continuously chases bad pitches, he may not understand the fundamentals of his strike zone, he may have sight limitations, or his mind may not be agile enough to distinguish between a strike and a ball. This will definitely affect his success as a hitter. Not swinging at bad pitches is a great talent. Remember a "walk" is every bit as effective as a single.

## Knowing Your Strike Zone

The most important elements in hitting a baseball is a combination of your stance or setup, knowing your strike zone, seeing the pitch, swinging properly, and getting the bat on the ball. I would like to take a moment right here to show you a simple method of hitting off a tee that will teach you the FUN-DA-MENTALS for learning your strike zone.

Take your stance in the batter's box where you can reach the outside edge of the plate with your arms comfortably, but not fully extended. Following the diagram below, place a ball on a tee knee high, to learn to recognize the bottom limit of your strike zone. Then move the tee to points at each corner of your strike zone. Please remember that the tee ball should always be within your strike zone, both up and down and in and out. So take the time to measure the exact distance from the ground to the bottom of your knees, and to the top of your belt in your stance. Set the height of the tee at those two maximum high and low levels every day and practice hitting the ball.

Now, using a 100 foot ball of string, tie one end of the string to the top of a stick at a point 5 feet above the ground where a pitcher would naturally release a pitch to the plate. Tie the other end to a stick in the ground on the inside corner of home plate. This will be the precise angle of a fastball being thrown knee high to you. Once you have done this, **set your tee** at various positions on the string line to visualize the exact limits of your strike zone.

You first recognize that a pitch may be entering your physical strike zone as it passes through an imaginary rectangle located approximately 15 feet in front of the plate. Much like reading the line of a putt on a golf green, there's no actual strike zone rectangle in the grass. But the commitment to swing at the pitch, getting the bat in the plane of the ball, and making contact now requires a cocking of the hips and shoulders, and lightning fast reflexes to get the bat started in motion through the contact zone.

When you have done this for a number of days, set the tee with a ball in place at the inside and outside limits of your natural swing plane and adjust your feet in the box to enable you to make contact with the ball in those locations. When you have spent 20 or 30 hours hitting pitches at the outer limits of your strike zone, you will be ready to take real batting practice. This type of practice will teach your eyes to reject bad pitches, and making solid contact will become your only focus. That's when you become a hitter.

Notice how far your hands and the bat must travel from your set position to make contact with the ball 4 inches from the end of the bat, when the ball is pitched on the inside, the middle, and outside corner of the plate. All three of these pitches are strikes but must be hit in different locations to get the meat of the bat on the ball with power. The following illustration will describe where the contact with that specific pitch must be made.

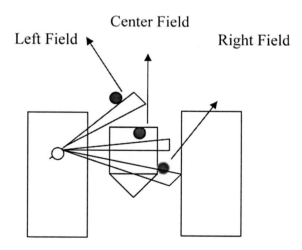

From the illustration above it should be apparent that to hit an inside fastball in the meat of the bat you must see the pitch early enough to make

THE FUNDAMENTALS OF BASEBALL

contact with it out in front of the plate. If you let this pitch get too far in, the ball will make contact on the wood bat below the label, "sawing it off" as they say, and you'll be standing there with just a stump! If you are using a metal bat, you might just hit it over the center field stands. Who knows with those things?

On a fastball thrown at the same speed on the **outside corner of the plate**, your bat will travel a shorter distance, as you make contact earlier in the arc of your swing. If you were to try to pull this ball into left field, you would have to change the angle of the bat as shown above to a much more pronounced angle with your hands in order to fly that pitch into left field. Big strong hitters can do this. If you choose to be a long ball pull hitter, you will have to set up to the plate, so you can reach the outside edge and make sure your hips and hands are very quick through the impact zone. A near full arm extension may be necessary to reach some of those pitches on the outside edge of the plate, especially if the ball is moving away from you.

**Choosing a Pitch to Hit**

We know that the total reaction time to hit a baseball thrown at 90+mph is near four tenths of one second. In that length of time the hitter must decide a number of things as the ball is in flight, they are as follows:

Within the first 15-20 feet of flight of the pitch:
- Load the right side of the body to swing
- Determine what pitch has been thrown by picking up the rotation of the seams

Within the next 15-20 feet of flight:
- Decide it is a good pitch to hit? Yes___ No___
- Decide the pitch is in the strike zone? Yes___ No___
- Decide where the pitch must be struck. Early / Mid plate / Late

Within the last 15-20 feet of flight of the pitch:
- Swing the bat in the trajectory of the pitch and hit the ball in the sweet spot of the bat

Note to Reader: Please remember that the pitcher is releasing the ball from his hand somewhere around 4.5 to 5.5 feet in front of the rubber, depending upon his height, so the distances above do not add up to 60'6". I used 55 feet as an average for this explanation.

## Eliminating Half of the Plate

An efficient and effective method for getting the pitch you want to hit is to eliminate half of the plate. When in the on-deck circle waiting for your turn at the plate, and after you have taken in all the immediate game conditions, follow the steps below to make up your mind what you are going to do when you enter the batter's box, then do it! This does not give you the right to disregard any sign the third base coach may give you during your time at bat. If he gives you a sign, follow it to the letter. To eliminate half of the plate the batter must:

1. Choose which half of the plate you are going to look for your pitch - **inside or outside**.
2. Choose the type of pitch you will look for - **fastball or breaking pitch**.
3. Take up to two strikes before protecting the plate, or until you see that pitch.
4. Shorten your swing stroke to protect the plate with two strikes

By choosing the type of pitch to hit, you are anticipating that the pitcher will throw you a specific pitch in a specific spot (over the plate) that will enable you to get the bat on the ball, and do with it what you want. One of those options would be to attempt a drag bunt to first or third off and inside or outside fastball respectively, if either the third or first baseman set up too deep in their positions. Another would be to pull an off-speed breaking pitch down the line with the infield/outfield bunched in the middle of the field. Finally, you must be ready to adjust away from this type-pitch-philosophy on a pitch-by-pitch basis, in the event you get a sign to hit the next pitch, no matter what or where it is thrown, to protect a **game important** runner who has the steal sign and must be advanced into scoring position. Should the third base coach flash you the Hit&Run or Run&Hit sign, you must swing at the next pitch no matter what the ball/strike count is, or where it is thrown, high, low, inside, outside, straight or breaking. It is important to recognize how fine the game can get at certain moments in time. The reason you must swing at this demand pitch is to keep the catcher back behind the plate to receive the pitch and throw it. It adds two or three hundredths of a second on the throw from the catcher to the base.

By choosing to swing only at pitches thrown over either the inside HALF or the outside HALF of the plate, you reduce the size of the strike zone, giving yourself an advantage of getting a pitch that you are looking to hit. If you choose to only swing at pitches thrown over one-half of the plate, you will become a much more focused hitter. Depending upon the game situation, you may look for YOUR PITCH until you have one strike called on you. Then, depending upon the overall ball and strike count, you may choose to widen the plate somewhat, until you are forced to swing at all close pitches with two strikes.

When you get to the point of protecting the plate with two strikes, you become more of a defensive hitter. This means you must be swinging at anything close enough to be called a strike, or risk taking a close pitch and being called out. When you are behind in the count, the pitcher has the advantage. But in the early part of this waiting-for-your-pitch scenario, you are making the pitcher throw more pitches, and you are getting a good look at all his stuff.

If the opposing pitcher or catcher recognizes that you are **"taking" all pitches on the outside half of the plate**, they will begin to throw all strikes over the outside half and show you pitches out of the strike zone inside to set you up. As a young hitter you don't want to be guessing what pitch is going to be thrown. But you do want to get into the pitcher's head. It's OK for later, when your reactions are quicker, but it might cause you to freeze mentally if the pitch is not what you expected to see. Mentally freezing on a pitch is a big NO NO. Your mind must be alert and aware at all times when hitting, and you must protect yourself at all times by wearing an approved high impact plastic hitting helmet every time you are in the batter's box, even clowning around. It only takes one errant pitch to severely injure you for the rest of your life.

**FUN-DA-MENTAL: NEVER enter the batter's box without wearing a high impact protective hitting helmet.**

Let's say you have hit against a particular pitcher in the past, and you know how he has tried to pitch to you. If you have been successful hitting him, he will probably change his routine of pitches to you. If he has been successful in getting you out, he will most likely continue with the same strategy. Remember that it is just as important for the defense to carry out their defensive plan against you, as it is for you to carry out your offensive plan against them. By looking for certain pitches in specific locations that you want to hit, you will be carrying out your offensive plan.

When you decide to eliminate half of the plate to get your pitch, you are betting the pitcher's control is not good enough to throw every pitch over the inside or outside half of the plate consistently enough to get you out. On this you would be correct. Most cannot, even in the big leagues. You can disguise your intentions, inning by inning, by changing back and forth from inside half to outside half as the game progresses. The more times you see his delivery, the easier it becomes to pick up certain pitches that you see better than others. When you are in the on-deck circle waiting to hit, you should make up your mind which half of the plate you will give the pitcher, and what pitch you will look to hit in your half of the plate.

Remember, that if the hitter ahead of you gets on base with no outs or one out, all the fundamentals for moving that runner to second come into play. So watch your third base coach for any signs to take, bunt, steal, run and hit, or hit and run.

The catcher and pitcher know this situation can affect them differently also, and will try to mess up whatever you are intending to do by pitching you in such a way that you can't accomplish your job of moving the runner along.

So let's move from the offense of hitting to the defense of pitching, and all that goes with that position. Try to get through this next chapter without falling face first into your cereal bowl, because there is a lot of stuff to cover here. Isn't this great!!! Mom and Dad, I hope you are hanging in there too. Doesn't this just beat going to a bad movie? Yeah!

⊘ ⊘ ⊘

# CHAPTER 17

## The Fundamentals of Pitching

Becoming a good pitcher is a lot of work. It begins with having genetically superior fine motor ability, mental toughness, and better than average physical coordination. Proper physical conditioning and the discipline to carry out daily exercise routines are the most important component in the making of a good pitcher. Anyone can throw baseballs from the mound to the catcher. Heck, its only 60'6"! But very few are blessed with the ability to throw the right pitch properly, at the right time, to the right location, and get you out, time, after time after time, that's pitching. Anything else is just throwing. Genetically gifted individuals, in excellent physical condition, able to think the game pitch by pitch, are the three primary differences between pitchers and throwers.

## Four Types of Pitchers

There are four general categories of pitchers. With reference to the Major Leagues for this explanation, each individual pitcher on every team is developed and utilized by the manager as a starter, a long reliever, a short reliever, or a closer. Hopefully, the following explanation will give you some insight as to why certain pitchers are brought into the game at certain times by the manager.

The starter knows that he will start every fourth or fifth game in rotation with four or five other starters. He is usually a more experienced pitcher who is able to throw up to 120 pitches in a single ball game and return, in rotation with the other starters, 4 to 5 days later to do it again, all season long. Occasionally, one pitcher might be scheduled over another due to his previous success against a particular opponent, but always with appropriate rest in between starts.

The long-reliever is a pitcher capable of throwing six or seven innings before losing his effectiveness. He is usually called upon to relieve a starter and throw a pre-designated number of pitches during his time in the game, and be able to come back two to three days later in a similar situation.

A short-relief pitcher is one who might be called on to enter the game to face a specific hitter, usually a left- or right-handed match-up scenario, to stop the hitting team from scoring. He will usually give way to the closer in the late innings even if he has thrown effectively for up to three or four innings, as he too must be able to return to the mound within two days, when either the starter or the long reliever gets into trouble.

Finally, the closer is a hard throwing individual with great stuff, like Eric Gagne, who is called upon to enter the game only in the eighth or ninth innings to stop any runs from scoring, ultimately closing out the game for a win. A closer must be able to throw wide open every night during the season. He is awarded a "Save" if he prevents the opposing team from winning the game.

Wouldn't it be cool to have the problem of too many pitchers? Most high school teams have one or two starters and a couple of up-and-comers who might be able to pitch in relief.

## Physical Conditioning and Care of the Arm

The process of winding up and throwing a baseball with deadly accuracy from the pitcher's mound to a catcher's target 60'6" away is a real talent. It is a position that is not for the "faint of heart." Sometimes the ball comes back at you faster than you threw it! That's always a surprise! To be successful at this position requires constant work, heavy physical conditioning, and complete mental focus on the mechanics involved in throwing a ball wide open to an exact location.

The body mechanics involved in throwing over 100 pitches wide open every four or five days takes a tremendous toll on the muscles, tendons and ligaments of the knees, quadriceps, hip flexors, groin, abdominal muscles, lower back, elbow, and the throwing shoulder capsule.

To keep everything synchronized over a full season of physical stress required to pitch, the player must run every day and stretch every fiber of his muscles to maintain the highest level of conditioning throughout his body. If one of the parts of the body weakens to a point where the other components are relegated to work harder to pick up the loss of its functionality or support, the remaining components become negatively affected, as they too, are running at their optimum levels. When one of the areas of the body noted above shows signs of weakness, such as a continuing soreness or stiffness, or a "dead tired" arm showing limited output, it would be in the best interest of the player to take a week or more off to completely rest, heal and rebuild the aggravated muscle tissue.

A healthy pitcher should be warming up with an easy 2-lap jog around the entire field, then a fifteen to twenty minute stretching program before picking up a ball. Following the completion of warming up his arm for 10 minutes, he should be ready to take on any physical assignment required of him, including additional running, shagging fly balls, throwing light batting practice, or fielding his position.

## Ice Packs versus Hot Water

To enhance the recovery of the arm so it will respond every four or five days throughout a full season without injury, today's trainers recommend wrapping the arm and shoulder in icepacks for 30 minutes immediately following a workout or a game. Some trainers prefer to stimulate the shoulder in a Jacuzzi at about 103 degrees as soon as the player enters the locker room, then apply the ice. In the fifties and sixties it was common to run hot shower water on the shoulder for 10 minutes after throwing. If you don't happen to have a trainer or a Jacuzzi, you're just flat out of luck. So bring your own ice!

Wrapping the shoulder in an ice pack immediately after throwing is preferred nowadays, as the ice tends to reduce the trauma in the muscle tissues. The recovery theory is that the healing of the tissues is enhanced when the ice is removed, allowing an increased volume of re-oxygenated blood to enter the tissues. Either method gives the arm the resultant healing that is needed to ready the arm for the next outing. Knees, hips and lower back soreness or stiffness can be worked out with applications of wet-hot towels, or a Jacuzzi. Dry heat from heating pads should not be used for muscle recovery after a workout, as they tend to "fry" the muscle tissue, rather than enhance the healing process.

## Warming up the Arm

Now that your body is warmed up from jogging and you have completed your full exercise program, you can put on your glove and begin to "crank up the cannon." Begin tossing the ball easy at a distance of 60 feet in an 8-10 foot arc to the catcher. As you make the first 10 of these lobbing throws, exaggerate your body motion slowly to loosen up all the throwing components from your ankles up through your knees and lower back.

After you have thrown about 10 arching throws, bring the trajectory down to eye level by picking up the speed for the next 10 warm ups. This will lengthen your release point. When you feel like you can pick up the tempo to 80% of wide open, let the catcher know by telling him or showing him with your glove that the next group of pitches will be faster. When you are ready to throw curve balls or sliders, let him know by turning your glove over for a curveball and sliding it to the left for the slider. Other pitches can have whatever signals you both agree upon. After forty or so warm up pitches, you should be throwing wide open. No pitcher should ever start or enter a ball game without being completely warmed up to throw wide open.

## Pitching a Baseball

Now let's get into the fundamentals of pitching that all players should know who decide that this position is the one they want to play. In previous chapters we have discussed that balls thrown in from the outfield and balls thrown around the infield are being made on flat ground. We also have learned that the trajectory of the throws coming in from the outfield, and those being made across the infield, are very different types of throws and must be executed in such a manner as to cover the distances each must carry to make it to its target. Infielders' throws should be quick and flat. Throws from the outfield must be released a little higher to carry the distance coming in from the outfield. But one thing is constant with each of these throws. They are all accomplished on the flat surface of the field. Not the pitcher!!!

Think about this for a second. A pitcher throws from a raised mound of dirt in the center of the infield. If that pitcher had to throw from the flat surface of the infield, without being 10" higher on the mound, as provided by the rules, his body would have a much shorter distance to "uncoil" as he delivered each pitch downward toward the plate. His left foot would make contact with the ground sooner, forcing him to go through his arm motion much faster to generate the same force on the ball. The increased speed of his delivery, throwing as hard as he could on each pitch, would add a great deal of stress to his legs, torso and arm, to endure over an entire game.

When you throw from a full windup off a raised mound, you drive off of the rubber with your right leg as your left foot drops ten additional inches downward toward the plate before it makes contact with the dirt. During this moment in time, you must be very careful not to open your hips and shoulders too early before making contact with the ground, because your arm would be late getting through this segment of the delivery motion, and would not be in sync with your lower body for the proper release point of the pitch to the plate. Throwing off of a raised mound requires that you hold onto the ball longer before releasing it, compared to throwing the same pitch on flat ground. The steeper the down slope angle of the mound, the further down the lead leg falls. The further down the leg falls before making contact with the ground, the longer you have to keep your hips and shoulders from fully opening to deliver the pitch to the plate. The longer you keep your hips and shoulders closed to the plate, the longer you have to hold on to the ball. But if you hold on to it too long you might end up throwing the ball into the dugout. Just kidding!

## Throwing from a Stretch Position

A pitcher throws from a **stretch position** to keep base runners closer to the base and prevent them from getting too large of a lead. A right-handed pitcher might also choose to hold a single runner closer to the base by throwing from a stretch position. But remember, "closer to the base" is relative to how far away the third baseman is from the base. The runner normally takes the same lead as the infielder and then listens for instructions from the coach at third.

Throwing from a stretch position means that the pitcher usually begins his windup with both feet in front of the rubber. His back foot must be in contact with the rubber before he can get his sign from the catcher. He will throw to the plate from a short set position without taking a full windup, therein, holding the runner closer to the bag. He must stop his motion in this set position for one full second before he can begin his delivery to plate. Holding the runner tight gives the catcher a better chance to throw out the runner if he attempts to steal. If the pitcher took a full windup with runners on first or second, or both, they could easily advance to the next base without any chance of the catcher's throw being there in time. Remember, base runners usually steal on the pitcher's motion, not the catcher's arm.

## Story Time

I'd like to tell you a true story about a very special pitcher, his release point, and a 15 inch high mound.

As I explained in the preface, upon our return home from Omaha in 1958 after winning the NCAA College World Series I signed with Baltimore and was sent to Wilson North Carolina with the Wilson Tobs. One of the players on this team was a twenty-year old left-handed pitcher named Steve Dalkowski. This story is about Steve and his release point. Our manager was a former Philadelphia Athletic and Cleveland Indian right-hand pitcher named Bob Hooper. He was a delightfully nice man, and a teammate of Bob Feller, Bob Lemon, Early Wynn, and Mike Garcia on the highly respected 1953 Cleveland Indians.

I arrived in Wilson about noon and met the team later in the day at the ballpark in Wilson as they returned from a road trip against the Greensboro Yankees. The team piled off the Tobs' bus and headed directly into the locker room to get ready for batting practice before that night's game. Coach Hooper introduced me as the new rookie, and I was given a wool uniform #8 to wear. It was so heavy I thought it must have been used to keep soldiers warm in Siberia in the winter. But when I put it on, I looked just like all the rest of the guys for which I was eternally grateful. I had a new glove, a new pair of Riddell Yellowback Kangaroo baseball shoes, and a new jock. The ultimate Rookie! But overall, I was excited and looking forward to my first professional baseball game.

I had just finished a four-year career with one of the premier baseball programs in the United States at the University of Southern California Trojans, winners of 12 NCAA Collegiate Baseball Championships from 1948 through the year 2005, where we were drilled to the limits of anyone's imagination. When I got to Wilson, I expected the same, wine and roses! Not! This was real life, minor league baseball! The real deal…the bush leagues.

As my first professional game progressed through the sixth inning I watched intently from the bench, taking in all that I could of the field, the player's arms and speed, and of course, the inning, the score, and the count on each hitter. In the seventh inning Hooper asked me go down to the bullpen and warm up Steve Dalkowski. Because I had caught batting practice a number of times and warmed up pitchers at USC over the years, I thought nothing of it, and proceeded to the bullpen. I didn't have a catcher's mask or any other equipment. I thought to myself, I could probably catch this, Dal.... whatever his name is, with my bare hands! I wonder if he knows he's about to get warmed up by Tommy Trojan! Well, what an awakening!

As I headed down the right field foul line I noticed that the bullpen was on perfectly flat ground and not very well maintained. I walked up to the bull-pen bench and asked the group of five or six pitchers for Steve Dalkowski. Up bounced a 5 foot 10 inch, 170 pound left-hander wearing a pair of glasses that could have been used as a forerunner to the Hubble Telescope. Now, I don't mean to be disrespectful in any way to Steve, but I thought he must have had a "**_20 / 8million_**" sight correction, and I bet his glasses didn't fully correct the problem. He walks back to a rubber plate in the dirt and turns around and looks at me. At this moment, I'm not sure if he sees me, or picks up my location by my aftershave lotion. But anyway, he begins to throw. After three or four pitches, I begin to experience a very aggressive and unique physical competence about him. He started his motion with a somewhat quick, hurky-jurky motion upwards until his hands split apart as they came down from over his head. Then, following a full turn to load up, he dropped down on his drive leg and launched his body toward the plate with an extremely explosive leg drive off the rubber, and an arm speed that I had never witnessed before. He threw a very light ball that was difficult to pick up in his motion, and I wasn't seeing it very well. The lights could have been better I thought to myself. I also took notice that each pitch hit my glove almost immediately after he released it! After I caught about 10 of these, I figured he was ready to go! Wrong! He hadn't even begun to get hot!

He then motioned to me with his glove that he was going to crank it up! I thought to myself, "Yeah sure... you can throw a lot harder than this, right?" Well, with an ever faster and more frighteningly quick and violent physical delivery, his fastball, in-flight just over a nanosecond, popped up over the top of my glove about 8" and caromed off the wall down behind home plate some 300 feet away ending up spinning in the dirt in front of the visitors' dugout. As it went by my left ear it sounded like a Cruise Mis-sile, or a platter of sizzling beef in a Chinese restaurant! The visitor's batboy picked up the ball and handed it to the umpire.

As the umpire threw it back to me, he suggested that I try catching the ball. I apologized, thinking to myself, "Heck, I've seen a lot of guys who could throw hard, but what was that thing that just went by me?" I'm sure that it had been thrown at a speed in the range of 110-115 mph… Or maybe it's that the lights in the ballpark were so poor I only **_heard_** the top half of the ball go by me! Or maybe I didn't get a good look at it. It was all of the above, or maybe none of the above! I had never seen, or heard, anything like it in my life!

Please remember, this is my first night in professional baseball and very embarrassing. So he throws two more fastballs that popped right over the top of my glove again, and two more times the umpire has to stop the game to retrieve the ball. The third time it came back to me with expletives, so I asked the umpire if he would like to trade places with me. He smiled and said, "Not even for one second!" I smiled back and returned to the bullpen just as Hooper came out of the dugout to remove Jack Fisher, who had run out of gas. Little did I know at that moment in time why the umpire responded as he did.

As the announcer belted out, "Now pitching…. Steve Dalkowski!" I began to walk back to the dugout. As I did so, I noticed all the people in the stands were moving out of the center section of seats at Fleming Field. The stands were positioned about 60 feet behind home plate and 8 feet above the playing field with a twenty foot high wire mesh screen on top of the wall that ran from dugout to dugout. By the time Dalkowski had jogged to the top of the mound, the entire center section of the stands behind home plate was empty, and our catcher, Cal Ripken Sr., was squatting down behind home plate with his head down as if he had gone to sleep.

I'm thinking to myself, "What in the world is going on here?" until I see his first warm up pitch scream 15 feet over the top of Ripken's head, tearing a massive hole in the ¼" steel-wire mesh protective safety screen behind home plate and ricochet off two or three seats before coming to rest in the seventh row. I looked back to Ripken behind the plate, and to my astonishment he still had not raised his head up to even look toward the mound. He knew that it was going to take Steve a few pitches to adjust to the height of the mound from the flat surface in the bullpen, and so did the fans! They had seen him do this before, and they were ready! I was totally blown away!

Had that particular pitch hit Ripken in the head it would have certainly killed him deader than a doornail.

Dalkowski got a new ball from the umpire, took his windup and threw a second warm up pitch. Like the first, it was somewhere near six feet over Ripken's head and tore a different hole in the backstop screen as it bounced all over the seats before coming to rest. Now Ripken stands up as a third ball is thrown out to Dalkowski. He winds up again and hits Ripken's glove about head high. The next warm up pitch was about belt high, and the final three or four were right down the pipe and totally off the speed meter, near 110-115 mph, I'm sure. By the way, Ripken caught Dalkowski's good pitches as if they were thrown at 40 miles per hour! A great receiver, he was.

For the reader's information, Steve Dalkowski is the fastest pitcher who has ever played the game of organized baseball. He was timed at the Aberdeen Proving Grounds in 1957, throwing pitches between two cameras mounted on large wooden platforms at speeds exceeding 110 mph with movement exceeding 8" upwards at 60'6." However, before he threw a strike through the timing devices, his wildness shattered the 2x4 inch shelving that held the cameras in place. Steve had to wait an hour and a half while they rebuilt the platforms, so he could try again to throw the ball through the clocking devices. He told me on numerous occasions that 110 mph was all he could muster because he had thrown seven innings the night before, and then he cooled down so much during the reconstruction of the camera platform, he got too tight. He said, "If I could have thrown yesterday, I would have broken 125mph." He was not being braggadocious in any way. It was just a matter of fact to him. With all due respect to all the hard throwers throughout the world, there has never been anyone even close to these speeds. I had the pleasure of being his roommate the entire 1960 season, along with our catcher, Ralph Larimore, and I spent the entire year in utter amazement of his unbelievable talent. I have many more mind-boggling stories about his athletic capacities, but maybe at another time. Let's get back to the reason for the story in the first place, which was his release point!

Steve wasn't able to throw consistent strikes for a number of reasons. To start with, his eyes were awful. His delivery motion for every pitch he threw can only be characterized as perfectly violent. His arm speed was so incredibly explosive that it was almost impossible for him to control his release point, as his fastball rose between 4 and 6 inches, every time he threw it, and, at speeds between 105 and 115mph. He had to start his fastballs at the ankles to get a knee high called strike. Because of his lack of control, he never made the "Big Show," as the Major Leagues are referred to. Thank you for allowing me to share this story about my incredible roommate. Now back to the reason I told this story!

Remember my first warm up session with Steve in the bullpen was on flat ground. As he delivered each of those pitches, his front foot landed much earlier than it would when he began to throw from the 15-inch high mound on the field. He had to adjust his release point downward toward the plate by hanging on to the ball longer. When he threw his first three warm-up pitches over Ripken's head, his front foot was falling 15 inches down the face of the mound, below the height of his drive foot pushing off the rubber before it made contact with the ground. This caused him to let go of the ball way too early (high) in his delivery motion. He brought his final four pitches down into the strike zone only after he was able to use the planting of his front foot on the ground as the lever to control the timing his arm motion. The timing of his foot hitting the ground creating the lever, combined with the location of his arm's forward motion in the delivery sequence, is similar to the force generated by a catapult. Because Ripken knew Steve wouldn't even be close for two or three pitches, he never looked up.

It took Dalkowski three or four pitches to correct his release point by hanging onto the ball until his right foot finally made contact with the ground. If you were to measure his pitching stride, it would be almost 90 percent of his height. This means that the distance from the front of the rubber to the toe of his landing foot was over sixty (60) inches. Impossible you say? How could he do that? The answer is that he exploded off the rubber with such low drive-leg power, that he landed his front foot almost 12" further out than a normal pitcher's stride. Remember, he was only 5 feet 10 inches tall. For you mathematicians, that's 70 inches. By the time his front foot landed in the hole, his fully extended rear leg was almost 12" from the rubber. He actually had to pull his front foot backwards following every pitch to maintain his balance. Do you think he had improper mechanics? You would be correct if you said yes! Steve wore out the left knee in his uniform in almost every game he pitched because he dragged it on the dirt between the rubber and his landing point due to his enormously low body drive. So what have we learned here? It doesn't matter how hard you throw if you can't throw strikes. The release point is everything when it comes to doing that. But, as Steve exhibited, to throw harder, you must generate faster arm speed. In order to do that, you must drive off the rubber with an explosive drive-leg surge. Now back to reality.

## Foot on the Pitching Rubber

The Rules of the Game require that **the pitcher have possession of the ball before he can step on the rubber, and that he must step onto the rubber before he can receive a signal from the catcher.** This alerts base runners that they can safely move off the base to take their leads and not get tagged out on the old "hidden ball trick."

## The Hidden Ball Trick

The hidden ball trick occurs when the ball is held secretly by an infielder, who then tags out a runner not paying attention as he takes his lead prematurely. It is the reason that base runners stay on the base until they either know that the pitcher has the ball or that the pitcher's foot or feet have made contact with the rubber. The base coach is also responsible for knowing exactly where the ball is at all times. If the defense tries to pull a hidden ball trick without the pitcher's foot on the rubber, it is considered a balk, and the runners are automatically advanced one base as a penalty before the next pitch is thrown.

## Dip and Drive versus Fall Method of Pitching

There are two mechanically different throwing motions that a player can decide to deploy when he determines that he wants to become a pitcher. The first is called the "Dip and Drive" method. The second is known as the "Fall" method.

## The Dip and Drive Method

The Dip and Drive method of pitching has been around from the beginning of the game. It is carried out as follows. As the pitcher reaches the top of his windup, he slides his right foot into the hole in front of the rubber, planting the outside rear spike of his right foot on the top of the rubber. This position of his foot provides the maximum drive potential off the ball of his right foot when the delivery side of the motion begins.

As the pitcher's left knee is raised upwards around his right drive leg, the pitcher's hands drop and separate behind his left thigh. When his hands come apart at the bottom, his left foot begins to drive down the slope toward the plate. At that exact moment the right knee flexes (bends) four or five inches, as the ball of the right foot pushes dynamically off the face of the rubber to exert maximum force and leg extension. This dip and drive procedure generates a faster upper-body-opening velocity for greater arm speed. This dynamic force can only be exerted against the face of the rubber when the ball of the back foot is positioned up against it in the beginning of the windup, with the outside cleat of the right heel hooked on top of the rubber.

## The Fall Method

In the Fall Method, the entire foot of the drive leg is set flat **into the trough in front of the rubber.** This positions the drive ankle straight up the leg without any flexion in the right knee, and in a static or stationary position. It also does not preset the drive foot angle back against the face of the rubber for maximum utilization of the large thigh muscles of the drive leg. In the Fall Method, the pitcher is taught to stand up as straight and tall as possible. He then raises his front or left knee as high as possible, up and in front of his chest, almost to his chin, with his arms hidden up and in behind his knee to hide the ball. **He then begins his motion to deliver the ball by actually falling toward the plate,** simultaneously driving his left foot down and toward the plate. He must keep his left side moving toward the plate until his lead foot hits the ground at which time his hips, upper torso, shoulders and arm follow in sync to deliver the pitch.

With the right foot flat in the hole in front of the rubber, the pitcher must begin his motion off the bottom of the entire length of his foot by falling toward the plate. This position is not only slow and awkward but offers no pressure against the face of the rubber at all. The difference in **drive-thrust** up through the legs is so much more efficient when the foot is placed at an angle against the face of the rubber during the wind up, that it takes an enormous amount of resistance off the arm during the delivery side of the motion. I'm pretty sure that the foot could be reset to utilize the ball of the drive foot without changing too much in the delivery side of the motion to the plate.

Please be aware that both methods of placement of the drive foot on the rubber are taught today. Which method is better for you depends on which of the two methods actually facilitate your physical throwing characteristics better than the other. Height and body type of the pitcher, arm strength, arm speed, flexibility, and the amount of torque able to be generated are some of the basic characteristics. However, arm speed is the primary factor in determining which method should be deployed. Whether or not the pitcher is able to generate faster arm speed, by getting his arm in the proper position for each of the assorted pitches that he is able to throw, without creating soreness from over stress due to inefficient position-mechanics is the question. Whew!!! That's a lot to think about. The more you test these ideas from the mound the more comfortable you will be with one or the other.

Here's my take on the subject. Delivering a pitch off of a **flat foot** down in the hole in front of the rubber provides little to no right leg drive to assist in supporting the right side through the delivery motion. For some players learning how to pitch, this may be very uncomfortable. This high leg lift sets the pitcher in his maximum counter-torque position from which his upper body must begin to fall toward the plate with no support from the static right drive-side foot. Because the drive leg is straight, it is impossible for him to do anything but fall toward the plate, driving the high left leg downward to open his hips, shoulders and arm toward the plate and drag the right side until it catches up.

There seems to be a higher potential for the pitcher's left foot to contact the ground too early in the delivery, with his left foot closed to the plate. This means that the left leg will stride "closed and short" of the proper landing point. Anytime the left foot lands closed to the plate, the pitcher has no other alternative but to drive his upper torso over the top of his left hip. That position automatically blocks the free flow of his hip rotation to a fully opened finish, ready to field a ball hit back at him. Closed and short landings can be career limiting by placing undue stress on the hip flexors, hip joint, quadriceps, and groin muscles, to say nothing of the un-natural torque of the arm at the instant of release when in an inappropriate position.

A pitcher throwing with a closed stride to the plate requires an off-balanced, stiff-legged bounce to maintain his balance. It will cause the right leg, or trail leg, to fly high in the air in an attempt to recover balance. The right leg will most likely land all the way around on the first base side of a line drawn from the rubber to the plate. The pitcher ends up looking at the first base dugout instead of the plate. A very dangerous position if a pitch is hit directly back at him, as he would have no way to protect himself, let alone make a play on a soft hit ball down the third base line. If any young player is throwing like this, please stop him before he ruins his arm, shoulder and hips, or gets hit in the head with a line drive that he wasn't in position to field.

If the delivery rotation of the upper body (from the belt up) causes the head and shoulders to rotate severely back and to the left, outside and over the left hip, finishing off-balance outside the left knee, then the overall delivery side of the motion must be corrected before it develops into a hip degenerating "bad habit" over the long run. The root cause of this short hip rotation is that the pitcher has opened his chest to the plate too early through the deliver stage of the motion. The problem is corrected by making a higher leg kick and a more definitive counter shoulder rotation before beginning the delivery stage. The addition of a higher left leg lift and a more concentrated rotation around the right hip will provide additional time for the hips and shoulders to open toward the plate as the arm nears its release point of the pitch.

To throw a ball correctly is not a difficult task, but it must be learned properly and practiced over and over until it becomes routine. To throw improperly, incorporating the motion problems described above, will put all of the stress of delivering the ball upon the muscles of the arm and the hip joint without full utilization of the right side drive support.

Besides the inefficiency of throwing a ball in such a way to cause the upper body to be out of balance over the outside of the left leg and hip, this physical action will cause hyper-extended hip flexors and shortened groin muscles, which can become a career limiting problem.

If you throw hard off a flat right foot, you will find that, although it feels like you are throwing wide open, the fact is your body is working harder than necessary to generate the same velocity if the toe of your right foot were positioned down in the hole with your toe spikes angled downwards and against the front face of the rubber. This position enables you to generate additional lower body drive toward the plate, finishing with your weight equally balanced between your feet, rather than out over your left hip. It also provides a smoother arm motion, which in turn creates a more consistent release point for the optimum control of all your pitches.

Ok, Ok! I've said it three or four times. But it is really important to understand the throwing motion.

Now that one or both of the pitcher's feet are in contact with the rubber, he can get his sign from the catcher. Normally, a pitcher will stand somewhere between looking straight in at the catcher, to a shoulder angle of about 45 degrees to home plate. Being right-handed or left-handed from here on is irrelevant, only reversed, as the case may be. The following instruction will assume a right-handed pitcher.

When the pitcher gets his sign from the catcher, he should put his hand on the ball in the pocket of the glove and grip the appropriate seams to throw that pitch. Remember, the ball should be hidden in the glove as long as possible as you go through your windup and delivery motion. The next movement you make starts your wind up for the delivery of that pitch. If you hesitate or stop your actual throwing motion and then start up again, you will be called for a "balk."

Please remember that there are three distinctly different body motions that take place during the act of pitching a ball to the plate. The first is the setting of the feet and relaxing, stepping and leaning slightly backward onto the left leg, and stretching the arms upward over head. The second is the lateral (horizontal) twisting and loading of the right drive foot into the hole in front of the rubber. The third is the flexion of the right knee and simultaneous unloading of the upper torso and arm toward the plate, ending with the release of the pitch.

## Getting the Sign from the Catcher

We have learned that the pitcher must have at least one foot on the rubber in order to receive his sign from the catcher. Pitchers have different stances when looking in to the plate. Some try to look dominating or mean. Some bend over at the waist with their hands on their knees to stretch their lower back muscles. Some stand with their hands down at their sides, ball in the throwing hand. Some twirl the ball with their throwing hand as they receive their sign so it is difficult for the opposing coaches to pick what seams they are holding. And finally, many hold the ball in the pocket of the glove to conceal it with their hands together up under their chin like Roger Clemens, Randy Johnson, and Andy Pettit. From either of these starting positions, the pitcher must do something to begin his wind up motion to throw the ball to the plate. Some begin their motion by pushing their hands directly up and over their heads. Some reset their foot on the top of the rubber and lean forward. Some pump their arms by dropping them to the rear and then back up over their heads. Any motion that is effective and comfortable for the pitcher is acceptable. It makes no difference if you throw strikes.

It has been said that too smooth a pitching rhythm is sometimes easier for the hitters to time. Some say that hurky-jurkey motions can be effective based upon the type pitches being thrown. The absolute truth of the matter is that no matter what the pitcher does in his wind up and delivery motion, he ultimately has to release the ball from his hand, and that's what the good hitters watch. Don't watch the motion. "Show me da'ball!"

**Position of the Feet on the Rubber**

Before getting the sign from the catcher, you should be standing on the rubber with the spikes of your right foot (or the ball of your foot) on the front edge of the rubber. The exact point on the rubber that one chooses to throw from is up to each individual. Some like to throw from the extreme left front corner, some in the middle of the rubber, and some prefer the extreme right corner of the rubber. The best location is the one from which you throw all of your pitches most accurately for strikes.

Once the sign is received, the glove should be positioned directly in front of your upper chest, placing your fingers on the appropriate seams of the ball to throw that pitch. Then in one continuous motion, the following steps of winding up and delivering the pitch are carried out accordingly.

**The Windup Motion**

The **windup motion** is the preparation of getting the motion of your body started with balance and rhythm, whatever that might look like. It always includes the preparation of the feet, legs, back and arms, and eyes, to throw the ball. The following paragraphs will try to explain, in detail, the timing of each of these motions that is required to complete one pitch. Then all you have to do is follow these instructions 130 times and credit yourself with a win! No big deal! So let's start with a micro-breakdown of the windup and delivery of a pitch to the plate.

With your hands together chest high, fingers on the ball appropriately to throw the pitch called, and the back of the glove hand facing the hitter to hide the ball, your first movement is to lean forward anywhere from 6" to

12" from the waist. At the same moment you begin the forward lean, your hands should drop, separate, and swing back behind your hips. During this action your arms should be relaxed and extended, with the ball in your throwing hand.

As the arms continue backwards, reaching their furthest comfortable position extended to the rear, your weight should now be 100% forward and over your right leg. In this forward lean position, your left foot is now free to slide back a comfortable distance (a few inches) to support the immediate weight shift back onto your left leg.

As the **non-stop motion of** both arms continues, they swing back down, forward and upwards directly overhead where your hands come together with the back of the glove facing the plate to hide the ball. When you have reached this position with your arms overhead, 100% of your weight should be over your left leg with your back in a slightly arched but comfortable position.

When the upward motion of your hands has stopped in the overhead position, and 100% of your weight has shifted back onto your left leg, <u>you are in position</u> to slide your right foot into the hole in front of the rubber. An instant before your arms and hands begin their downward motion, your right foot should be positioned with the right toe in the hole in front of the rubber at a 45 degree angle with the ball of the foot pressing against the front face of the rubber. If there isn't a 1" deep trench there, carve one out before getting the sign from the catcher. It's quite easy to do, but very difficult to visualize. Once you do it, you will have no problem doing it automatically every time you wind up. The right foot is set in its final drive position as 100% of the weight on the left leg now shifts smoothly to the right side to begin loading the delivery side of the motion. The **delivery motion** begins when the right foot slides into the hole at the proper angle, and all of your weight is transferred forward onto your right leg.

## The Delivery

The **delivery motion is the other half of the windup motion.** When you reach the end of your delivery motion you will have released the ball toward home plate. The delivery side begins with your hands starting downward from overhead and all the weight from the left leg transferred to a point directly balanced over a flexed right leg. Your hands should come down and separate as they pass behind your left knee coming up in front, and around the right hip, twisting the entire torso clockwise. The purpose of this motion is to reach a maximum torqued or coiled position, so that you can ultimately unwind with force to fire the ball toward the plate.

The stopping point for the rotating left knee and upper body is a comfortable point around and just beyond the right hip point, with the hips, chest and shoulders making the same degree of full turn. At this point you must have both eyes on the target. This is where you *almost* show the hitter the number on your back. But remember, if you can't see the catcher's glove with both eyes, you have rotated too far. Now that you have reached this ultimate torque position, you have loaded all the appropriate body components to begin to deliver the pitch. This is pitching, baby!

As your left knee stops its rotation around the right hip, wherever that maximum point is for each individual, the right-hand holding the ball should be extended down and in back of the right thigh. At this exact instant, your left elbow should be bent across your chest pointing toward shortstop with your glove hand positioned in front of your right shoulder. The position of the glove hand at the right shoulder is very important as it gives the shoulders the needed torque to stay in sync with your hip rotation due to the resistance coming from your left knee. Your belly button should be pointing into left or left center field for your body to be in the right position. I call this the moment of truth. By the time you reach this point in your delivery, you have made up your mind to throw this particular pitch, you know where you're going to throw it, you've wound up your body like a corkscrew, your eyes are focused on the target, and there is nothing else to do now but "Turn it loose!" So let's get there!

Remember that the windup and delivery of a baseball to the plate is a continuing and flowing motion with very little hesitation from start to finish. However, the faster you can uncoil your body from this tightly wound position to drive it towards the plate, the faster you can train your arm to go. The faster you can make your arm go, the faster the pitch will travel. **The problem with trying to throw "fast" or hard without all of these components working together is that the arm ends up being early or late in the sequence, therefore absorbing all of the stress because it is constantly trying to catch up to the speed of the opening of the hips and upper body rotation, or vice versa.** This is the primary reason that young players have sore or dead arms after they throw only a few pitches. Until the mechanics of throwing a baseball are fully understood and performed without stress, no young pitcher should ever be allowed to throw above 50% velocity. That's half speed, man! No More!

When the upper body has fully coiled upwards and around the right hip, the left leg with bent knee, should be raised up to a position as high in front of the chest as is comfortable. If the knee is not raised any higher than the hip, there will be a tendency to slide the left foot toward the plate in a gentle swinging motion. What is needed here is a dynamic driving of the left foot downward and toward the plate from the top of the knee's highest point in the windup. With the left foot driving downward and the toward the plate, the left side can be opened easier and with a much more dynamic thrust, setting up the drive from the right leg and upper body for a faster arm motion. A low swinging leg motion, as stated above, could cause the foot to hit short and closed to the plate, with a natural tendency to throw up and over the closed foot and left hip.

**The Glove Hand Motion**

During the loading of the right side, the left arm assists the torso in turning the shoulders as the hands come apart to begin the delivery motion. The glove hand leads the opening of the upper body as the back of the left elbow is thrust laterally back to the left side. This action aids the opening of the shoulders to the plate and must coordinate simultaneously with the opening of the hips. Accelerated by the back leg pushing off the rubber, the left hip starts the body opening toward the plate, followed by the left shoulder, followed by the left elbow pulling across the chest. Remember to keep your head moving downward and in front, leading your shoulders (slightly closed) to the target until the arm catches up in the delivery side of the motion. If you allow your head to fall over the outside left of your shoulder, you will have a tendency to cross your drive leg over and in front of your planted front foot to regain your balance. This is a common error when learning how to throw. It should be corrected immediately and not allowed to become a habit. Bob Gibson, a 1981 Hall of Fame inductee and pitcher on the St. Louis Cardinals 1968 World Series Team, was one who crossed over like this, but it sure didn't affect his results! Just goes to show you that there are exceptions to every rule!!! So if you can throw like Bob Gibson, it's OK to cross over. If you can't, don't.

**The Motion of the Throwing Arm**

By the time the left knee stops at its final coiling point up and around the right leg, both arms should have moved downward as a counter balance. The right arm, with ball in hand, should now be out of the glove, below the waist, and extended downward and behind the right hip. The instant the left hip, left elbow and right drive leg dip and drive to open the body to the plate, the throwing arm should rotate to a palms-up position with the wrist laid back and relaxed. That position allows the right **elbow to rise up in front of the shoulder and lead the forearm**, wrist and fingers toward the plate in a natural downward trajectory. That is the moment the wrist, hand, and fingers are super accelerated through the release point for the specific pitch being thrown. Remember, the elbow MUST be in front of a trailing forearm and wrist until the forward motion of the arm naturally rotates the forearm and wrist over the top like a catapult.

Continuing the fluid forward motion of the delivery, the forearm and hand, with wrist laid back for a splitter, passes over and in front of the elbow, violently finishing with the delivery of the ball at the appropriate release point for that specific pitch. As the fingers release the ball the arm must continue through the release point, ending in a full follow through down and around to the outside of the left knee.

The more force exerted against the front face of the rubber by your right side, simultaneously opening your hips, shoulders, and left elbow, the longer your arm and shoulder will last. Remember to keep your head and chest driving toward the plate and your back as flat as possible, finishing your follow through with your feet, hips and shoulders squared off to the plate, your glove under your chin, and your eyes on the ball as it crosses the plate.

As you release the pitch toward the plate, your glove hand will most likely be somewhere down and outside your left hip. As you finish your stride squared off to the plate it is vital to your safety to move your glove hand back up in front of your chin with the palm of the glove open to the plate. Once you have released the pitch toward the plate, you become the fifth infielder. And sooner or later someone is going to hit a line drive back at you so hard you may not have time to react. With the glove up under your chin you provide yourself some protection. Your hands will always react faster than your eyes. But you MUST keep your eyes on the ball to allow your glove to either stop or deflect the ball from hitting you in the face. Remember you are only about 55 feet from a ball being hit back at you off one of those aluminum things.

Let's go back to the feet for a minute. As the upper body opens to a point where the legs take over, your back leg begins its dynamic drive off the rubber. Sometimes the TOP of the toes of the right foot will actually drag out of the hole, not the side of the big toe, as you might imagine. The lead or left foot should land on the ball of your foot approximately 10 to 12 inches short of your height. If you are landing on your heel you may be over striding. If you are landing short and casting over your left leg you are landing short. Both are improper strides.

So, if you are 6 feet (72 inches) tall, a normal stride would be between 62 inches and 64 inches from the rubber without any super maximum effort to do anything differently. In fact, if you are really driving your body towards the plate, the knee of your push off leg might even drag the dirt at the moment of full extension. Some of the contact might be caused by the angle of the slope of the mound from the rubber to the plate as all mounds are prepared and maintained differently.

Prior to 1969 the mound was 15 inches high with a much steeper slope. This made it easier for a pitcher to drag his back knee on the ground at full extension releasing the ball. MLB established that the front slope of the mound be maintained at one inch per foot from 6 inches in front of the rubber toward the plate. That meant that a 6 foot pitcher's front foot would contact the ground about 5 inches below the back one. With the height of the mound lowered to 10 inches, dragging a knee qualifies as a maximum drive effort and decreases the chance of scrubbing the knee similar to the delivery of Tom Seaver of the New York Mets in the 60's.

The FUN-DA-MENTAL here is that it doesn't matter how far you stride if that point is where you have the best velocity and control of your pitches without incurring any unusual stress in your legs or arm. Watch Randy Johnson throw as complete support for this statement. He throws in the mid to high 90 mph range from a modified straight up whipping action of his arm and a relatively short stride for his height. He is 6'10" and has tremendous leverage due to the length of his arms and legs. Needless to say, each pitcher should be trained and coached according to his or her individual physical makeup.

A cautionary note to the reader: a pitcher never wants to over-stride when pitching, but equally, a pitcher should never under-stride either. Mechanics man, it's all about the mechanics.

For the reader's edification, you might be wondering why a pitcher would want to land on the ball of his foot and not flat-footed or on his heel. The answer is that many pitchers land first on their heel when throwing off-speed pitches without slowing the speed of their arm. When landing on the heel the pitcher automatically scrubs off the maximum velocity of any pitch and is a great way to disguise the change of pace. Landing on the ball of the foot stabilizes the left side of the body by acting as a lever for the right side to release the pitch. Landing on the heel prevents the right side from being able to continue wide open through the delivery side of the motion, holding up the speed of the pitch.

Many pitchers who have learned to throw more with their arm than with their legs will stride more casually toward the plate. This lazy leg and slow lower body action forces the arm to provide all the impetus of the pitch. Over time this type of throwing will kill their arm, and the poor guy will end up throwing wide open at about 15 mph.

**FUN-DA-MENTAL: This entire chapter is fundamental to the success of anyone deciding to be a pitcher. Every detail in each area above is mandatory for the pitching motion to be without weakness.**

**FUN-DA-MENTAL: Vigorous support from the legs is mandatory when making any throw, especially by a pitcher. Run, run, run, run, as much as you can every day. The strength of your arm is in direct proportion to the condition of your legs.**

⚾ ⚾ ⚾

# CHAPTER 18

## The Micro-mechanics of Holding and Releasing Various Pitches

This chapter is dedicated to the micro-mechanics of how you hold and release various pitches to the plate. It will teach you the proper gripping of the ball and the correct position of the wrist at the release point. First, let's learn what part the wrist plays in the preparation and release of the ball.

## Position of the Wrist

The position of the wrist during the actual throwing sequence is vital to the effectiveness of the delivery of each pitch thrown. In the last chapter, we covered how your hands come apart on the front side of your windup and the throwing arm extends downward and back toward second base. From this position, the arm must immediately begin its path upward and forward at the precise moment that the upper body can best support and coordinate its action. During this initial stage of the arm moving down and then back up to begin the delivery of the ball to the plate, the wrist should be loose and relaxed, because you don't throw the ball to the plate from here. The wrist "sets" into its final position, depending upon the pitch being thrown, the instant the elbow begins to come forward toward the plate. Any sooner, the arm would be flexed too early. Any later, the wrist would not be in the correct position for the release of the pitch.

Since the wrist plays a major role in the delivery of every pitch it is vital to learn to "feel" the various positions and angles of the wrist that you must pre-set for each different pitch. You may wish to utilize multiple fastball spins during a game so as not to be too consistent in the eyes of the hitter. The message here is to start all fastballs in the delivery motion the same way until the final downward movement toward the release point. You might be able to hear your fingertips snap against your thumb if you are releasing them with enough down force.

## The Fastball

The fastball can be held in a number of different ways to achieve the desired rotation of the seams as it approaches the batter. The sequence below shows a two seam fastball being thrown from the overhand, ¾ and sidearm positions. But in every case, the fastball is thrown with the palm of the hand coming directly to the plate and the fingers releasing off the back of the ball. It doesn't matter if you are using a two seam or four seam grip. The fastball is released with a strong but relaxed wrist forcing the fingertips off the back of the ball.

Varying positions of the arm and wrist at the release point will produce everything from vertical to horizontal rotation of the seams. Rotation of a **two seam overhand fastball** causes the ball to spin vertically and track slightly down and in to a right-hand hitter. A three-quarter arm position on a **two seam rotation** can cause a pitch to move anywhere from flat in, to down and in, depending upon the amount of fingertip pressure applied by the big middle finger at release. A flat out sidearm **two seam** release motion generates a horizontal seam rotation, causing the fastball to move anywhere from flat in to down and in.

Examples are shown below:

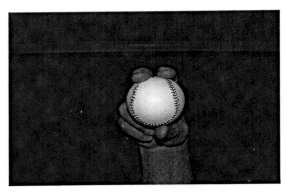
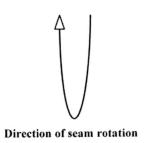

Direction of seam rotation

**Straight Up overhand fastball position**

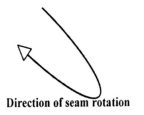

Direction of seam rotation

**3/4 arm position fastball**

Direction of seam rotation

**Sidearm position fastball**

## Holding the Fastball for the Best Results

A fastball held **across the four long seams** and thrown from a ¾ motion will **move into** a right-hand hitter. The harder it is thrown, the greater the movement. Isn't this a kick! As you become more aware of the movement of the ball and experiment by holding the fastball in a number of different ways on or across the seams, you will begin to develop your pitching persona. It is perfectly acceptable to throw two, even three different fastballs by the creation of these different spin characteristics. It will also tend to confuse the hitter who is watching for specific seam rotation.

The most effective position of the wrist for a fastball is with the palm of the hand laid back and upwards as the arm begins to move forward in the overhand delivery sequence. As the naturally coordinated motion of the elbow leads the forearm toward the plate, the wrist follows in a laid back position. As the arm motion nears the final release of the ball, the wrist should be accelerating downward to the release point of the pitch. At the release point, you should hear a "snap" when your fingers come off the back of the ball. The snapping sound occurs when the thumb and fingers snap together as the ball is released from the fingertips. If you don't hear the snapping sound, the ball may be held too far back into the fingers. Make sure this pitch is held with only the first and second joints of the fingers making contact with the seams of the ball. The bigger and stronger your hands are, the more efficiently you will throw this pitch. If your wrist is stiff at the release point, the ball will tend to go as straight as a string pulled tight with almost no movement as it crosses the plate. This is batting practice pitching.

## The Slider

In the opinion of many great hitters, the slider is the toughest pitch to hit. It's a great strikeout-pitch, and it's a great set-up pitch to get the hitter leaning. Because the slider is thrown with almost the same velocity as a fastball, it looks like a fastball until it gets about 10 feet out from the plate.

From that point to the catcher's glove, it actually "slides" away from the hitter and has a tendency to move slightly downward. By the time the hitter sees the "dot" on the front of the ball formed by the tight spin of the top two seams rotating on an axis, it has already begun to move off the corner of the plate.

To develop a faster breaking slider you can put additional pressure on the fingertip of your middle finger at the release point. This added pressure will generate faster seam rotation creating faster air flow under and over the ball.

**FUN-DA-MENTAL: The slider must be thrown down and on the outside corner of the plate to a right-hand hitter. Take extra precautions when throwing a slider inside unless you know it's going to be a wasted pitch, or a set up pitch, for a ball. Many inside sliders that have broken over the plate are still in the air...somewhere!**

If you are the hitter, you will initially see the speed of the slider as a fastball upon release from the pitcher's fingers. But once the ball is in flight about 40 feet you will pick up the circular rotation of the seams. You must then adjust the timing of your swing to hit the pitch away and later if it is in the strike zone, which is very difficult to do. That is what makes it the most difficult pitch to hit with any consistency.

In contrast, the seams of a **fastball** rotate straight under or three-quarter sideways depending upon how it is released. The seams of a **slider** always spin in a clockwise circular motion as seen by the pitcher. The hitter will see it spinning counterclockwise The slider is going to be moving **away** from a right-hand hitter **and slightly down,** but only the last 10 feet of its path.

To throw a slider properly without snapping the elbow to accomplish the rotation required, **the slider must be thrown like throwing a foot-ball,** with the little finger edge of the throwing hand moving downwards toward the plate like a karate chop, finishing across and underneath the ball. As the arm begins downward from the top of the delivery motion, the wrist should be straight up in the air with the side of the hand continuing to move downward to the release point. At the release point, the palm of the hand should pull across the chest and underneath the ball as the fingers come off the seams, like throwing a football.

The action of coming off the seams by rotating your wrist underneath the ball and pulling the seams downward and across in front of your body generates an extremely rapid circular rotation of the seams that forces the ball to break quicker and later. This motion takes all of the stress of spinning the ball off the wrist, elbow and shoulder, and is accomplished by merely moving your arm across in front of your chest with your palm facing upwards. The tip of the big middle finger pressed tightly down on the long seam is the final control point before release. The rotation is automatic.

But look out for this! When a slider is thrown incorrectly, big bad things can happen. First of all, a slider released at the inside of the plate will break out over the center of the plate. DUCK! This is not a good thing! It ends up hanging over the plate and is quite easy to hit. Secondly, a slider released with the fingers **off the back of the ball** will cause it to "backup" or move back into the hitter, like a screwball. This is because the rotation is not spinning in a circular motion as it should be, but semi-horizontally like a 3/4 fastball. If your target was the outside edge of the plate, this release error will cause the ball to move back into to the hitter over the center of the plate. And, guess what, **CABOOM**, gone, into the parking lot.

The slider may be held with two different grips on the seams. The first is with two fingers across the long seams, almost to the curve in the bottom of the loop. The first finger and middle finger should be positioned so that the seams are comfortably under the first joint of both fingers, with the first finger showing just a little white area at the large curve of the seams. You should be looking at the two top seams of the ball between your thumb and forefinger. The thumb should be placed on the seam underneath right in the crease of the first joint. Unlike the fastball that is griped rather lightly, you have to hang on to the slider to make it break with authority. Your release motion should cause the ball to spin clockwise with the top two sets of seams forming a dot on the front and the back of the ball, as if it were spinning around a shaft in flight from your hand to the plate.

The second way to hold a slider is to place your right middle finger all along the left side of the long seam going into with the index finger loose next to it. The palm of the hand covers the entire TOP of the ball where the two seams are close together. The thumb is positioned right in the center of the large loop. This finger position requires you to release the ball by forcing both of your fingertips downward, and pointing to the plate at the release which causes the ball to rotate with a flat spin. Take sufficient care when throwing it this way because there is a tendency to snap the fingers downward at the release point with the arm already in a hyper-extended position. That is exactly how bone chips are caused by an improper release. Extreme caution should be taken when learning this pitch.

**The Curveball**

The curveball is a pitch that causes the most controversy among parents and coaches as to when a young player might begin to learn how to throw it without causing arm trouble. The truth of the matter is, a player can learn to throw it **properly** at any age and not injure his arm, or he can learn it **improperly** at any age and injure his arm.

I am aware of the human anatomy's physical growth period of the elbow during the ages 9 to 14 years old. Without getting overly technical, young players under daily supervision can learn to throw any pitch without incurring any soreness or pain if they are taught to throw each pitch correctly, and <u>never more than half speed</u>. They must learn to throw each pitch with the proper seam rotation and exhibit an absolute understanding of their wrist position and release point for each pitch before being allowed to throw over half speed.

At 9 or 10 years old most children's hands are still too small to be able to grip breaking pitches with sufficient strength, so that rules them out automatically. They should learn to throw strikes with two different fastballs. Twelve year olds, taking into consideration their individual physical maturity, can begin to learn the proper mechanics of throwing breaking pitches for the first time, but only at half speed. It may take a few weeks, it may take a year, or a beginner may never learn them due to a natural lack of fine motor control.

If it takes you too long to learn how to master the release and control of various pitches, have your coach hit you a million fly balls and become an outfielder. Please don't force pitching on any individual who lacks the physical abilities or the desire to work at such a position. A natural pitcher is a gifted athlete. Now onward and upward!

The secret to throwing a curveball without straining the tendons in the elbow, developing bone chips, compressing the bursa sac in the shoulder, or tearing the rotator cuff includes three things:

1. **A delivery motion supported by lower leg drive and upper body rotation**
2. **Perfect arm position throughout the delivery side of the motion**
3. **Most importantly, perfect wrist position at the moment of release**

An educated guess on my part would be that a great many coaches and parents involved in teaching young players the mechanics of how to throw a curveball properly have no clue what they are talking about. With the deepest respect for the effort by Moms and Dads trying to help out a beginner, they may never have learned how to throw a curveball properly to be able to teach it properly. So it goes without saying that improper throwing habits learned early can develop into debilitating problems in later years. Have you ever seen a parent, sitting in the stands, screaming at his 10 year old to snap his wrist at the end of his curveball delivery motion? That is precisely where the bone chips are developed. It would be the same scenario if any novice attempted to teach astrophysics at the college level without sufficient education to do so. It's not an ego thing, just a fact!

Unlike any other pitch, the curveball must be thrown with the wrist bent inward approximately 60 degrees toward the forearm through the complete dynamic of releasing the pitch. The ball must roll over the top of the first and second knuckle of the index finger to be thrown properly. How one gets to that position and how the ball comes out is what we are going to learn right now. Are you ready?

Remember the mechanics of the delivery segment of the pitching motion, where the arms drop from overhead and come apart behind the left knee as it comes up and around the right hip? The right arm loops downwards and in back of the right hip with the ball held firmly in the fingers. As the lower body begins its uncoiling motion back toward the plate, the right leg bends slightly at the knee to achieve a dynamic drive thrust from the right leg against the front face of the rubber.

Simultaneously, the left elbow (glove hand) pulls horizontally across the chest to the left side to add speed to the hips and upper body now beginning to uncoil toward the plate. Within this same action, the path of the throwing arm begins upwards just like throwing a fastball, only with the curveball, the position of the **wrist turns inward at the top of the delivery motion to about 60 degrees.**

If it could be seen in slow motion, the pitcher would be looking into the palm of his hand just before releasing the ball to the plate. With the back of the hand facing the plate and a firm grip on the seams, the ball is released by pulling the bent wrist downward, causing the ball to **ROLL OUT OVER the TOP OF THE INDEX FINGER** as the arm continues downward to finish the delivery motion. There is no snapping, just pulling the hand downward. The release of the ball is almost automatic.

**Curveball Grip**

Bent Wrist Release Begins

Final Release Point over Index Finger

The curveball should be released about half way through the downward motion of the arm for it to ultimately cross over the plate as a strike. It is a matter of throwing hundreds of them to be confident and comfortable with the release point. In game conditions, the curveball should be thrown at about 80% of the speed of a fastball. You must allow the air currents over and under the ball to take effect. It is very easy to over throw any breaking pitch. Back off the arm speed a little bit and allow "Mother Nature" to help your pitches break.

In this position, a pitcher cannot release the curveball from a fully extended arm position because of the bent wrist, so there is absolutely no snapping of the wrist at the release point, and therefore, little to zero probability of incurring an injury. "It's the same motion as pulling down a curtain," they used to say in the old days. With the right side of the pitcher's body being supported by a strong right leg drive off the rubber, the stress incurred by the rotator cuff is insignificant, and the elbow is relaxed at the point of release.

I have heard many unknowing coaching associates suggest to their young pitchers to "get the ball out in front and then snap your wrist to make the ball spin." This is the immediate formula for bone chips and tendonitis. Stressing the muscles and tendons of the elbow and shoulder from an already hyper-extended position is the reason arm trouble develops in the first place. Through the bending of the wrist, the arm and shoulder are protected by the pull-down motion of the hand and arm at the release point. Nothing to it!

**One point of caution:** If you want to learn to throw curveballs early in your career, please remember to learn the rotation of the seams and the release point by lobbing a maximum of 25 curveballs every other day for at least two weeks. When you are learning, never throw faster than half speed curveballs, even if you think you know what you are doing, and never without adult coaching supervision.

**FUN-DA-MENTAL: Never, never, never throw curveballs at more than half speed until you fully understand the dynamics of the wrist motion through the release of the ball and can make the seams rotate properly!**

Controlling the break of the curveball is a matter of how you are holding the ball and where you release it in your throwing motion. The faster you are able to make the ball spin, the <u>harder</u> it will break at the plate. The longer you can hold on to it and still throw it for a strike, the <u>later</u> it will break in flight towards the plate. Speed is not as important as making the pitch break.

**FUN-DA-MENTAL:   Ideally, the delivery motion should be exactly the same for every pitch you throw. What will vary is the way you grip each pitch, the wrist position at the moment of release for each of your pitches, and your arm speed for each of the pitches.**

Ok. We now know the fundamentals for throwing a fastball, a curveball, and a slider. Let's move on to a very effective off-speed pitch known as the SPLIT FINGER FASTBALL. Like the slider, it can be thrown as either a set up pitch or a strike out pitch.

## The Split Finger Fastball

If you are a beginner, the split finger fastball may be difficult to hold in your small hands. But here is a little history on the pitch for you to know. The "forkball" began as a significant out pitch in the late 50's and early 60's when a young pitcher by the name of Elroy Face, a left-handed MLB Hall of Fame pitcher from the Pittsburgh Pirates, made it famous. The tumbling rotation of the seams caused the ball to sink or dive as it neared the plate. The current split finger fastball is a slightly modified forkball, because the forkball was pushed wider between the fingers than the current split finger fastball. The splitter also seems to be thrown harder today than the forkball was then.

Face held his forkball up between the index and middle fingers that split them widely apart. The thumb was placed under the ball. As this pitch was delivered to the plate, the palm of the hand was open to the plate at the release point, but the wrist continued downward in the follow through as if it were a fastball. As it neared the plate the bottom dropped out it. In 1959, Elroy Face won 22 consecutive games as a relief pitcher before suffering his first loss of the season and posted an 18-1 record that year. He was without question one of the most successful pitchers in the history of the game.

The split finger fastball is thrown by placing the entire length of the index and middle fingers **on the outside edges of the top two seams** where they widen downward into the big loop with the thumb tucked underneath the ball. Some pitchers rotate the ball slightly clockwise to position only the index finger on the seam and the middle finger in the middle of big loop. It's all a matter of personal preference.

The proper arm speed for a split finger fastball is pretty close to wide open, but as with most breaking pitches, they will automatically get to the plate somewhere near 90% of wide open. There is a natural tendency to over-throw breaking pitches in an attempt to make them break harder or faster as they approach the plate. The best advice here is to practice throwing the split finger fastball with a fastball arm motion, but note that the best movement will occur at about 90% of the speed of the fastball. The air currents must be able to pick up the rotation of the seams for the ball to dump, sail, or slide. Be aware that the tumbling effect of a split finger fastball into the wind will cause the ball to move more dramatically. The direction of the prevailing wind during the flight of each of these pitches will have a direct influence on the movement of the ball. So it may be necessary for the pitcher to adjust his speed and location when throwing these types of pitches on windy days to keep them in the strike zone.

Another nasty, off speed pitch is the knuckleball.

## The Knuckleball

The knuckleball is the most technically difficult pitch to learn to throw consistently for strikes. It's a great weapon if you can control its movement, but that is the problem. Because the knuckleball's seams remain almost static from the release point to the plate, meaning it might rotate 1 time in 60 feet, it is affected far differently by the air currents in flight to the plate. It may rise and drop, it may sail upwards, it may drop and slide or it may even go dead straight and flat if it is overthrown. Most catchers have very real problems trying to cope with its inconsistencies. Charlie Hough, Hall of Fame Pitcher, who played most of his career with the Dodgers and Texas Rangers, threw 73 passed balls one year, 65 of which were credited to him as <u>wild pitches</u>, and not to the catcher as passed balls.

A zero to one and a half seam-rotation pitch like a knuckleball will have more movement when thrown directly into a prevailing breeze than it would if it were thrown into a cross wind or directly downwind. When thrown into the wind, the limited rotation of the seams of a knuckleball causes the ball to break more dramatically when thrown in the 30 mph range rather than trying to force it to break at higher speeds.

It takes time and patience to learn to throw this pitch effectively, and there are many theories about the best way to hold the ball to keep it "quiet." First of all, a knuckleball is not thrown using the knuckles. It is held with the fingernails of the index and middle finger tips. I was taught to hold it with the fingertips (fingernails) of my index and middle fingers in the center of the wide-open area of the big loop. I placed my thumb in the middle of the center of the loop on the left side of the ball, and my third finger was positioned comfortably in the center portion of the loop on the right side of the ball. The ball was held lightly in the fingers and would either touch or almost touch the palm of my hand.

Now that you are comfortable with the grip (for the moment anyway) you must now hold your wrist straight all the way through the delivery motion, and release the ball with hand, wrist, and forearm perfectly straight, almost stiff, with as little wrist motion as possible. Whew!!! Forget it!

The ball will effectively slip out from between your thumb and ring finger, being pushed by the palm of your hand. The two fingertips on the base of the seams in the middle of the big loop merely hold the ball with some degree of confidence. The effect of this motion causes the ball to exit your hand with virtually zero to one or two full rotations of the ball from your release point to the catcher's glove. The movement of the ball is unreal when it is thrown correctly. Many a great hitter has stepped out of the box to both admire and wonder how that movement is even possible! It's an absolute gas to throw. But you have to throw it a lot to be good at it, and it does tend to develop shorter shoulder muscles if thrown as a primary use pitch. Do not over throw the knuckleball. It won't help it at all.

It can be thrown over hand, three quarters, sidearm, or even underarm (below sidearm) effectively. The most important thing to remember is that is must be thrown with a straight arm from elbow to fingertip. Otherwise, it will rotate too many times and be a sitting duck to hit.

## The Circle Change Up

An easier change up to learn is the circle change up. It is one of many variations of change up pitches thrown in the big leagues. It incorporates the touching of the fingertip of the index fingertip with the tip of the thumb, creating a circle on the left side of the ball in the neck area between the top of the ball and the loop. The middle and third fingers should be positioned on the long seams on top of the loop, with the little finger placed down on the right side of the ball. Although it seems a bit awkward to hold, especially for a pitcher with smaller hands, this setup seems to have good results for those who throw it. I have no thoughts about it as I have no experience throwing such a pitch in competition. If you can throw it for strikes and get people out, use it!

Visualizing how I might deliver the circle change, I can imagine throwing it with a lot of arm motion without the ball going very fast…ever! It is truly a pitch for a specific situation. When thrown in the right place at the right time, this pitch, as with any change of speed pitch, can be very effective. The more creative the selection of pitches, the more off balanced and confused, the pitcher can keep his opponents. I'm always for that concept. Oh, yeah, Baby! Keep em' off balance!

## The Straight Change Up

Another good pitch to learn is a straight change up. This version of change merely utilizes the exact same arm speed and motion as a regular fastball, but this change is held back against the palm of the hand. To get this pitch on its way to the plate, throw it as if it were a fastball. Because you have the ball pressed back against the palm of your hand it can not and will not go as fast as a fastball when released from the palm of the hand.

As it loses speed in its flight to the plate, the bottom drops out of it at about 56 feet, and it tumbles downward across the plate. Because you have so much of your hand touching the surface, it is impossible to throw it as hard as you could if you were to move it further out toward the ends of your fingertips. It is easier to learn than the circle change.

**The Screwball**

A screwball is thrown at about 85% velocity. It is a pitch that is released with a three quarter vertical and counterclockwise under rotation causing it to move in to a right-hand hitter. It can be thrown hard but should be thrown at the speed it works the best for you. When thrown properly, it will work in on the hitter's hands. It is a good set-up pitch to a left-hand hitter off the outside edge of the plate or for an inside fastball strike out attempt, because it causes the batter to lean forward as he swings or takes the pitch. Good hitters take advantage of off speed pitches if they are thrown up in the strike zone, so it is critical to keep this pitch down and working inside. It can be thrown inside to a left-hand hitter, but it must be thrown off the plate inside and deep enough to catch the back inside corner of the plate. But a mistake here, allowing the ball to break out over the plate, is a great pitch to hit.

A screwball is thrown by holding the ball across the bottom of the loop, with the index finger exposing only a small portion of the loop. The middle finger is moderately spread and positioned with the crease of the finger over the seam in the wide part of the loop. Again, it is the action of the arm, wrist and finger position at the release point that is critical in making the seams rotate under, counterclockwise, and at a 45 degree angle.

The under counterclockwise rotation is generated by rotating the wrist inward along the left side of the ball through the downward segment of the delivery motion. The delivery of a screwball generates a very stressful action on the elbow and shoulder capsule due to the inside counter direction of the wrist at the point of release. With the wrist straight but twisting inward from the elbow, the thumb of the right-hand should be pointed downward and to the right as the fingers come off the left side of the ball as the arm continues downward in front of the chest to complete its follow through. The 45 degree under rotation makes the ball move into the right-hand hitter and away from the left-hand hitter. This pitch takes a lot of work to learn and throw efficiently and effectively, and extreme caution should be taken when learning to throw it. The screwball exerts the most torque on the elbow and shoulder at release of any pitch and therefore should be taught with the utmost caution and attention to mechanical details. An experienced suggestion would be to postpone learning this pitch until the player's arm is more mature and he is able to carry out the critical physical mechanics to deliver the screwball properly.

## The Palmball

The palmball is thrown at about 60% of maximum arm velocity to allow the air currents to pick up the slow downward rotation of the seams. A properly thrown palmball will tumble toward the plate with an erratic seam rotation. It's fun to learn how to throw this pitch. It resembles the straight change shown above, but the palmball is truly thrown out of the palm of the hand, where the straight change is released at the back of the three fingers, not all the way back against the palm.

Place the ball back against the palm of your hand with all of your fingers across the four long seams. By holding the ball in this manner, you should recognize immediately that it is an off speed pitch, because the more contact your hand has with the ball's surface the slower it's going to go. Your right thumb is the most important point of contact on the ball's surface. The first joint of the thumb should be placed on the long seam underneath and half-way into the loop.

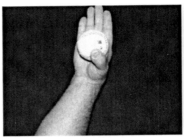 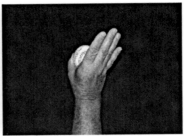

Front View                    Back View

As with all pitches you throw, you must remember to hide this one in your glove as long as possible before exposing it in your forward motion to the plate. It will feel slightly awkward in your hand as you begin to throw it, and it will have much the same movement as a split finger fastball, only much slower. It must always be thrown low in the strike zone, even in the dirt with no one on base, for obvious reasons. If it is thrown up to a good hitter, it will move into his power zone. When thrown between mid-thigh and the knee, it should sink below the knee before it gets to the plate, if you are releasing it correctly.

The effect the Palmball will have on a hitter is two-fold: (1) It will appear to the hitter initially as a split finger fastball, but because so much pace has been taken off, it will cause the hitter to get out over his front leg, and (2) it will set him up for a hard fastball inside following the lunge.

The Palmball is released with the palm of the hand flat, open to the plate. As the arm reaches the top of the delivery motion, all four fingers come up and off the ball with only the palm and thumb maintaining contact with the ball's surface. As the ball is released toward the plate, the seams will tend to tumble or rotate slowly over the top of the ball. At about 50 feet it will begin to tumble in a downward direction and slightly in or out depending upon the exact seam rotation created by the wrist position as it comes out of the palm of the hand. It can be thrown directly overhand, giving the ball a more downward direction at the plate, or from a ¾ motion which will cause it to sink in or out. Don't forget, this is an off speed pitch and is not designed to be thrown at more than 60% of the velocity of your fastball. This pitch can be used in place of an off speed fastball because of its tumbling trajectory.

## Shaking off Catcher's Signs and Changing Speeds

What if you don't want to throw the pitch the catcher has called for? What do you do? There is a significant difference between a thrower who tries to pitch and a pitcher who actually pitches. The difference is that the "thrower" doesn't necessarily think about the choice of the pitch, the speed, or even the location of the pitch he is about to serve up. A "pitcher" thinks about those three things on every pitch. There will be times that a catcher will call for a pitch that just doesn't feel right in that situation. You may lack the confidence to throw a particular pitch in a specific situation, like a curveball at 3 and 2. You may see something the hitter is doing in the box that calls for a different pitch. You have to have a feel for how you are pitching to each hitter. How effective or how ineffective you might be throwing is very important in the scheme of setting up hitters. When you are not comfortable with the pitch called, it's OK to shake off the call and give the catcher the chance to call another pitch. If the same sign is put back down, throw it, or call the catcher out and talk it over with him. It's your ball game to throw, but he knows how to set up the hitters as well as you do. Don't argue, and don't be a buffoon. If you throw a different pitch and the hitter rips it, you had better have a good reason for shaking off his first sign. The catcher is your best friend when you are pitching.

On some ball clubs the Managers will call all the pitches during a game. I have never understood why they do this, other than to exert extreme control over their players or to take all the thinking away from the catcher so he can concentrate on the game. But any catcher or pitcher playing under a system like this will be years behind in building their own levels of expertise and confidence in the real world when they advance to higher levels. How is it possible for someone on the bench to see slight shifts made by hitters in the box who are adapting their stances to adjust to a specific game situation? The catcher is the only one close enough to see those adjustments and should be given the responsibility for calling the pitches. Such responsibility also gives the pitcher added confidence each time they work together, especially when they win. They become a team within themselves.

When the pitches are called from the bench, a pitcher may be under strict instructions to throw what the catcher calls. In this scenario, the pitcher has one variable at his disposal. That is the changing of speeds. Changing speeds is the next best thing to a 96 mph fastball.

**FUN-DA-MENTAL: The most important fundamental to learn when pitching is that you have four advantages over the hitter when you are standing on the mound. The first is the assortment of different pitches you are able to throw for strikes, namely the fastball, curveball, slider, change, splitter, knuckleball, and whatever others. The second is the variation in speeds that you will deliver each of these pitches, from wide open to off speed. The third is the location of each of these pitches that you throw, such as low and out, up and in, down in-high out. The fourth is the strategy that you will use when pitching to each hitter you face. You know what, where and how you are going to throw each of these pitches, and the hitter doesn't! It is absolutely mandatory that you appreciate these points. Whether you are learning to pitch, or teaching someone else how to pitch, anything short of using all four of the advantages described above on every pitch will develop a "thrower" rather than a pitcher.**

### Balk

After receiving your sign from the catcher, you will normally wind up and throw to the plate, or come to a set position with runners on base, check the runners, then throw either to a base, or to the plate. If you make any unnatural physical movement that is not part of your natural set position, like a head jerk, a shoulder twitch, or any quick and unnatural motion with your hands or legs, you have committed a **BALK**. When a balk is called on the pitcher, the base runner(s) automatically advance(s) to the next base.

Left-handed pitchers are notorious for such rules violations. Pat Gillick, one of the most brilliant General Managers in Major League Baseball today, had one of the best pick off moves to first base I have ever seen. I don't know how he got away with it. He looked as if he was in motion to home plate, and bingo, the runner was caught flat-footed! I was sure glad he was on my team and not the other guys. He concealed his move so well that he would freeze runners in place, dumbfounded that they had not seen it coming! Pat and I were teammates on the 1958 University of Southern California Trojans NCAA Championship Team, and a year later in the Baltimore organization. He became the General Manager of the Toronto Blue Jays, Baltimore Orioles, Seattle Mariners, and is currently General Manager of the Philadelphia Phillies. Congratulations, Tiger!

## Covering First Base

The first of two very important responsibilities of every pitcher is to cover first base on a ball hit to the right side of the infield. When the ball is hit in that direction, the pitcher must get a good jump, run at a 45 degree angle to the foul line toward first base, continue up the line to the base on the infield grass, and make the play. If the first baseman can make the play, the pitcher merely turns into the field of play and gets out of the way.

On a **bunt play**, which will be explained later in the book, the pitcher has a completely different responsibility. Never get into the mind set that all this guy has to do is throw the ball to the catcher. The pitcher becomes the 6th infielder (catcher included) the moment he releases the pitch.

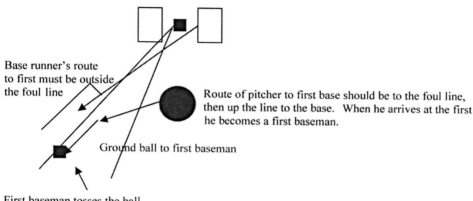

Base runner's route to first must be outside the foul line

Route of pitcher to first base should be to the foul line, then up the line to the base. When he arrives at the first he becomes a first baseman.

Ground ball to first baseman

First baseman tosses the ball to the pitcher for putout

When the pitcher gets a good jump to the line and then up the line to the base, not even the fastest man in the world can beat him to first. Arriving at first base the pitcher has two choices. The first is to keep running inside the baseline as he catches the throw from the infielder, tagging the base on the dead run, and turning into the field of play. The other is to get to the base quickly and receive the throw in a stationary position on the infield side of the foul line. In a majority of cases, the pitcher would continue to run over the base unless the ground ball was bobbled by the infielder, causing a delay in getting the ball to him for the out.

## Covering Home Plate on Passed Ball or Wild Pitch

Covering home plate on a passed ball or wild pitch with a runner trying to score from third is slightly more difficult to accomplish than the play at first. At first base the out is a "force out," meaning that the out is recorded when a defensive player, with possession of the ball, touches the base before the runner gets there, no tag being required by the pitcher covering the base. There is an exception to that rule, and that is where the throw to first from the infielder is wild requiring the pitcher to catch the errant throw and tag the runner physically before the he gets to the base.

In the case of a play at home plate, the pitcher must physically tag the runner attempting to score from third. This requires the pitcher to get to the plate, set up to catch a very quick throw from the catcher, usually at some odd angle, and make a blind tag on the runner. The exception here would be if a third-strike on the hitter gets away from the catcher, the hitter would try to get to first before being thrown out. With the bases loaded, the catcher might throw to the pitcher covering home plate for a force out, requiring no tag on the runner trying to score.

# CHAPTER 19

## How to Learn to Pitch

In order to throw often enough to actually learn how to pitch, it is imperative that a workout schedule be established for each individual. The schedule should include the following:

- o The days you learn the mechanics of how to release various pitches
- o The days you learn to play your position defensively
- o The days you only run, exercise, and stretch
- o The days you rest – No activity of any sort
- o Specific days that you throw a pre-established number of pitches learned

If you don't adhere to a strict schedule like this, you will have a tendency to throw too often, throw too many pitches improperly, and ultimately burn yourself out or develop a sore arm.

Most importantly, an accurate count of the number of pitches you throw each day should be kept. It should include what pitches you threw, how many of each pitch were thrown, and how hard you threw each set.

In the early days of learning, your focus should be directed at proper throwing mechanics and learning how to make the seams of the ball rotate perfectly for each type pitch. It doesn't help anyone if you throw pitches that are not effective, or are not thrown for strikes. Learning at half speed will protect your arm as you develop its strength and flexibility to release the various pitches shown in the previous chapter. Take care of your arm, it's your future! The following table might help you get off to a successful start.

*Caution: The following pitching schedule is designed for a beginning player with a young and untrained arm. A more mature and well-conditioned player may wish to throw a little harder in a shorter period of time. If he knows what he is doing that may be practical. If he is in shape to throw hard, he can be led through the routine faster. However, it is imperative that he throw each of these pitches with the proper arm and body motion, and that he is able to make the seams rotate as they are supposed to before he throws hard. Warming up the arm at a distance of 60 feet or 90 feet should be established by age, arm strength, and level of play. Pitching off the mound from 45 feet or 60 feet should be determined by age and level of play.*

## Week One:

Day 1:  Run 2 laps around entire perimeter of field / Stretch 20 Minutes
**Play catch** ONLY at (60 feet or 90 feet) for 20 minutes on flat ground
Practice fielding bunts off mound and throwing to all three bases
Practice covering first base on balls hit to first baseman
Run 2 laps around entire field
Cool Down – Stretch

Day 2:  Run 2 laps / Stretch 20 Minutes
**Play catch** ONLY at (60 feet or 90 feet) for 20 minutes on flat ground
Practice fielding bunts off mound and throwing to all three bases
Practice covering first base on ball hit to first baseman
Run 2 laps around entire field
Cool Down – Stretch

Day 3:  Run 2 laps / Stretch 20 Minutes
**Warm Up Arm** (60 feet or 90 feet) for 10 minutes on flat ground
Practice pick offs to all three bases with infielders
Practice backing up home plate, and third base with infielders
Run 2 laps around entire field
Cool Down – Stretch

Day 4:  Run 2 laps / Stretch 20 Minutes
**Warm Up Arm** (60 feet or 90 feet) for 10 minutes on flat ground
**Throw 20 Fastballs @ Half Speed** (45 feet or 60 feet depending upon age)
Throw 10 with the top two seams, and 10 across the four long seams

**Lob 25 Curveballs @ Half Speed** (45 feet or 60 feet depending upon age)
Make sure wrist is cocked inward as arm comes down to release point
Run 2 laps around entire field
Cool Down - Stretch

Day 5:   Run 2 laps / Stretch 20 minutes
Rest Arm – Day Off – No throwing of any sort
Cool Down – Stretch

Day 6:   Run 2 laps / Stretch 20 minutes
**Throw 15 Fastballs @ 3/4 Speed** – Work on location – Inside/Outside
**Throw 10 Curveballs @ Half speed** - Work on seam rotation
**Lob 15 Sliders** - Work on seam rotation
Release slider with side of hand moving downward and underneath ball
Run 2 laps around entire field
Stretch 20 minutes – Go to a movie!

Day 7:   Day Off - No Running - No throwing of any sort - No Nada

**Week Two:   Pitch off the mound only from here on.**

Day 8:   Run 2 laps / Stretch - Warm up Arm for 20 minutes
**Throw 20 Fastballs @ 3/4 Speed** – Work on two and four seam fastball location
**Throw 15 Curveballs @ 3/4 Speed** – Work on seam rotation
**Throw 20 Sliders @ Half Speed** – Work on seam rotation
Run 2 laps around entire field
Cool Down - Stretch

Day 9: Run 2 laps / Stretch and Warm up 20 minutes
**Play Catch Only** @ 90 feet for 10 minutes — Do not over-throw
Practice covering first base on ball hit to first baseman — Run to line, then up line
Learn and practice bunt play mechanics
Run 2 laps around entire field
Cool Down — Stretch

Day 10: Run 2 laps / Stretch and Warm up Arm for 20 minutes
**Throw 20 Curveballs @ Half Speed** — Work on seam rotation
**Throw 20 Sliders @ Half Speed** - Work on seam rotation
**Throw 10 Fastballs Wide Open — Work on location**
Run 2 laps around entire field
Cool Down - Stretch

Day 11: Run 2 laps / Stretch and Warm up Arm for 20 Minutes
Play Catch Only at 90 feet
Practice bunt play mechanics
Practice pick off play to first, second, and third
Run 2 laps around entire field
Cool Down — Stretch

Day 12: Run 2 laps / Stretch for 20 minutes
Rest Arm Completely — No throwing of any sort
Cool Down - Stretch

Day 13: Run 2 laps / Stretch and Warm up Arm for 20 minutes
**Throw 20 Curveballs @ Half Speed**
**Throw 20 Sliders @ Half Speed**
**Throw 20 Fastballs Wide Open**
Run 2 laps around entire field
Cool Down — Stretch

Day 14: Day Off
No running - No exercising - No throwing of any sort

## Week Three:

Day 15:  Run 2 laps / Warm up 20 minutes
Play light catch - 10 minutes Maximum
Go home. Take a shower and go out for a pizza!

Day 16:  Run 2 laps / Warm up 20 minutes
**Throw 20 Fastballs @ 3/4 Speed**
**Throw 20 Curveballs @ 3/4 Speed**
**Throw 20 Sliders @ 3/4 Speed**
Run 2 laps around entire field
Cool Down – Stretch

Day 17:  Run 2 laps – Stretch 20 minutes - No throwing of any sort

Day 18:  Run 2 laps / Stretch 20 minutes – Warm up arm for 10 minutes
**Lob 10 Split finger Fastballs @ 1/2 Speed** – Work on rotation at 60 feet
**Lob 10 Palmballs @ 1/2 Speed** – Work on rotation at 60 feet
**Lob 10 Circle Change Ups @ 1/2 Speed** - Work on rotation at 60 feet
Run 2 Laps around entire field
Cool Down – Stretch

Day 19:  Day Off
No throwing of any sort

Day 20:  Run 2 laps / Stretch 20 minutes – Warm up arm thoroughly
**Alternate Fastball, Curveball, and Slider Wide Open 10 times / 30 pitches total**
**Alternate Split Finger Fastball, Palmball, and Circle Change 10 times / 30 pitches total**
Run 2 laps around entire field
Cool Down – Stretch

Day 21:  Day off – No throwing

Day 22:  Run 2 laps / Stretch 20 minutes
Play catch @ 90 feet for 10 minutes **Lob Only** – No hard throwing
Cool Down – Stretch

Day 23:  Run 2 Laps / Stretch 20 minutes
        No throwing at all – Complete rest day for final exam tomorrow
        Cool Down – Stretch

Day 24:  Run 2 Laps / Stretch 20 Minutes
**FINAL**  Warm up arm for game condition start!
**EXAM**  **Throw 20 Fastballs wide open to catcher with hitter in**
**DAY**   **batter's box**
        **Throw 20 Curveballs 3/4 Speed"**
        **Throw 20 Sliders wide open"**
        **Throw 20 Changeups @ 3/4 Speed"**
        Cool Down - Stretch

When beginning pitchers have completed this rigorous physical conditioning program and developed the ability to throw at least three pitches with some degree of consistency and accuracy, they should be ready to begin pitching competitively. By throwing up to 80 of the various pitches learned above, they can be scheduled for regular rotation weekly. If there are any complaints of soreness, or that their arm is feeling "dead," this individual may be throwing too much or throwing incorrectly. Some stiffness accompanied by a little soreness is perfectly normal after throwing 75 to 100 pitches. But when a young player complains that their arm feels sore after a normal workout, as scheduled above, they must be given time to fully recover before resuming their throwing routine. They must also be cutback on the number of pitches that they are allowed to throw until the soreness disappears. Remember to ice your arm after throwing more than 50 pitches wide open.

## Warm Up Pitches and a Caution

Here are two pearls of wisdom for every pitcher who takes the mound. Number one: Always take as many warm-up pitches as you need to properly prepare your arm to throw at maximum speeds. And number two: Always watch the catcher throw your last warm up down to second base. The reason for this is to avoid getting hit in the back of the head by your own catcher. After all, catchers have to throw right over the top of the mound, and about six feet high, to get the ball to second base. That happens to be right about where your head is positioned. Clear off the mound and watch the ball all the way to second base.

If the above schedule is too strenuous for the young player (10-14 years old), reduce the throwing to two days a week. If the schedule is not heavy enough for a **more mature player** (15-18 years old), increase the velocity of the pitches a few days earlier in the schedule but keep the number of pitches thrown the same. Because it's not how many pitches are thrown, it's how many are thrown correctly, and for strikes. If a beginner can throw 60 pitches for strikes, he can probably throw 100 without causing any harm to his arm. Keep in mind he is only learning how to throw at this early point in his career. We don't want to leave his career on the mound at the age of 15 years old. Be very cautious not to overwork him just because he doesn't seem to be making any progress, or he claims he is not tired. Over work is not the solution when learning how to pitch. Discipline is! Enough said!

# CHAPTER 20

## The Art of Bunting

In this chapter we are going to direct our thoughts to the hitting team, or the offense, for the purpose of learning about the art of bunting. In this chapter you will learn the benefits of bunting and why the bunt is so important in the overall game of baseball. One of the most important skills in all of baseball is for everyone on the team to be able to bunt a ball on the ground towards third and first base when called upon to do so. The use of the bunt has become somewhat of a lost art over the last 20 years, being used only late in games rather than every time a high percentage situation presented itself. With the amount of money being paid to players nowadays, the last thing a team's management wants to see is their big RBI hitters sacrificing themselves, to put a runner in scoring position, when they are being paid to come through in these types of situations with base hits, or even home runs. Play for the big inning! That's what the fans come out to see! In other words, bunting doesn't sell tickets as well as a long ball hit for a home run. That may be a true statement, but it says nothing for high percentage winning mechanics of the game itself.

It can be argued that sacrifice bunting will win more games throughout the season by putting runners in scoring position than playing for the big inning. However, in direct contrast, during Casey Stengel's era as manager of the New York Yankees from 1941 to 1960, he managed the Yankees under the philosophy that they would score more runs in one inning than the other team would score in all nine innings. Well, with the direct support from the likes of Joe DiMaggio, Mickey Mantle, Roger Maris, Yogi Berra, Hank Bauer, Billy Martin, Bill "Moose" Skowran, Enos Slaughter, Phil Rizzuto, Johnny Lindell, Frankie Crosetti, Tommy Henrich, Charlie Keller, Andy Carey, Bob Cerv, and Elston Howard, to name a few, he was probably right. He seldom asked any one of these hitters to bunt. He was blessed to have this many great hitters on the same team, and his philosophy proved to be correct. However, most managers and coaches only wish they had this level of talent on their team. Most don't, so they play the percentages to win games. That statement means that when the lead off hitter in any inning of the game reaches first base with no outs, the next batter shall sacrifice himself by bunting the ball to safely advance that runner to second base and into scoring position.

The fundamental here is that the team with the best win/loss record at the end of the season wins the pennant. The losers go home and cut the lawn. So it is more important to win games than to promote one or two players who may or may not be successful in getting strategic hits in tight situations, ultimately losing the game because of such failures. Remember, the high average hitters are only successful 3.5 times out of ten plate appearances. Coaches must also recognize, in general terms, that pitchers toughen up when there are runners on base. So the next hitter coming to the plate in these situations will not necessarily see pitches that he might hit well or out. Pitchers tend to get stingy with their placement and, even more critically, throw different speed pitches, hoping for a double-play ground ball, or a ground ball force out on the lead runner.

Bunting a pitched ball takes a lot of practice. The sacrifice bunt is designed to put the ball in play, on the ground, long enough for a base runner to advance to the next base without being thrown out or becoming the first out of a double play on a hard hit ball to an infielder.

When playing true "percentage ball," the bunt is called for <u>almost</u> every time the offensive team has a runner on first, or first and second and no outs in the inning. Remember that we are talking about a "Sacrifice Bunt" here, one where the hitter actually turns and faces the pitcher as he begins his motion to the plate. Many teams call for the sacrifice bunt only in the later innings, playing for the big inning early in the game.

## How to Hold the Bat to Sacrifice Bunt

There are two different schools of thought as to how to position one's self to carry out a sacrifice bunt. The old school teaches the hitter to turn and face the mound with his shoulders squared off to the pitcher. The bat should be **perfectly level** with the logo on the bat facing straight upwards. The right thumb should be placed just into the logo on the backside top of the bat, and the index finger should be positioned underneath the bat pinching the bat between the thumb and forefinger. The remaining fingers should be in a held like a fist below the index finger. Gripping the bat in this manner, hold the bat out in front of you with arms extended about 60%, elbows bent slightly. At the same time, lower your head down directly behind the bat to eye level, viewing the incoming pitch just over the top of the bat. The bat should be **perfectly level** and extended out over the front of the plate as shown below.

The hitter is giving himself up or sacrificing himself to move the on-base runner to the next base. His job is to bunt the ball firmly enough onto the infield grass to make the third baseman, pitcher, or first baseman field the ball, but only in time to throw to first base. The hitter's actual physical vulnerability facing the pitcher straight away makes it very difficult for him to protect himself from being "plunked" on an inside pitch.

As the ball is delivered by the pitcher and with the bat **perfectly level**, lower or raise your hands simultaneously with your eyes, moving the entire upper body as one unit as you follow the incoming flight of the pitch to make contact. To bunt the ball down the third base line, pull the left-hand backwards to set that bat angle. As the ball makes contact with the barrel of the bat keep your grip firm on the bat to make the ball roll a minimum of 15 or 20 feet down the third base line. To bunt the ball down the first base line, push the handle of the bat forward with the left-hand to create the proper angle for a bunt down the first base line. Keep the bat level at all times, and your eyes level with the bat at all times.

The new school of thought regarding the hitter's sacrifice bunt position is for the hitter to turn shoulders slightly open to the mound with his front foot pulled back a few inches and his weight on the back leg. This position offers good balance with the ability to move faster and control the bat. The left-hand stays down on the knob of the bat, and the right-hand is slid up barrel to the label and held with a pistol grip. This means pinching the bat with the thumb and forefinger with the remainder of the fingers in a fist below the index finger. The barrel of the bat in this stance is not level, but pointed out toward the second baseman and **at a 45 degree angle upwards.** The bunter must have plate coverage no matter which stance he assumes in the box. In this stance, if the pitch is above the end of the bat it is a ball. If it is below the end of the bat the bunter merely bends his legs and drops the bat on the ball. It has been accepted over the last twenty years that a ball bunted with the **bat held at 45 degrees** will cause the ball to go downwards to the ground more often than holding the bat level as described in the old school description above. Try both methods and experiment with them under pressure until you find out which is more consistent for you.

**FUN-DA-MENTAL: Bunting is an art and takes lots and lots of practice to be good at it. To control the impact of the ball against the surface of the bat and attain the best direction of the bunted ball, the left-hand is pushed slightly forward for a bunt down the first base line, or pulled slightly backwards for a bunt down the third base line.**

For your information, when a bunted ball starts down the line in fair territory but rolls across the line into foul territory inside first or third base, it must be immediately picked up or pushed farther into foul territory so it doesn't come back into fair territory. If the bunted ball rolls back into fair territory inside the bases before the infielder can kick it outside the line, the bunt is considered a fair ball. In this case, the infielder must pick up the ball and look to any base for a potential out.

### The Drag Bunt

The drag bunt is a different animal. The batter disguises the fact that he is going to attempt to bunt a pitch by waiting until the pitch is actually on the way to the plate before dropping the barrel of the bat straight off the shoulder to make contact with the ball. This is usually tried when the defense is set up deep in their positions.

To perform a drag bunt the hitter must wait until the ball is in flight before moving his feet in the box. By waiting until the ball is in flight, he won't tip off the first or third basemen that he is going to try to bunt for a base hit until it is too late for them to react. In one motion, the hitter takes a half step back with the back or (right) foot and drops the head of the bat level and at the appropriate angle for the ball to make contact with the bat to rebound in the desired direction. His right or top hand slides down the barrel of the bat to the logo. His left-hand remains behind above his right hip in a fixed position. When contact with the ball is made, the lower body should already be in motion forward but **must still be in the box** until such contact is made. If the bunter's feet move out of the box before contacting the ball, he is automatically out. With both eyes on the ball and the angle of the bat appropriately set to drop the ball down one of the lines, the bunter tries to get a step advantage in order to beat the throw by the infielder. The moment of surprise wins if the infielders are playing deep in their positions. Of course, the bunter needs to have good speed to "leg" a drag bunt safely. The drag bunt should roll as close to the foul line as possible and must travel a distance of about forty feet to have any chance of being successful.

**The Suicide Squeeze**

Another means for scoring a run utilizing the bunt is called a "suicide squeeze." The suicide squeeze is called for when a team is desperately in need of one run to win the game or is the home team and needs one run to tie the game to go into extra innings. It is an offensive play or tactic that has two components: the runner being given the steal sign and the hitter being given the bunt sign, on that same pitch.

The suicide squeeze is usually saved for a situation that includes a man on third base, with either no outs or one out, late in the game, and the score either tied or the hitting team being down by one run. But it can be run anytime with less than two outs if the speed of the runner on third is good and the probability of the batter bunting the ball on the ground is high.

The suicide squeeze is executed as like this. With the steal sign given to the runner on third, he will be coming down the line to steal home as soon as the pitcher's motion begins toward the plate. To protect the runner, the batter must turn and face the pitcher, assume the proper bunting position, and bunt the ball **somewhere** in fair territory on the ground. Then he must get out of the way before the runner sliding into home plate wipes him out. When done properly, the run scores, and the hitter is either safe or out at first base. But the task of scoring the one run necessary to remain in the game has been achieved. A player's ability to bunt successfully is a real asset. In the case above, a pitch that is bunted into the air and caught is an automatic double play at third, as there is no way the base runner can make it back to third before being forced out.

**The Bunt Play: A Defensive Action to Prevent a Successful Sacrifice Bunt**

We have now been exposed to bunting and how teams utilize the bunt to move runners into scoring position, catch the defense asleep for a base hit, and even score a run when they have little, to no other, choice. Teams that practice this formula for moving base runners are said to be playing percentage baseball.

When the hitting team has a runner on first base, or first and second, with no outs, the defensive team will try to counter a sacrifice bunt attempt by calling a defensive play known as the **bunt play**.

The bunt play is executed through pre-established coordination of the pitcher, catcher, and infielders carrying out a strict set of sequential steps in an attempt to prevent the sacrifice bunt from being successful. Those steps are as follows:

**Step #1: The first pitch to the hitter must be a fastball, and it must be a Pitch Out. There are two reasons for these actions.**
- A. To see if the hitter gives any indication that he is going to bunt.
- B. To set up a quick "catcher to first" pick off throw should the runner commit too big of a lead toward second on this first pitch. The first baseman remains back to hold the runner close and receive either a pick off attempt from the pitcher, or a pick off attempt by the catcher.

**Step #2:** The second pitch to the hitter must be a fastball thrown right down the center of the plate because we want the batter to bunt this pitch. Everyone in the infield moves as follows: _Before the pitcher begins his motion to the plate,_ the first baseman and third basemen charge in to field the bunt. The second baseman covers first; the shortstop covers second. In the diagram below each of the participating players has a zone of coverage during the execution of a bunt play. The pitcher covers zone #1 after he delivers a perfect strike.

A. The first baseman **(#3) charges the plate on the second pitch** to field any bunt hit to the first base side of the pitcher's mound (down the first base line) quickly enough to make a play on the **lead runner** at second or third as the case may be. If not possible to force the runner at third, he will look to second for a force out there and finally throw to the second baseman covering first, for one sure out. This all happens in less than three and a half seconds. **The FUN-DA-MENTAL here is to make sure you get one out somewhere...**

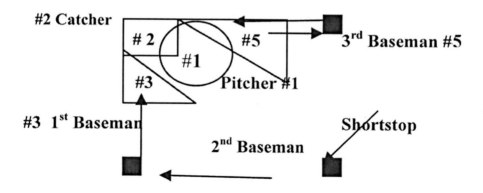

**#2 Catcher**     # 2     #5     3<sup>rd</sup> **Baseman #5**

#1

#3     Pitcher #1

**#3  1<sup>st</sup> Baseman**     **Shortstop**

**2<sup>nd</sup> Baseman**

B. The pitcher **(#1)** covers bunts hit from directly back at him to half way down the third base line. After fielding the bunted ball, he will look to see if the third baseman has returned to the base in time to receive his throw to force the lead runner. If not, he will look for a force out at second. If too late at second, he will make sure to get one out at first.

C. The catcher **(#2)** takes all super short bunts in front of the plate. He will make sure of one out to any of the three bases. He has the entire play in front of him. He will go after all pop ups in back, around, and in front of the plate, should the attempted bunt be fouled up in the air.

D. The second baseman covers first base to catch a "one-out-for-sure" throw from the player fielding the bunt.

E. The shortstop covers second to start a possible double play from the player fielding the bunt.

F. The third baseman **(#5) <u>charges the plate on the second pitch</u>** just like the first baseman. BUT, he must read instantly whether or not he has any chance to field the bunt or return to third for a possible play on the lead runner. He will field **ONLY** a bunt hit hard enough down the line that goes by the pitcher. He will first look to second to start a double play or make the throw to first for the absolute "one out."

G. If the pitcher fields the bunt, **the third baseman must get back to third to take the throw on the lead runner if there is a play there.** The runner coming from second can be forced out. A runner coming all the way around from first base must be tagged out at third. This is where verbal communication between the pitcher and the third baseman is critical in making the play work. If the pitcher can yell-off the third baseman early enough, he can get back to third to take the throw for the force out of the lead runner. That is the entire reason for initiating this play! We know what they are going to do, so let's take it away from them.

H. After catching the sure out at first, the infielder will run the ball across the infield to prevent any runners from advancing, and thus eliminating the chance of a wild throw across the diamond. The runner moving from second to third will most likely make a wide turn at third and/or attempt to score in a tight game as the play is being made to first base. A throw to home plate may be necessary if the runner tries to score. Throw a strike to the catcher, so the runner can be tagged out!

From a defensive standpoint, the bunt play is the best tool ever devised to prevent the start, or continuation, of a big scoring onslaught. The secret to its success is to follow each step during its execution, exactly. The most important part of its execution is to make sure that the defensive team gets one out somewhere, preferably the lead runner, but absolutely the bunter at first base.

Please take some time to study the mechanics of the bunt play. It is easy to execute and, without question, the best strategy to get your team out of trouble. When the bunt play defense is executed properly and you get the lead runner, it takes all the wind out of the hitting team. The following diagram shows the defensive options for all the players when a Bunt Play is called.

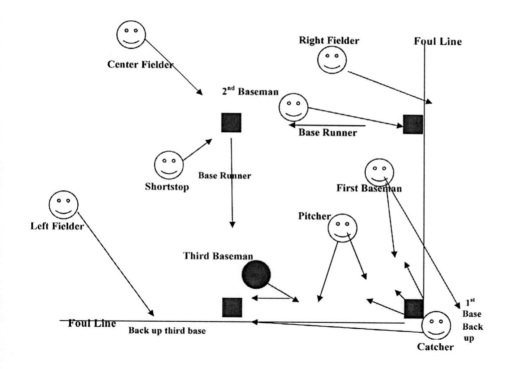

The illustration above shows the immediate field coverage for each of the players the moment the batter squares around to bunt. In this particular scenario, there are no outs, runners at first and second, with the tying or winning run on second. To attempt to sacrifice these runners over to second and third with no outs would be routine for any team playing high percentage baseball, whether early or late in the game. The primary purpose of the defensive team is to field the bunt quickly to force out the lead runner trying to advance from second to third base. Then you are set up for a natural double play to end the inning.

If the bunt is fielded by the catcher, pitcher, or first baseman, the third baseman would cover third, the shortstop would cover second, the second baseman would cover first, because the first baseman is too far out of position to get back to the bag to receive the throw from either of them. The first basemen should be about 20 feet from the plate and still coming when the bunt actually hits the ground. Depending upon how far up the third base line the bunt rolls, the third baseman will either make a play to second or first for the one sure out.

Once again, if the bunt is fielded by the third baseman, he has the option of throwing to the shortstop covering second to start a double play, or, if too late, would throw to first base for **one sure out**. During the time it takes for the throw to go from the third baseman to first, the runner advancing will see third base open, and might not stop at third but continue on to try to score. In this case, the second baseman covering first must make the sure out then throw a perfect strike to the catcher for the double play tag out at home plate. This entire scenario happens in about four seconds. So you have to know exactly what to do when these different options arise. Study this sequence of events over and over, as it is extremely important that you understand and practice your own responsibility in carrying out the bunt play to perfection. It's all timing and quickness of the feet and mind.

# CHAPTER 21

## Running the Bases, Lead-offs, and Stealing Bases

### Running to First Base Outside the Foul Line

First of all, you have to get on base to be able to run the bases. In doing so, there is one rule that is very important to learn early. When you leave the batter's box to run down the first base line in an attempt to beat the throw, you must run **<u>outside the foul line</u>** in the last 30 feet as you approach first base. In better ballparks the grounds keepers will outline this box in the grass in foul territory. On normal sandlot fields, the runner just has to know to run outside the foul line when approaching first base. The reason for this is to protect the runner from being hit in the back of the head by a throw from the catcher or pitcher fielding the ball. Running outside the line also provides a little more room for the first baseman to move around the base as he tries to catch offline throws without getting into a catastrophic collision with the oncoming runner. Don't fight it, just do it!

**FUN-DA-MENTAL: Hit the ball, start down the line any way you want, but get outside the foul line in the last thirty feet before the bag. Your career will last longer if you learn this fundamental early.**

### Proper Lead from First Base

Now that you have arrived at first, there is a lead off procedure that has been "the standard" for many years. Specifically, it is three steps off the base plus one half-step if the pitcher has only a fair move to first. This places the average runner with good reactions between eight or nine feet off the base. Experienced base runners with great speed and super reaction time will push this distance out to four steps or nearly 10 feet. If the pitcher has a great move to first, even three steps may be too far out.

**FUN-DA-MENTAL: The proper lead off first base is to take whatever distance you can get away with and still make it back to the base without getting picked off. This is usually three and one-half steps, or four if you are really quick.**

And it's ok to dive back on your stomach. However, being flat on your face doesn't help you too much in advancing to second, should the pickoff attempt get by the first baseman. The consistent stealing of a base is accomplished more by getting a good jump on the pitcher's motion rather than getting too long of a lead off the base and have to protect it by putting your body in a negative lean (back to first) position. You negate a good jump when you are not perfectly balanced over your feet to take the first crossover step when you break for second.

**How Important Is Your Run?**

There are a number of very critical things you must know when you become a base runner. They include the following:

1. What is the score?
2. What inning is it?
3. What does my run mean in the game?
4. What sign should I be looking for in this situation?
5. Who is the hitter now in the box?
6. Are we going to bunt in this situation?
7. Is the pitcher right- or left-handed?
8. Does he have a good move to first base?
9. What is a safest distance to lead off without getting picked off?
10. How strong and accurate is the catcher's arm to first and second?
11. How has the defense set up for the next hitter?

The score of the game determines whether or not your run means anything at this moment or to the final outcome of the game. For example, if you are the runner on first base with no outs in the ninth inning and one of the scenarios below occurs, you should do the following:

- If your team needs three runs to tie up the game in the ninth inning, your one run means nothing. With no outs, take a safe lead and don't get picked off. Be alert for a hit and run, or a run and hit. Don't get doubled off on a line drive. Move back to the base on a line drive. Run hard on a ground ball to break up the double play if possible. Go half way (a safe distance) on a ball hit to the outfield. You might consider tagging up at first if the ball is hit deep to the wall and the outfielder must make a running catch moving away from you. If the ball comes off the wall and you are half way, you can make third safely. If you tag up, and the ball is caught you might be able to advance to second. But when you are halfway to second and the ball is caught on the run, there is no way you will be able to return to first base, tag up, and advance to second. It becomes a judgment call as to how and where the ball is hit. Remember, down three runs with no outs, your run means nothing without base runners behind you. Don't be a hero. Every game situation requires some risk, some caution, or complete safety. As a young player you must be involved in each to begin to understand when to take a risk and when to play it safe.

- When you are the home team you play for a tie in the ninth inning because you bat last in every inning at home. If you are a base runner representing the tying run late in a game, the amount of lead you take in a bunt scenario is very critical, because you need to reach second, no matter what, when the ball is bunted by your teammate. You must also appreciate that you cannot afford to get picked off by either the pitcher, or the catcher on a pitch out, on the first pitch of a defensive bunt play. Be alert!

- When you are the visiting team you must take chances to try to win the game in the ninth inning. When you are the Visiting Team, your last time at bat is the top of the inning, so you must throw caution to the wind, take a good but safe lead so you don't get picked off, and take every reasonable risk to advance to the next base. Run hard and watch / listen to your third base coach for instructions as to what to do. Then do it without hesitation.

Appreciating the fact that some of this information does not apply to those of you playing in the younger levels of the game where you must wait until the ball crosses the plate before you can attempt to steal any base. But it's perfectly OK to learn it correctly now so you will be ready to play at the higher level. With that in mind, let's take a moment to learn about base running speed, in particular, going from home to first.

## Player Speed to First Base from Home

The following speed chart shows the actual distance in feet/per second that a base runner will cover sprinting from home to first base, based on his own specific speed.

For Example: A player running from home to first in 3.6 seconds is covering the 90 foot distance at a rate of 25.0 feet/sec. This is an extremely quick time. How fast are you from home to first?

| Stopwatch Time | = | Feet / Second Covered |
|---|---|---|
| 3.6 Seconds | = | 25.0 Feet / Second |
| 3.7 | = | 24.3 |
| 3.8 | = | 23.7 |
| 3.9 | = | 23.1 |
| 4.0 | = | 22.5 |
| 4.1 | = | 21.9 |
| 4.2 | = | 21.4 |
| 43 | = | 20.9 |
| 4.4 | = | 20.5 |
| 4.5 Seconds | = | 20.0 Feet / Second |

You may ask why this is important to know. Here is the explanation.

**SITUATION:** You are the only base runner. You have reached third base with no outs or one out, late in the game. Your team is down by one run when a fly ball is hit approximately <u>275 feet</u> into the outfield.

**QUESTION:** If the ball is caught by the outfielder, do you have the speed to tag up and make it home safely, or should you bluff trying to score looking for a wild throw that gets away from the catcher, or should you go back to third to wait for the next hitter to drive you in?

**INFORMATION:** The knowledge you gained watching your opponent's outfielders throw during their infield drill before the game showed you each of their arm strengths. In this situation, the left fielder will catch the ball 275 feet away from home plate and attempt to throw you out. Let's estimate that he can throw the ball at a speed of 75 mph or 110 feet per second. His throw will cover the distance in 2.5 seconds. It will take him an additional one-half second to set and throw the ball into home plate. <u>Of course, his accuracy plays a big part here also.</u>

Adding the time it takes for the catcher to actually catch the ball and make the tag on you will take another second to second and a half for a total of 4.0 to 4.5 seconds to make the play on you if the throw is perfect. If not perfect, add another second for a total of 5.0 to 5.5 seconds.

You, on the other hand, cover the distance of 90 feet from a fully tagged up position at a rate of 21.4 feet per second. This equates to 4.2 seconds. The play on you at home on a perfect throw will be very close, but with a wide throw you will be safe by over one second. If you get a bad jump from third, and the outfielder makes a good throw, you would be out. If the outfielder throws off target, pulling the catcher away from the plate, you're safe by a mile.

In this scenario, down in runs late in the game, you must always try to score. Put all the pressure on the outfielder to make that perfect throw to get you out. In high school, very few throws will be so accurate that you can't slide away from the tag by the catcher to score the tying or go ahead run.

Good high school outfielders throw about four times the speed that a base runner can run. So if he can throw 75 mph and you can run 18 mph, whether or not you will be safe or out at the plate is purely a matter of how far away from home plate the outfielder catches the fly ball, and how fast he gets it on the way to home.

Now, back to leading off from first base. For the more advanced player there are a number of ways to lead off at first base. The most FUN-DA-MENTAL and popular lead is to take three full side steps plus one half step. Another is to take a walking lead by starting off the bag as the pitcher begins his stretch. When he looks to check your distance from the base, he will see that you are pretty close and not a threat. But by the time the pitcher actually releases the ball your walking lead can take you out 8 or 9 feet from the base. If the pitcher holds his set position long enough, it will force you to stop, or even shorten up. This is the way a smart pitcher prevents you from getting too far off the bag. Be aware that a right-handed pitcher will hardly ever look directly at you. They have learned to look over their shoulder into the grass to pick up your lead off distance peripherally. Any unnatural movement of the pitcher's shoulders while holding you close, without throwing over to first, is a balk. A left-handed pitcher will be looking right at you. Be extremely careful until you learn all of his moves. If you are a fan in the stands watching the game, keep your eyes peeled on the distance the base runner leads off first base, and how far out the pitcher will let him go before a pick off throw is made.

Getting a good jump is essential if you are going to attempt to steal second. But when you need to get back, you have to really hustle, because many catchers have strong enough arms to pick you off if you are caught leaning in the wrong direction with a big lead. Without the steal sign being given, the fundamental for every base runner is to be in motion toward second as the ball passes over the plate to take advantage of a wild pitch, a passed ball, a base hit, or a ground ball.

**FUN-DA-MENTAL: ALWAYS move back to the base on a line drive until you are sure it will not be caught by anyone, then advance, or not, accordingly.**

All great base stealers study every movement that pitchers make in their routines on the rubber, especially the left-handers. The right-handed pitcher must lift his back foot off the rubber in order to throw to first, unless he tries to pick you off before he touches the rubber to get his sign. His motion is not as deceptive as the left-hander's. Many left-handers will try to pick you off even before looking in to get their sign from the catcher, not waiting to get to the set position. Some left-handed pitchers have two moves. One that just makes you retreat to the base, and a "quick" nasty one that he will use when you are least expecting it. It might come over sidearm, or even without a step motion. Never take your eyes off of a left-handed pitcher.

Supposedly, the left-handed pitcher must throw the ball to home if his right knee passes open in front of his left knee toward the plate. Watching his head or shoulders will only freeze you, because he does not have to move his left foot out of the hole like the right-handed pitcher. So he can be very sneaky and get away with a lot of cheating unless you (and the first base umpire) are watching very closely. Most good moves will include a look to home and throw to first in the same motion.

## First Step When Stealing Second

When you have taken your lead, your first step from this set position is the most critical. With your weight evenly balanced over both feet set slightly wider than shoulder width, the left side is launched over the right leg with a big crossover step with your left foot. By shifting all of your weight onto your right side and opening your shoulders straightaway to second base, your right foot pushes off the outside edge of the foot and is in an immediate position to push and lift for the second step. An inexperienced base stealer will pick up his right foot first and replant it in the direction of second, then push off his left side for his first step. When he does this he is already one step behind the runner above, in the previous sentence.

Normally, it takes between 13 and 14 strides to run from first to second with a normal lead off at first base. The distance from first to second is ninety feet. In a set lead off position 8'off first base, means that you have to run 82' to reach second base before the catcher can receive the pitch and make the throw to second in time for the shortstop or second baseman to catch it and make the tag on you for the out. If the catcher were to get a quick pitch from the pitcher each time a base runner decided to steal, a very high percentage of the runners would be out. But a quick pitch is not the pitcher's natural motion, and he would most likely be called for a balk. Remember that most catchers have powerful, quick and accurate arms which enables them to throw the ball somewhere in the mid-80 mph range. The point I am making here is that unless a base runner takes a good lead, gets a good jump on the pitcher's motion, and has good speed, he will most likely be thrown out. Some catchers are wild and do not throw well when forced to do so under pressure. Base runners can take advantage of their inaccuracy more than they can the power of their arms.

Bases are not usually stolen on the catcher. They are stolen on the pitcher's motion who takes too long to deliver the ball to the plate. If you have better than average speed, take an aggressive lead and get a good jump, you will most likely be safe more times than you will be called out. Maury Wills and Ricky Henderson both studied the opposing pitcher's delivery motions on every pitch throughout the entire game to learn when it was possible to break for second and be safe when they got the opportunity. Wills did not have blazing speed but got exceptional jumps. Henderson has good speed and has always been successful because he knew exactly what the pitcher's actions were and could judge when to take advantage of them.

**FUN-DA-MENTAL: Successful base stealers most often steal the base on the pitcher, not the catcher. You must take a good lead, get a good jump on the pitcher's motion, and crossover on your first step away from first base. The rest is pure speed.**

When a base runner is forced to get back to the base, on either a throw over from the pitcher, or a pick off attempt by the catcher, he must get back to the base safely and present the smallest target for the first baseman to tag.

Many base runners who take substantial leads tend to dive back to the base on their chest touching the corner of the base with their hand. This is fine unless the first baseman has to adjust his footing to catch an errant throw and inadvertently steps on the runner's fingers or hand. It doesn't happen often, but it happens.

Finally, when the pick off is not a high-speed attempt, the runner can pivot 180 degrees as he reaches the base with his left foot on the bag, simultaneously spinning his body clockwise back onto his right side and behind the first baseman, keeping his left foot in place on the base. This type return requires a sweep of the glove by the first baseman to make the tag. It also allows more time for the runner to be safe. From this return position the base runner is in perfect position to advance to the next base on a wild throw that gets by the first baseman.

**Proper Lead from Second Base**

Now let's discuss how to take an appropriate lead at second base. The next time you watch a major league game notice the variation of leads that are taken by the runners who reach second. Fundamentally, the shortest distance between two points is a straight line, right? So why do so many runners stand 5 or 6 feet toward the outfield when they lead off? The answer is that they never learned how to properly run the bases when they were young, so they think that if they can start with a better angle rounding third base from being higher at second they will be able to make the turn at third easier. WRONG!!! This position also puts the runner much closer to the shortstop than is necessary. The greater the distance from the infielder, the safer it is for the runner.

An appropriate lead from second is whatever the shortstop and second baseman will give you, as long as you appreciate that they may be setting you up for either a pick off attempt by the pitcher or a throw down by the catcher. The secret is to know where both of the infielders are at all times.

As a base runner, when you see the second baseman on the grass thirty feet from you, it is obvious that he will not be a factor on the next pitch. Since you have your back to the shortstop, it becomes mandatory for you to listen to your coach tell you that your current lead is OK! When he says "BACK," you go back. He will only tell you that when he sees the shortstop breaking in behind you. Many shortstops will try to fake you back to the bag, especially on certain pitches that the batter might hit the opposite way, enabling you to advance or even score. His purpose is to get you to step back toward second as the pitch crosses home plate. This minor delay might cause you to be held up at third due to a bad jump on the hit to right field. Isn't this great? Everything done on a baseball field is for a reason!

The shortest distance between two points is a straight line! Your lead from second should be straight off the bag. The length of your lead can be as far off as the closest infielder. With a right-handed pull hitter at the plate, the shortstop will probably be playing deep and a step or two towards the hole at third, so it's obvious that any pick off attempt at second base will be started with the second baseman shortening his distance to the bag. All you have to do is watch him as you increase your lead. One thing is absolutely critical when you are a base runner, and that is when the ball is crossing over the plate you must be physically in motion toward the next base. If you allow the defense to fake you back to the base, they will have a much better shot at throwing you out if you try to advance.

## Making the Proper Turn at Third

When rounding the bag at third, the fastest way around the base is to hit the inside left corner of the base with the arch of your LEFT foot and cross your right leg over the top like a football player who is trying to avoid being tackled. This action will prevent taking too wide of a turn, causing you to lose valuable time. The secret in making this turn easy and fast is to run directly at the base until you are about 18 feet from it, then make a three stride arc out to the right and then right back at the left inside corner of the base. I'll try to illustrate it for you below. Many coaches want their runners to hit the center of the top of the base so there is no doubt that the base was touched.

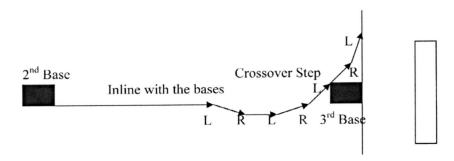

Here are a couple of Cardinal Rules for every base runner who reaches second base.

### Rule #1: **Always Hustle Back** to the base on a line drive.

Never get doubled off on a line drive hit to one of the infielders.

### Rule #2: **Never Advance** on a ground ball hit in front of you with less than two outs, unless it goes through the infield, or you have a runner behind you at first.

When you are on second base <u>with no runner behind you</u>, the last thing you want to do is run into an out at the base you are trying to get to. A good shortstop will merely throw to the advanced base, and you will be tagged out. Oh, that's embarrassing!

## Proper Lead from Third Base

When a runner reaches third base, it is normal to take a lead that is approximately the same distance as the third baseman is away from the base. If the pitcher is right-handed and throwing from a stretch, he will be looking right at the runner when he comes to his set position. He may be throwing from a stretch position to try to prevent the runner from getting too big a jump on an infield ground ball on which he may try to score. In this case, the runner should start off a step shorter from the bag until the pitcher's motion actually begins, then be in motion down the line as the ball crosses the plate.

If the pitcher throws from a full windup and the runner's run means little at this point in the game, the only real important distance to remember here is how far away the third baseman is setting up. Naturally, the pitcher is not going to throw over without the third baseman being there to catch it, right? So if the third baseman is 10 feet away as the pitch is going over the plate, the runner can also take a 10 foot lead off down the line.

In a tight ballgame, you certainly don't want to get picked off by the catcher on a pitchout. As you watch the ball cross the plate without the hitter swinging at it, you have nowhere to go but back to the bag as quickly as you can. If you don't, you're a dead dude! This is because the catcher can throw 90' on a pitch out faster than you can run 10 feet to get back to the bag safely. Listen to your coach, return to the base quickly after the ball passes the plate, and be sure to return to third running inside the base line. A pick-off throw by the catcher is an easy move for him, especially with a left-hand hitter in the box. The ball shows up down there very quickly. Your third base coach must be very attentive in watching the movements of the third baseman. You should be looking for a wild pitch or a passed ball to score. They may try to pick you off to get out of the inning.

**The basic thing to remember here is to be moving toward home plate as the ball crosses it.** Starting from a 6 to 8 foot lead set yourself to gain the pitcher's confidence that you are not going to steal on this pitch. Let him throw the ball to the plate and be ready to either run on a ball hit to the right side of the infield, tag up on a fly ball to the outfield, move back on a line drive, or go full blast if you have been given the green light to score at all costs.

⚾ ⚾ ⚾

# CHAPTER 22

## The Run-Down or Pickle

When you are trapped between bases with no place to go but back and forth until you are tagged out, you are considered to be in a "pickle." With no place to go, you try not to get tagged out as long as possible, hoping someone will drop the ball so you can get to one of the two bases you have been caught between. You also make time for the runner behind you to advance to the next base.

The defensive team, on the other hand, wants to tag out this runner trapped between the bases as quickly as possible, and then if it is the case, make a second play on the runner trying to advance to second base during the run down. There is a detailed play that the defensive team must initiate to tag out this "pickled" runner. It is called the "Run-Down Play."

The "pickle" might be created when a runner hesitates running the bases on a base hit to the outfield. He might make a big turn at second and get half way to third before he realizes he can't possibly make it without being thrown out. So he stops and tries to get back to second. Woops, gotcha!

Under normal game conditions, with no outs or one out, a runner on first base, and the score not yet a factor, it is FUN-DA-MENTAL for an outfielder to field a base hit and throw it into second base to split up the runners, rather than trying to make a perfect throw to third and possibly miss a close tag on the lead runner. By throwing the ball to third base, the hitter has a free pass to make the turn at first base and move on to second while the play is being made at third. A throw into second base holds the hitter to a single and keeps the double play option alive. This is playing the percentages.

As the ball is being handled at second, the runner who has advanced to third might try to go all the way to the plate and score. A good throw from the second baseman to the catcher usually can be made in plenty of time to tag the runner out by a large distance. In some cases a runner will stop in the base line before being tagged out at home, allow himself to get into a run-down, and try to keep it going until the hitter ends up at second base, or even third. This is where it is imperative for the catcher to run the base runner back to third base. He will be sure to get at least one out with two runners standing on the same base. The runner stays in the pickle as long as he can before getting tagged out to allow his teammates to advance behind him. That's what you need to learn here.

Infielders practice run-downs in spring training until their tongues hang out. The purpose of the run-down is to prevent a runner from getting out of the pickle, period! So let's learn how the trap is set.

When a runner is caught between bases, the infielder with the ball should run right at the stranded base runner until the runner commits to one direction or the other. In the case where the runner is much closer to third base than second, the ball should be thrown to the third baseman immediately to start the play back toward second. The infielder fielding the ground ball should hold the ball high up in the air over his head so all his teammates can see it clearly, ready to toss it. If the runner makes a move toward third base, the infielder should chase the runner toward third base. Simultaneously, the third baseman should begin running right at the base runner to close the distance on him as quickly as possible. As the third baseman closes the distance to about ten feet, the infielder with the ball held high, **tosses** it to the third baseman for an immediate tag out. No base runner in the world is fast enough to stop in the base line, turn around, and run in the opposite direction to get away from a player that is running wide open toward him, within 5 or 10 feet.

## One Throw, One Out, That's What It's All About!

As illustrated below, the third baseman with ball held high above his head should run wide open at the base runner. As the pickled runner turns to go back toward second base, either the shortstop, or second baseman, whichever is in position, should **immediately** run right at the oncoming runner to close the trap. When the shortstop is within 10 feet of the runner, the third baseman should toss (not throw) the ball held from high over his head to the shortstop, who makes the catch and tags the runner out before he can stop and start back towards third. When this play is run correctly, there should be only one throw made, and the runner should be out every time. If there is a scenario requiring more than one throw, start the play again by running the pickled runner in the other direction and have another teammate close the distance on him to receive the toss for the out.

# THE RUN DOWN OR PICKLE

If you have been a part of the run-down and thrown the ball to your team-mate for the tag, make sure that you immediately move in behind him as a backup in case he misses and the runner gets around him in the other direction. In that case, the chase, the trap, and the final throw starts again just as if it were the first time. No panic. The runner is getting real tired!

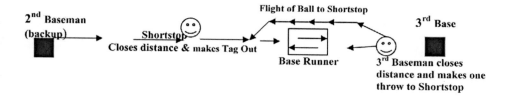

# CHAPTER 23

## The Outfielders

The defensive position of an outfielder on a baseball team is a really neat place to play this game. All you have to do to be an outfielder is enjoy being alone, talk to yourself a lot, run like a cheetah, possess an arm like a bazooka, have no fear of running into fences, jump 10' high against the wall on the dead run to steal base hits or home runs from opposing hitters, hit over .300, and drive in 100 or more runs every year. No problem. Easy deal, except for the last six things!

## Decision Making –Where do I throw the ball when it comes to me?

The most important decision that an outfielder has to make defensively is which base he will throw to if the ball is hit to him. Throwing to a specific base for the right reason during a critical game situation is the result of rapidly processing all the information available in front of him at the moment, and making the play.

For example: Let's set a game scenario in the bottom of the 9th inning, in which the Visiting Team is ahead, 5-3, needing just three outs to win the game. The Home Team, on the other hand, is at bat and has put runners on first and second with no outs. The base runner at first is the catcher who has only fair speed. The base runner at second is the shortstop who is very quick.

**Questions: To which base should an outfielder throw the ball on a base hit to his field?**
**What did the outfielder have to know before he fielded the base hit into his field?**

1.  **He had to know the inning, the number of outs, and the score of the game.**
    **Answer:** Last of the 9th inning; No outs; Score 5-3 his team (Visitors) ahead

2.  **He had to know which of the base runners represented the tying and go ahead runs.**

**Answers:** Runner at second = No Problem
Runner on first = Tying run
Hitter at plate = Winning run

3. **He had to know how fast each of the base runners was on first and second.**
   **Answer:** Base runner on second is a shortstop - Runs very well and will most likely score on any base hit.
   His run would bring the score to 5-4. Base runner on first is the catcher with only fair speed – Tying run. Must attempt to keep him at second and the hitter at first for potential double play.
   Hitter represents winning run – Must not let him get into scoring position.

**Options: If it is a hard hit line drive straight-away** - Might possibly have a play at home, might not...too risky to consider. **Worst decision.**
**Reason:** To throw to home would allow both runners behind him to advance to second and third, taking the defense out of a double play possibility, still with no outs. Even if the run scores, it means nothing. Score: 5-4, still no outs.
**If the ball is hit through the hole at short**, the left fielder would have no play at home on the speedy runner from second. (Score: 5-4.) No problem.

**BEST DECISION:** Throw to second base. If a play on the catcher going to third is not absolute, throw to second base to split up the runners. Keep the hitter at first base, at all costs.

Second option, if ball is hit down line or in the alley, the only decision would be to throw ball to cutoff man for any play. Even with a good jump on the base hit, the catcher would most likely stop at second, not wanting to risk being thrown out at third and take the tying run off the bases. Slow runner at second, winning run at first, still no outs. Score remains 5-4.
**Bad Decision to throw to third.**

**The BEST decision the outfielder can make is to throw the ball into second base and split the runners up for a double play, allowing the tying run to score and move the game**

**into extra innings. He cannot risk something happening at third base that negates the out and puts the winning run in scoring position.**

**Actual (Hypothetical) Game Scenario: Here's what (might have happened) happened.**

The home team manager gave the sacrifice bunt sign twice to the #4 hitter. On two attempts he failed to get the ball down on the ground and struck out on a close third strike. In his failure to move the runners up, he hurt his team by keeping them in a double play situation, needing two runs to tie and three to win. Now with one out, runners still at first and second, score still 5-3, the visitors have a much higher potential to get out of the inning without giving up anymore runs.

What does this all have to do with the decisions of the outfielders? Everything! Each of them must start all over justifying to which base they are going to throw the ball with one out, instead of no outs. Tying run is on second with fair speed, winning run is on first.

As the #5 hitter steps into the batter's box the sacrifice bunt is no longer an option. The hitter can be expected to hit away, or hit and run, to move the runners along in an effort to stay out of double play. Because he is a left-hand pull hitter, the visitors are going to pitch him outside and try to get a ground ball in the middle of the infield for the double play. This brings the center and right fielder into the action. As it turns out, he drives a liner between the first and second baseman for a single.

Are you wondering if the right fielder had done **his homework**? Well... let's find out. As it turns out, the speedy runner from second scored easily. Score 5-4. The right fielder picked up the ball and fired it to third base, missing his cutoff man as he tried for the out on the slower catcher going from first to third. The runner was safe at third, but the hitter remained at first base. Score Now: 5-4, but the hitter remaining at first base puts them back into a double play situation, lucky for the outfielder. The safe runner at third is only the tying run for the home team. The winning run did not want to risk being thrown out at second, trying to stretch his single into a double. Had the right fielder done his homework, he would have thrown the ball directly to second base to split the runners and set the table for a possible double play with one out already recorded. The tying run on third base is of little consequence when it comes to setting up for the final two outs. The double play gets the visitors out of the inning. The winning run must always be stopped from getting into scoring position late in the game. The throw should have gone into second base, with the pitcher now facing the #6 hitter in the lineup with one out and runners on first and third.

Are you still with me??? Early on in this book I mentioned that if you wear a baseball uniform you are on the team. If you are on the team, you are obligated to know how to play this game, so you won't make the wrong decision, at the wrong time, and take away your team's chance to win. It will happen, but if you think the game properly you won't make the wrong decision very often. That's all anyone can ask of you.

**FUN-DA-MENTAL: It is extremely important to know where you are going to throw the ball on every pitch in a game. Because there is an advantage or disadvantage to each team on every pitch, you must be sure you make the smartest play for your team.**

### The Offensive Blunder of the Game

Please appreciate that I purposely picked a situation late in the game where a **sacrifice bunt** was the highest percentage tactic for the offensive team to try. The number four hitter failed in two attempts and then struck out for the first out of the ninth inning. The home team needed two runs to tie the game and go into extra innings.

As you read these game situations, you will recognize the importance of being able to do the job when you are called upon and play high percentage baseball throughout the game, both offensively and defensively.

As this game played out, the home team scored only the one run on the single to right. The catcher died at third as the #6 hitter hit into a double play to end the inning. The home team lost the game because the #4 hitter failed to successfully sacrifice his teammates to second and third. The home team might have won the game on a mental error by the right fielder throwing to the wrong base for the wrong reason, but the #6 hitter ended the game with the double play ball, 6-4-3.

## Difference Between Mental Errors and Physical Errors

A mental error is a mistake that could have been avoided through better thought preparation. Throwing to the wrong base is a mental error. Not tagging up at second with no outs is a mental error. Getting picked off a base is a mental error. A pitcher not covering first on a ground ball to the right side of the infield is a mental error. Missing a sign from the coach is a mental error. Not sliding into a base on a close play is a mental error. Over time, mental errors will beat you more often than physical errors.

A physical error is a mistake that points to the physical ability of the individual. Throwing the ball poorly to second base on a double play is a physical error. Poor throws to first base are physical errors. Booting an easy ground ball is a physical error. Booting a ground ball that takes a bad hop is a physical error. A wild pitch is a physical error. Physical errors can happen to anyone from the sandlots to the big leagues. More practice, less errors. Softer hands, less errors. More throwing practice, more accurate throws. Catching with two hands, fewer dropped balls. It all gets back to the fundamentals of the game. If you don't learn the fundamentals, you can never expect to play this game at a high level.

## Communications Between Outfielders

There must be loud and definite communications between the outfielders as they both run after the same ball during a game. I'm sure you have seen two outfielders crash into each other trying to catch the same ball. Sometimes the collision includes an infielder that thinks he might also have a chance to make a play on it. So here comes all three of them wide-open to catch the same fly ball, in the same spot in the field, and all three are only watching the flight of the ball. What o' what do you think is going to happen? You guessed it! CRASH!

Without talking to each other as this play develops, and without following a strict set of rules that are in place to protect each of them against crashing into each other, the ultimate collision takes place. Following the fundamental rules of the game, all three of them think that they, individually, can make the play and all yell to each other, "I've got it." But if all three yell, I've got it, and each one independently fails to follow the rules, the eminent crash takes place.

## Rules for Calling-Off Teammates on Fly Balls

The fundamental rules for catching a fly ball hit in between various players anywhere on the playing field or in foul territory is as follows:

- When an infielder goes out after a pop fly that might drop in for a base hit, he must LISTEN for any other player in the vicinity of the potential catch to call him off the chase. When he hears the outfielder say "I've got it," he is to pull up immediately and peel off from the direction of the flight of the ball. He is the first one out of the chase, EVEN IF HE HAS CALLED "I'VE GOT IT," especially with men on base. The reasoning here is that if he makes the catch running at full speed, he is in the worst possible position to make a good throw on a runner tagging up when he has his back to the infield. INFIELDERS GET OUT OF THE WAY FIRST!

- Now, for this example only, we have two outfielders running wide open toward the same pop fly, and both of them are yelling, "I've got it!" Someone has to give in here, or there is going to be that big crash we talked about. The rule is that if the center fielder calls for the catch, everyone gets out of the way. He's da man! When he says "I've got it," he means it! At that instant, **any other pursuing players pull away** from the crash site and let "da man" make da play. This procedure prevents any unpleasant physical contact between them. Usually, an outfielder running in to catch the ball has the right away over any infielder running out to make the catch.

- In some cases, either the shortstop or second baseman trailing the play will be the one responsible for calling the name of the fielder best suited to catch this particular pop fly. When each of the players gets used to listening and reacting to each other's voices as the play develops, the potential for one player running into another is significantly reduced.

  **If the center fielder does not call for the ball,** the other outfielder has the right to keep coming and do whatever it takes to make the play, unobstructed by the center fielder, who has realized that he can't make the play. The center fielder then yells, "You take it!" Both outfielders are running in toward the infield, so both have the play in front of them. If close in, the one who catches the ball should continue to run the ball all the way into the infield to control the movement of any base runners.

If a runner on base happens to be too far off base waiting to see if the ball is going to be caught or not, the outfielder should continue into the infield, running right at him to start a run-down play by throwing the ball to the player closing the fastest on the runner. And all this fun and hustle happened because the outfielder who was supposed to catch the ball did so, through perfect communications with his teammates! "Don't you love it when a plan comes together?" as quoted from The A-Team Series on television.

If the ball is hit between the outfielders, the center fielder again has the right of way and continues after the ball until he realizes he can make the play. At that instant, he calls out, "I got it" and makes the play. The most important thing to learn here is that somebody has to be in charge, so everyone else can do their job. It's called communication, and it is vital to the success of any organization, whether it is a baseball team, a business, or at home.

# CHAPTER 24

## Advantage / Disadvantage between Pitcher / Hitter

Throughout this book, references have been made to an advantage/disadvantage scenario occurring on each pitch during a game. It is the constant and continuing battle between the pitcher and the hitter, from the first pitch in the game to the last. It's all about specific pitches that a hitter can look for when he is ahead in the count. And in reverse, it is all about the type of pitches that a pitcher can throw to the hitter when he is ahead in the count.

The further in front of the hitter the pitcher is in the count, the wider the selection of pitches he can expect to see, and the further off the plate the pitches will be thrown. The further behind the pitcher is in the count, the more limited his pitch selection will become, and the better the location of those pitches will be to hit. That is one of the reasons why taking the first pitch to see how the pitcher is going to throw to you is very important. More pitches, more looks, better pitch to hit!

**FUN-DA-MENTAL: Every pitch creates an advantage or disadvantage simultaneously for both teams. Learn how to take advantage when the advantage is yours.**

In the early innings of a ball game, it is smart baseball for every hitter going to the plate to take at least one pitch to see the motion of the pitcher and get a feel for his delivery and release. If that first pitch is a ball, it would be prudent to think that the pitcher surely doesn't want to walk the first hitter in the game. So if you are the hitter with a one ball count, you might look for the next pitch to be a pitch in exactly the spot that you have decided in the on-deck circle that you want to hit. If the next pitch is in that spot, you should hit it unless the take sign is on. If it is not in that *exact spot* in your strike zone, you should take it, even if it is a strike. Now you have seen two pitches, but you are behind in the count, one ball, and one strike. **Advantage Pitcher:** He has three pitches to get you out, and you have two pitches to swing at. However, his advantage is only a slight one at this moment in time.

If the second pitch had been a ball, you would have been in the driver's seat with a two ball and no strike count, but it wasn't. Count one ball, one strike. **Still Advantage Pitcher.** Now you look to the coach for a sign. If you don't get it, you focus on looking for the exact pitch of your dreams. If you get it, you swing; if you don't, you take it. Count two balls, one strike. **Advantage Even.** You both have two pitches left. Next pitch is ball three. Count three balls, one strike. **Advantage Hitter.** Now he can make only one pitch to you at this time, and that is to throw a strike. If it is not in your strike zone, you should take it for ball four and a free pass to first base with no outs. This type of patience makes the pitcher work to get ahead of you in the count, or lose you. When you are ahead in the count you have the advantage, when you are behind in the count he has the advantage.

Look at your coach for the take sign at 3-1. Let's imagine that this time you get the take sign! That's good baseball percentages! The umpire calls, "Strike Two!" Now the count is 3-2. **Advantage Even.** The pitcher has now thrown five pitches and all have been just off the corners of the plate. You've seen a couple of fastballs, maybe a slider, and maybe two breaking pitches of some sort. Being that you are the leadoff hitter, your 3-2 pitch must be close enough to hit, because he really doesn't want to put your speed on the bases with no outs. So here it comes! Bang, a line drive into left center. Nice going, you just ruined his no-hitter! This was a great start for your next time at bat. See how simple baseball can be. You're one for one batting .1000.

**Advantage/Disadvantage Between Offensive Team / Defensive Team**

OK. During the pitching and hitting sequence above, the same advantage and disadvantage was taking place between the offensive team and the defensive team. In the following explanation, we will put a runner on first base to more effectively explain the point. Let's assume it's the seventh inning, the hitting team has a man on first, the score is 5 to 3 in favor of the defensive team, and there are no outs. That means that the hitting team has the tying run at the plate. **Advantage Offense.**

In this scenario, let's say the batter now at the plate is the #3 hitter in the lineup. We know he can pull the ball, we know he has power, and we know he can run. We also know that he is a poor breaking ball hitter. So we are going to show him fastballs out of the strike zone, and we are going to try to get him off balance by throwing an assortment of breaking pitches away for strikes. Up and in fastballs, down and away breaking stuff, very simple…right?

At the same time the pitcher is getting his sign for a **breaking ball** for the first pitch to begin the down and away, up and in, down and away sequence, the shortstop and second baseman are picking up the catcher's signs also. When they see two fingers down, they immediately signal to the outfielders what the pitch will be. They might signal by not doing anything if it is a fastball and put their glove behind them if it is going to be a breaking pitch. Now all the pitcher has to do is throw the pitches where he is supposed to throw them. All the fastballs will be up, inside, and out of the strike zone. All breaking, or off speed pitches, will be on the outside half of the plate.

The first pitch to the #3 hitter is a breaking ball down and away for a strike. Since this hitter is a known pull hitter, the shortstop signaled to the second baseman prior to this pitch that the second baseman should cover second if the runner at first attempts to steal on this pitch. He does this by holding his glove up to his right cheek and opening his mouth wide if he wants the second baseman to cover the bag, or he will keep his mouth shut if he wants to take the throw from the catcher on a possible hit and run. Who covers the bag is dependent upon the pitch and the count on the hitter.

**Advantage/ Disadvantage, remember!! A breaking pitch is usually an off speed pitch, meaning that a pull hitter will either be out in front of it and pull it, or he will take the pitch because he is looking for a fastball in this situation until he gets to two strikes. So the shortstop signals to the second baseman to cover second on this pitch. Since the pitch was a strike, it puts the pitcher ahead in the count so he can set up the hitter with an up and in fastball off the plate remaining with his scheme.**

Since the next pitch called for is a fastball in, the shortstop signals second to take the throw by opening his mouth wide. It is anticipated that the hitter will get out in front of the pitch, even if it's off the plate. So the shortstop must shade toward the hole a step or two leaving 2nd base to be covered by the second baseman.

Second pitch is a fastball up and in for ball one. **Advantage Pitcher.** The count moves to 1 ball, 1 strike. The next pitch called for is a circle change up thrown on the outside half of the plate as scheduled. When a good hitter is hitting against a pitcher with good control, a 1 and 1 pitch is a very important pitch to gain the advantage or lose it, from both players' perspectives. It is a pivotal pitch, because **if it is a ball, it takes away the pitcher's advantage in the count; if it's a strike, it gives the defensive team the advantage.**

Sure enough, the runner goes, but the hitter swings and fouls the ball into the stands for a 1 ball 2 strike count. **Advantage Pitcher.** Now the shortstop can play double play depth but a step toward the hole, and the second baseman can play a step closer to the bag to start the double play on a ground ball to the left side of the infield. The reason for the adjustments is that the pitcher now has the advantage of throwing the hitter three of his best pitches off the edges of the plate, while the hitter can only look to protect it by being more defensive.

The next pitch called for is a fastball up and in. Good location, because hitter has to move his feet. Count moves to 2 balls – 2 strikes, man on first, no outs. **Advantage Pitcher.**

The 2 and 2 pitch is known as the pitcher's strike out pitch. In this case it is a hard slider out and down. The ball just misses the corner of the plate and is called a ball. The count moves to 3 balls and 2 strikes. **Advantage Hitter.** The next pitch has to be a strike, most likely a fastball or a hard slider away, since the pitcher just missed his out pitch.

The 3 and 2 pitch called for is another slider away. The pitcher does not want to walk this hitter with no outs. The hitter is looking for a fastball in his strike zone. The pitch is fouled off to continue at 3 and 2. **Advantage Hitter.**

Now what? So far, the pitcher has done his job well, and the hitter has taken him out to a full count. The runner is still on first base, and that's a good thing! Ok, ok, ok, don't panic!

The next pitch called is a two seam fastball over the plate. Its downward movement is a great pitch to get a ground ball. On this pitch the runner has been given the steal sign. Since we haven't yet made a move to first base, we will this time to keep the runner a half step closer to the bag as we set up the hitter for a ground ball double play. The pitch comes in sinking as it crosses the plate, and the hitter hits a slow ground ball to third. The third baseman fields the ball, the second baseman covers second, but the runner who got a good jump from first, is already there, so the throw has to be for one out at first base. Now there is one out with a runner at second. **Advantage Offense.**

**Still Advantage Offense**

I hope you get the idea. Although this is a rather simplistic explanation of how the advantage changes back and forth, every pitch forces both teams to consider all their alternatives to prevent the other team from accomplishing its job. No wonder they call this the greatest game on earth.

# CHAPTER 25

## Sliding into Bases

Now that you have learned how to play your position, where you are hitting in the lineup, and what you are going to do at the plate, you get your first base hit. You also know how big of a lead to take off first base, so it is very important to know how to slide into a base if there is a close play on you. The act of sliding into a base is easy to learn. So let's get to it!

There are three basic slides that every ball player should learn, and one that you may want to add at a later time. The three versions are known as the **figure-four slide, the hook slide,** and **the stand up slide.** An additional slide you may add later is the head first slide, but it is not recommended by the writer. All four of these slides are initiated when running at full speed, and specifically determined by the situation as it develops at the base.

For example, the figure-four slide is a **straight in slide** that allows you to touch the base going into it with a straight leg. It is used when there is no deception or dodging required by the runner to avoid the tag. This slide would be used when a defensive infielder had set up on the outfield side of the bag, waiting for the throw to make the tag, with nothing in front of the runner but the base. It is accomplished by leaping feet first, with either leg, tucking the trailing foot underneath the opposite leg at the knee, which is extended straight at the base. The runner's lead leg, hip and/or butt makes the first contact with the ground. He then sits down on his seat pockets and leans back fully stretched out onto his back until the slide ends at the base. Both hands should be up in the air to avoid being stepped on. Running at full speed, the runner's feet should leave the ground 8 to 10 feet out from the base.

THE FUNDAMENTALS OF BASEBALL

When there is a potential tag impending at the base, a different slide may be required to present a smaller target. In this case, the runner might use a hook slide to slide into the oncoming throw to disrupt the infielder's ability to catch it and make the tag. In another case, it might be used to slide away from the potential tag, presenting only a sliding foot as a target.

The hook slide is the one most used when stealing bases or trying to score on a close play at the plate. As with the figure four slide above, the hook slide is also initiated running at full speed, but instead of tucking the trailing leg under the knee, the hook slide begins by leaning backwards and thrusting the lead leg in a direction three feet to one side of the base or the other. As the slide begins to take form, the trailing leg merely bends inbound, as in a hurdling position, to enable only the foot to capture a corner of the base. The runner should leave the ground about 10 feet out from the base and end up with only the toe of the trailing foot "hooking" the corner of the base furthest from the infielder.

To better visualize the actual position of the base runner would be like watching a track athlete going over a hurdle in race. His trail leg is flat out to the side, with his lead leg pointing directly down the lane. But unlike the hurdler's upper body positioned forward, the hook slide requires the base runner to twist his upper torso out around the base to get it out of the way as a target for the tag. Here is my stickman doing a hook slide to the inside of the bag to avoid a tag from an outfield throw! The runner can also slide to the outfield side of the base by reversing the take off leg, to avoid a tag on a throw by the catcher.

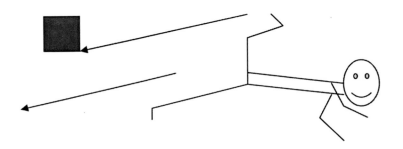

The last slide is called a stand up slide. It is used in two situations. The first is when an errant throw gets away from the infielder and rolls 30 or

40 feet away. The second is when he risks overrunning a base. In each of these situations the runner may be just one step from beginning one of the slides noted above. Rather than overrunning the base or making a full slide when it isn't necessary, the runner performs a standup slide.

The standup slide is carried out in full stride by taking off as if to carryout a figure-four slide, and instead of laying back to continue the slide toward the base, the runner merely pushes himself right back up using the base as a stop for his lead foot. With good speed going in to the base, his entire body will merely pop right back up to a stand up position to either remain on the bag or advance to the next depending upon how far away the ball has rolled. The total distance of this slide is about three feet, no more. You start late, hit the ground late, and pop right back up to a standing position.

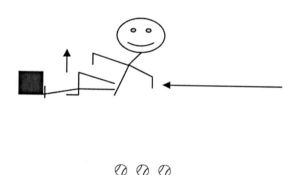

# CHAPTER 26

## Signs

Hand signals, or signs, as they are known in the game of baseball are flashed to batters and base runners alike to manage the offensive scheme, much like plays in football. They are usually given by the third base coach. Signs are traded between the catcher and pitcher, catcher and the infielders, between infielders, between the manger and the catcher, and the infielders to the outfielders. The third base coach gets his orders by hand signals from the manager on the bench. The coach relays the sign to the hitter and/or runners on base to be carried out on the next pitch.

There are an infinite number of ways to give signs. The faster and more efficiently the third base coach can disguise them, the less chance there is that the opposition can pick them off and know what the hitter or runner is going to do on the next pitch. So signs are usually flashed in very rapid sequence with the signal for the next pitch somewhere in that routine! Since we are talking fundamentals here, let's begin by explaining some basic signs that a younger player can pick up easily, and then step up to the more sophisticated variety that is used in higher classifications of ball.

Remember, earlier in the book, we learned about anticipating **WHICH** sign might be given (what to look for) depending upon the game conditions, the score, the inning, number of outs, speed on the bases, and so on. So here you are up at bat! The third base coach watches the manager for signals from the bench and then he relays that sign, or multiple signs, to the hitter, the base runner, or both.

As the third base coach begins his routine, touching one or both hands to his face, arms, cap, ear, chest, belt buckle, etc., it is important for the hitter to continue to watch until he has finished. The signal(s) flashed will tell the hitter, the base runner, or both, what to do, or what not to do, on the next pitch. So both must be watching very closely!

For the player not familiar with looking for signs from the coach, let's begin with three basic signals for the hitter, and one for the base runner. For the hitter, they would be the Hit Sign, Take Sign, and Bunt Sign. For the base runner(s), it would be the Steal Sign. So you won't be bored to sleep reading paragraph after paragraph of individual game situations that would create the necessity for every one of these signs to be given, let's go with the quick and obvious ones for demonstration.

First of all, the following signs will be oversimplified to allow younger players to understand what they are and how to recognize them in the sequence.

H- Hit Sign will be when the coach touches his **right-hand only** to his CAP

T- Take Sign will be signaled by touching **right-hand only** to the CHEST

B- Bunt Sign will be signaled by touching **both hands** to PANTS

S- Steal Sign will be signaled by touching **any skin to skin** (FACE OR ARMS)

When a hitter is in the on-deck circle getting ready to take his turn at bat, he must anticipate what sign to look for based upon the conditions of the game. When it is his turn to hit, he will walk to the batter's box, stop short of entering the box, and look at the third base coach for a sign. With no runners on base, no score, no outs, early in the game for example, he would only be looking for the **TAKE** sign at 3 balls - 0 strikes. Hitting away <u>up to</u> 3-0 would be almost automatic, and would not require a hit sign to be flashed. But the hitter should still look at his coach after every pitch and watch the entire routine to its end.

In a more complicated situation, let's put runners on first and second with no outs. The hitter would be looking for the **BUNT** sign, **both hands to the pants,** or the **HIT** sign, **right-hand Only to the cap.** He might also be given the **HIT** sign, as the runners are given the **STEAL** sign, which would be **any skin to skin** through the entire routine. This is the hit and run combination sign.

Playing high percentage baseball with no outs in the inning, the bunt sign would be given in an effort to advance both runners and stay out of a possible double play situation. However, an aggressive Manager might flash a **HIT and RUN (Right-hand to cap for the hitter)** and **(both hands to the pants for the base runner)** to give the runners a better jump and protect the base runners by making the batter swing at the next pitch. In this scenario, the offense team would be playing for the big inning and the defense would be playing in double play depth. By putting on the bunt sign the offense would be playing high percentage baseball. To try and take it away, the defense would put on their bunt play to counteract the offensive move. It just doesn't get any better than this does it!!??

So the third base coach starts his routine of signs to the batter by touching his left-hand to pants, then left-hand to cap, **left-hand to chest, both hands to pants, right-hand to left arm.** Only **both hands to pants, and right-hand to left arm** means anything. Now you know that the manager wants you to advance the base runners by bunting the next pitch, and preferably down the third base line if at all possible. So you step in the box, here comes the pitch, and you lay down a perfect bunt that requires the third baseman to field it and throw to first base for the out. The bunt allowed both base runners to advance to second and third as planned. Now there are two runners in scoring position with only one out. Great job, and you get big time HIGH FIVE for doing your job correctly. **Advantage Offense.**

But what if you are **not** thinking, and have **not prepared** properly in the on-deck circle, and you go through the same scenario with the coach but **miss** the bunt sign because you looked away too soon, or you just didn't remember what the bunt sign was for that moment. On the next pitch, you hit a ground ball that is turned into a double play. You missed the sign and took your team right out of a potentially big inning. Missing the sign was a mental error. Mental errors are unacceptable! You have to think!

When you get back to dugout this time, your coach let's you know that you missed the sign, you don't get any high fives, and your team loses the game by one run. Everyone on the team knew what was going on but you. You're the goat, and that's not a good thing! Being the goat more than once means less playing time until you can prove that you are capable of helping the team in those kinds of situations. It would have been acceptable to have tried to bunt and missed the bunt attempt. Physical errors are acceptable mistakes, although not very well liked. But mental errors, like missing the sign in a tight situation, are unacceptable. Baseball is not a game for dummies!

To get more deceptive, the coach might include an **INDICATOR** in his routine of signs. An indicator is just another hand or arm signal given by the third base coach somewhere in his routine that is followed by the sign he wants you to carry out. On any given day, the real sign may be the first, or second sign after the **INDICATOR is flashed**. Using an indicator allows the normal H-T-B-S signs above to remain constant. **The only thing that changes is the indicator from day to day.**

For example: The indicator for today is **Left-hand ACROSS CHEST**. This means that when the coach wipes his chest with his left-hand....the next sign will be what he wants you to do. So his sign routine might look like this: The coach touches his cap with both hands, wipes his chest with left-hand only **(indicator)**, then **touches his pants with both hands**, then touches his chest with both hands, and finishes by clapping his hands. The bunt sign is on!

Every team will have a different set of signals for each game. If a team uses the same signs for every game, every team in the league will know them. To adjust the signs you merely adjust the indicator. This can get very progressive, as you might well imagine. The most important thing is to keep the signs simple enough that your players see them and don't have to stop the game to ask if they just saw a steal sign given. That's a no, no.

⚾ ⚾ ⚾

# CHAPTER 27

## Handling the Fans and Parents

If you think the game of baseball is a difficult and complicated topic, it pales when compared to the problems that unruly mothers and dads can create during a ballgame.

Sometimes you just want to trade places with the parents who continue to rant and rave about their son or daughter not playing every inning of every game. And you hear about it...every game, over and over and over.

My best advice is to ignore the parents and give all the extra time you have available to this type player to build his/her confidence. Teaching is a science. You don't have to have twenty years of major league baseball experience to teach it. But you must know what you are talking about if you expect to be successful. If you are teaching young players how to play the game of baseball, you are already a success in life. It is the best training that you could ever have for building mental self-tolerance! Don't ever acknowledge the existence of anyone in the stands, ever, ever! Stay cool and keep your head in the game until it's over!

For the moment, this is over. I hope you were able to learn something from this book, and I wish you the best success in playing or teaching baseball, the greatest game in the world, America's Favorite Pastime.

⊘ ⊘ ⊘

# ADDENDUM I

## The FUN-DA-MENTALS of Baseball by Chapter

Chapter 1
    History of Baseball

Chapter 2
    Specifications of a baseball field

Chapter 3
    How to play the game

**FUN-DA-MENTAL**: Upon striking the ball into fair territory, the base runner has two options to consider as he gets close to first base. If the play is going to be close, he usually runs over the base and continues down the line before turning into foul territory to come back to first base. Should the throw to first get by the first baseman, the runner may turn into the field of play and try to advance to second if he so chooses. The fundamental here is that if he turns into the field of play but does not continue on to second, he may be tagged out at first base by the player covering first. Interesting, huh? Remember also that the base runner must run outside the line, in foul territory, when approaching first base. If he runs on the field of play, inside the foul line, he can be called out for obstruction if there is a close play on him.

Chapter 4
    Analysis of each Player Position and General Responsibilities

**FUN-DA-MENTAL**: When pitching, work smart, work quickly, and throw strikes! What is meant here is to get the ball over the plate so the game does not drag on.

**FUN-DA-MENTAL**: Field the position like an infielder, but get out of the way on a high pop fly around the mound.

**FUN-DA-MENTAL**: Catcher's signs to pitcher.

| # Fingers | Finger / Direction / Motion |
|---|---|
| 1 = Fastball | Right index finger / downward / hand to R/L thigh for in or out location |
| 2= Curveball | Right index and middle finger /downward / R/L thigh for location |
| 3= Slider | Circle right index finger / downward / Right thigh for location |
| 4= Changeup | Wiggle all four fingers / downward / R/L thigh for location (May include circle change, screwball, sinker, or palmball / R/L thigh) |
| Thumb Flip | High inside knockdown pitch / Location is automatic up and in |
| Fist | Pitch out |

**FUN-DA-MENTAL**: In the event a ball is hit to <u>any one of the outfielders</u> with runners on base, the most important thing for him to accomplish is to prevent the ball from getting by him for extra bases. The most common mistake an outfielder can make is to try to field the ball on the dead run with his entire body off to the side of the oncoming ball. The outfielder must become an "infielder" when attempting to catch a hot ground ball by keeping the ball directly in front of him if at all possible. When fielding a ground ball base hit, the outfielder should attempt to catch the ball with his right leg forward if he is right-handed, or vice versa, if he is left-handed. It then only requires one step onto his opposite foot to release the throw back into the infield. Taking two or three steps to release the throw in this situation allows the base runner to cover too much ground between bases.

Chapter 5
 How to think the Game of Baseball

**FUN-DA-MENTAL**: Get your head in the game! At all times, know the score, know how many outs there are, who is on base, what inning it is, what you would do if you were hitting at this very moment, what signs you might be given by the coach, and what pitches you might expect to see in this exact circumstance. Watch every pitch! You may be up next!!

**FUN-DA-MENTAL**: Anticipate all the situations that might present themselves before entering the batter's box. Be ready to execute any sign given by the third base coach. If you have the hit sign, choose the type pitch and location of the pitch you are looking to hit until you get to a two-strike count.

**FUN-DA-MENTAL**: Never miss looking at your third base coach for a sign on every pitch as a matter of habit, especially when there are runners on base.

**FUN-DA-MENTAL**: Be patient at the plate!! Look for the exact pitch you want to hit until you get two strikes then protect the plate. There are just as many base hits in right field as there are in left.

**FUN-DA-MENTAL**: NEVER look back at a play behind you when running the bases! ALWAYS look ahead and follow your third base coach's instructions. TRUST YOUR COACHES. That's what they are there for!

**FUN-DA-MENTAL**: Learn to hook slide to the left and to the right by beginning your slides off both feet. Caution: Always slide early enough so you don't get hit in the head with the throw to first by the shortstop or second baseman. The defensive player has just as many rights to protect himself as you do to prevent him from completing the double play.

**FUN-DA-MENTAL**: GENERAL RULES
FOR RUNNING BASES
With no outs, tag up at second and third on any fly ball to the outfield, and advance if the ball is hit deep enough to advance safely. The question is: is the risk worth the reward? If you must risk being thrown out at home plate to win the game, go for it! The coach should be telling you exactly what to do. Listen and react accordingly!

With one out, a runner on second moves nearly half way between second and third and waits to see the outcome of the play in the outfield. Half way is a relative term. He must go to the furthest point between the bases that will allow him to get back to second safely if the ball is caught for an out. If the ball drops in or is bobbled, he can advance to third. When a runner goes nearly half way between bases, he may be a target for an outfielder with a great arm to try to throw behind him for a tag or force out. Be careful and vary your "half way distance" by the situation right in front of you.

With no outs or one out, the runner on third automatically tags up and scores on deep fly ball to outfield. On a shallow fly ball hit into the outfield, the runner tags up and listens to coach for directions. Remember, if there is a runner behind you on first base, he will be reacting to what you do, so don't confuse him by going back and forth between the bases. Stay calm and do what the situation allows you to do! More than one runner at the same base can be very embarrassing, and very OUT!

With two outs, all base runners run wide open upon the batter's contact with the ball and follow the directions of the third base coach whether or not to hold at third or make the turn and try to score. By saying this, that does not mean that you run straight into an out on a ball hit in front of you. You must protect your potential run by making the infielder throw the hitter out at first base.

A base runner must also be careful not to overrun the base runner ahead of him. It's pretty busy at the base when there are two base runners and a third baseman with the ball in hand. Woops!

Chapter 6
The Team Offensive and Defensive Strategy

**FUN-DA-MENTAL**: Have a game plan. Every team should have both an offensive and defensive strategy for each opponent they play. A pre-set pitching strategy is always more effective than just showing up and going through the motions.

Chapter 7
   Proper Stretching Exercises

**FUN-DA-MENTAL**:To lessen the chances of pulling muscles, tearing rotator cuffs, or acquiring tendonitis in the knees hips,
   shoulders or elbows every player must stretch sufficiently
   before even thinking about throwing a baseball.

**FUN-DA-MENTAL**: The better the condition of a player's legs,
   the longer and stronger his arm will perform throughout
   a full season. Running and stretching are the secrets to a
   strong and injury free arm. Don't ever forget this as long as
   you play. It is more important to exercise and stretch repetitively than it is to throw repetitively during the season.

Chapter 8
   Bursitis and its Effect on Joints

Chapter 9
   The Baseball

Chapter 10
   How to Hold and Throw a Baseball

**FUN-DA-MENTAL**: If you are right-handed, take the ball in your
   hands and place your right index or first finger on the left
   seam of the two on the TOP of the ball. Now place your
   middle or second finger on the right seam next to it. Place
   your thumb straight under the bottom of the ball in the
   open spot between the two close seams. This is known as a
   Two Seam Fastball grip.

**FUN-DA-MENTAL**: Now rotate the ball in your hand to the right
   so the two close-together seams on the TOP of the ball are
   seen coming out to the left from between your thumb and
   forefinger as if you were about to eat the name right off the
   ball. This hand position places your fingers across two of the
   four long seams that continue under and beyond your index
   and middle finger into the loop. Place the first joint of the
   index and middle finger over the seam. Your thumb should

be located comfortably under the ball directly below your fingers, with the crease in your thumb on the seam about half way into the bottom of the loop. This is known as a Four Seam Fastball Grip.

**FUN-DA-MENTAL**: How you hold the ball and how and where you release it from your hand will cause the ball to fly in that specific direction or trajectory. The entire body, from foot to head, must be in sync for the ball to carry to its intended target with sufficient velocity and accuracy.

Chapter 11
   The Release Point and Why it is so Important

**FUN-DA-MENTAL**: The release point of any throw is the precise moment in the throwing motion when the ball comes off the fingertips of the hand toward its intended target. The release point governs the trajectory of the ball to a specific target.

**FUN-DA-MENTAL**: To develop a strong and accurate throwing arm you must throw long distances at a high velocity (rate of speed) to learn your release point.

**FUN-DA-MENTAL**: Never take your eyes off your target when catching or throwing a baseball. Your eyes are your arms GPS system.

Chapter 12
   The Act of Catching a Baseball

**FUN-DA-MENTAL**: For the maturing player, you will develop faster hands by catching, gripping, and releasing all of the throws that come to you by pushing out the center of the pocket of your glove with the palm of your hand to almost flat at the moment the ball strikes the leather, catching the ricochet in your throwing hand.

**FUN-DA-MENTAL**: Quickly resetting your feet to position your body in front of the ball is the first component in catching a ball efficiently and effectively. The second is to extend your arms out in front of you so you can see the ball into the glove. It is difficult to see the ball into your glove when the glove is held too close to your body.

**FUN-DA-MENTAL**: Move your feet in front of every incoming throw to position your body and hands in the best location to catch the ball. Lazy feet cause a lazy and inaccurate arm.

**FUN-DA-MENTAL**: The faster your feet move to set up your body position for the on-going throw, the faster your hands will be able to catch, grip, and release the ball to its intended target.

Chapter 13
The Act of Fielding a Ground Ball

**FUN-DA-MENTAL**: Expect the UNexpected! Anticipate that the ground ball coming at you will take a weird hop and train your eyes and hands to be quick to react. Remember, charging a ground ball will set up a better hop than staying back and letting the ball play you. Bend your knees; spread your feet apart; keep your seat down, your back flat, your arms extended out in front of you at ground level, and your eyes on the ball all the way into your glove.

**FUN-DA-MENTAL**: Charge every ground ball that you can and carry out a same-foot hop prior to planting your feet, bending your knees, and extending your arms down to the ground and out in front of you as the ball arrives. Relax your hands and absorb the ball into your glove.

**FUN-DA-MENTAL**: On a slow hit ground ball in the infield never take your eyes off of the ball. You must field it bare-handed and throw it immediately from whatever body position you are in.

**FUN-DA-MENTAL**: Infielders must throw the ball hard and accurately every time they take infield. Try to hit your teammate in the chest with the ball on every throw. Be quick and be accurate. Outfielders must throw hard and hit their respective cutoff men.

Chapter 14
The Proper Way to Make the Double Play Pivot at Second Base

**FUN-DA-MENTAL**: Practice making every double play IN ONE CONTINUOUS MOTION, catching the ball, touching the base, pivoting and throwing to first base, simultaneously, to be perfectly redundant, again!

**FUN-DA-MENTAL**: When making the pivot on a double play, always relay the throw to first from the position you caught the ball. For example, if you catch the ball low and outside the base, you must relay the ball to first from that same low position. Normally, you just don't have time to straighten up to throw the ball to first base in time to catch the runner.

Chapter 15
How to Learn to Hit a Baseball

**FUN-DA-MENTAL**: Get in front of a mirror and practice swinging your bat for as long as you can hold up your arms. Make the above motion a perfect and simple transfer of weight from over both feet, back to the right side, and immediately back to the left side, unloading the built up torque around the straight left leg.

**FUN-DA-MENTAL**: The secret to hitting is to swing the bat at the same angle upwards as the ball is coming to the plate downwards. Keep the bat in the plane of the pitch as long as you can through the contact zone. When you accomplish this, you will have increased your chances of making contact more often.

**FUN-DA-MENTAL**: The Equal and Opposing Angle Theory of hitting requires the bat to be in the same trajectory as the pitched ball through the contact zone. Remember that the hands are always in front of the head of the bat through the contact zone. So to hit a pitch early enough to pull it, the hands must travel further around in front of the body before making contact with the ball early in the contact zone. On a pitch thrown over the center of the plate, the hands should again lead the barrel of the bat to make contact with the ball over the center of the plate. On a pitch over the outside edge of the plate, the hands again lead the handle of the bat, but the barrel of the bat makes contact later in the contact zone to drive the ball to the opposite field. Hitting is all about bat speed, bat trajectory and timing through the contact zone. The hitter must have his bat moving through the contact zone at the same time the ball is passing through the contact zone. Being late or early through the hitting zone is the difference between missing the pitch completely, hitting the ball hard, or not waiting long enough and hitting it with much less power.

When you understand this paragraph, you will be on your way to becoming a great hitter. Until you do, you won't!

Chapter 16
What is a strike zone and why is it important to know yours?

**FUN-DA-MENTAL**: NEVER enter the batter's box without wearing a high impact protective hitting helmet.

**FUN-DA-MENTAL**: The vertical strike zone runs from the bottom of the hitter's kneecaps to the bottom of the letters on his uniform or just above his belt buckle when he is in his stance at the plate. The horizontal area of the strike zone is the exact perimeter of home plate, plus one additional ball width each for the inside and outside edges. To the average six-foot baseball player in a normal hitting stance, the strike zone is a little over 4 square feet.

Chapter 17
Pitching and All That is Involved

**FUN-DA-MENTAL**: This entire chapter is fundamental to the success of anyone deciding to be a pitcher. Every detail in each area above is imperative for the pitching motion to be without weakness.

**FUN-DA-MENTAL**: Vigorous support from the legs is mandatory when making any throw, but especially by a pitcher.

Chapter 18
> The Micro-mechanics of Holding and Releasing various Pitches

> This chapter is dedicated to the mechanics of holding and releasing various pitches to the plate. It will teach the beginner the proper gripping of the ball and the correct position of his wrist at the release point. The entire chapter is fundamental to all pitching.

**FUN-DA-MENTAL**: The slider must be thrown down and on the outside corner of the plate to a right-hand hitter. Take extra precautions when throwing a slider inside unless you know it's going to be a waste pitch or a set up pitch for a strike out. Many inside sliders that have broken over the plate are still in the air...somewhere!

**FUN-DA-MENTAL**: Never, never, never throw curveballs at more than half-speed until you fully understand the dynamics of the wrist motion through the release point, and are able to make the seams rotate properly!

**FUN-DA-MENTAL**: Ideally, the delivery motion should be exactly the same for every pitch you throw. What will vary is the way you grip each pitch, the wrist position at the moment of release for each of your pitches, and your release point based on the arm speed for each of the pitches thrown.

Chapter 19
> How to Learn to Pitch

**FUN-DA-MENTAL**: The entire chapter is fundamental to the success of learning how to pitch.

Chapter 20
> The Art of Bunting

**FUN-DA-MENTAL**: Bunting is an art and takes lots and lots of practice to be good at it. To control the impact of the ball against the surface of the bat and attain the desired direction of the bunted ball, the bat must be held level with the left-hand pushed forward to preset the angle of the bat for a bunt down the first base line or pulled backwards to preset the angle for a bunt down the third base line.

Chapter 21
> Running the Bases, Lead-offs, Stealing Bases

**FUN-DA-MENTAL**: Hit the ball, start down the line any way you want, but get outside the foul line in the last thirty feet before the bag. Your career will last longer if you learn this fundamental early.

**FUN-DA-MENTAL**: The proper lead off first base is to take whatever distance you can get away with and still make it back to the base without getting picked off. A normal lead is three and one-half steps, or four steps if you are really quick.

**FUN-DA-MENTAL**: With less than two outs ALWAYS move back to the base on a line drive until you are sure it will not be caught by anyone, then advance, or not, accordingly.

**FUN-DA-MENTAL**: Successful base stealers most often steal the base on the pitcher, not the catcher. You must take a good lead, get a good jump on the pitcher's motion, and crossover on your first step away from first base. The rest is pure speed.

**FUN-DA-MENTAL**: Always be moving toward home plate as the ball crosses it.

Chapter 22
> The Run-Down or Pickle

**FUN-DA-MENTAL:** The entire chapter is fundamental to the success of learning how to complete a one-toss run down.

Chapter 23
  The Outfielders

**FUN-DA-MENTAL:** It is extremely important to know where you are going to throw the ball on every pitch in a game. Because there is an advantage or disadvantage to each team on every pitch, you must be sure you make the smartest play for your team.

Chapter 24
  Advantage / Disadvantage between Pitcher / Hitter

**FUN-DA-MENTAL:** Every pitch creates an advantage or disadvantage simultaneously for both teams. Learn how to take advantage when the advantage is yours.

**FUN-DA-MENTAL:** Advantage/ Disadvantage, remember!! A breaking pitch is usually an off speed pitch, meaning that a pull hitter will either be out in front of it and pull it, or he will take the pitch because he is looking for a fastball in this situation until he gets to two strikes.

Chapter 25
  Sliding into Bases

**FUN-DA-MENTAL:** Entire chapter is fundamental in becoming a good base runner.

Chapter 26
  Signs

**FUN-DA-MENTAL:** Entire chapter is fundamental in learning to receive signs.

Chapter 27
  Handling the Fans and Parents

⊘ ⊘ ⊘

# ADDENDUM II

## The History of the Game of Baseball

# Early bat and ball games

## by Thomas R. Heitz and John Thorn

**1085** Stool ball, a primitive stick and ball game and a forerunner of rounders and cricket, is mentioned in the Domesday Book.

**1200s** "The scholars of every school have their ball, or baton, in their hands; the ancient and wealthy men of the city come forth on horseback to see the sport of the young men..." *From Sports and Pastimes Of Old Time Used In This City*, Fitzstephen.

**1200s-1300s** Primitive bat and ball games are used in religious observances in Eastern France.

**1621** Christmas Day: Governor Bradford finds the men of Plymouth Plantation "frolicking in ye street, at play openly; some at Virginia pitching ye ball, some at stoole ball and shuch-like sport."

**1700** In his memoirs, the Rev Thomas Wilson, a Puritan divine in Maidstone, England, states: "I have seen Morris-dancing, cudgel-playing, baseball and cricketts, and many other sports on the Lord's Day."

**1744** John Newbery's *A Little Pretty Pocket-Book* contains a wood-cut illustration showing boys playing "baseball" and a rhymed description of the game.

**1748** Lady Hervey describes in a letter the activities of the family of Frederick, Prince of Wales:"... diverting themselves with baseball, a play all who are or have been schoolboys are well acquainted with."

**1778** George Ewing, a Revolutionary War soldier, tells of playing a game of "Base" at Valley Forge: "Exercisd in the afternoon in the intervals playd at base."

**1786** Games of "Baste Ball" are played by students on the campus of Princeton University. (A year later, the faculty prohibits ball "on account of its being dangerous as well as beneath the propriety of a gentleman.")

**1797** Daniel Webster, in private correspondence, writes of "playing ball" while a student at Dartmouth College.

**1798** Jane Austen mentions "base-ball" in her novel *Northanger Abbey*.

**1803** An informal group called the "New York Cricket Club" is head-quartered in New York City at the Bunch of Grapes Tavern, No. 11 Nassau Street. The club flourishes for a year, then dies.

**1806** Louisiana Purchase explorers Meriwether Lewis and William Clark attempt to teach the Nez Perce Indians to play the "game of base."

**1809** The first formally organized cricket club is established in Boston, Massachusetts.

**1810** The rules for "Poisoned Ball" are described in a French book of boys' games. "In a court, or in a large square space, four points are marked: one for the home base, the others for bases which must be touched by the runners in succession, etc."

**1812** Peter Van Smoot, an Army private present at the Battle of New Orleans, writes in his diary: "I found a soft ball in my knapsack, that I forgot I had put there and started playing catch with it."

**1816** June 6: Trustees of the Village of Cooperstown, NY enact an ordinance: "That no person shall play at Ball in Second or West Street [now Pioneer and Main Streets], under a penalty of one dollar, for each and every offense."

**1824** Henry Wadsworth Longfellow, a student at Bowdoin College in Brunswick, Maine, writes:"... there is nothing now heard of, in our leisure hours, but ball, ball, ball."

**1825** The following notice appears in the July 13, 1825 Hamden, NY edition of the *Delhi Gazette:*"The undersigned, all residents of the new town of Hamden, with the exception of Asa Howland, who has recently removed to Delhi, challenge an equal number of persons of any town in the County of Delaware, to meet them at any time at the house of Edward B Chace, in said town, to play the game of Bass-Ball, for the sum of one dollar each per game."

**1828** *The Boy's Own Book* is published in London and contains a set of rules for rounders, an early version of baseball.

**1820s** A group of Philadelphians who will eventually organize as the Olympic Town Ball Club begin playing town ball but are prohibited from doing so within the city limits by ordinances dating to Puritan times. A site in Camden, New Jersey is used to avoid breaking the laws in Philadelphia.

**1832** Baseball - not rounders or town ball - is played in New York City by two clubs. One club is comprised of players from the first ward (lower Manhattan). The second club includes players from the ninth and fifteenth wards (upper Manhattan). The club from lower Manhattan evolves into the New York Club (see entry for 1843) and later splits into the Knickerbockers and Gothams. The club from upper Manhattan evolves into the Washington Club, which in turn gives way to the Gothams.

**1834** Rules for "Base" or "Goal Ball" are published in *The Boy's and Girl's Book of Sports* by Robin Carver. Carver's book copies the rules for rounders published in *The Boy's Own Book.* A line drawing of boys "Playing Ball" on Boston Common is included.

**1838** James Fenimore Cooper, a resident of Cooperstown, describes in his novel *Home As Found* the return of the Effingham family to Templeton and their ancestral home. There they find a gang of boys playing ball on the lawn. The passage is thought to be based on a similar incident in Cooper's life in 1834.

**1838** June 4: Residents of Oxford County gather near Beachville, Ontario, to play the first recorded game of baseball in Canada. The Canadian version uses five bases, three strikes and three outs to a side. An oblique, irregular foul line delineates buildings at the playing site, creating an out-of-bounds area.

**1839** Abner Doubleday, later to become a Civil War hero, is said to have "invented baseball" at Cooperstown, New York, according to the findings of the Mills Commission (1904-1908), a group of baseball magnates appointed by the American and National League Presidents to investigate the origins of baseball. The Commission bases its findings on letters received from Abner Graves, a resident of Cooperstown in his childhood. The Commission's findings are soon discredited by historians who proclaim the "Doubleday Invention" to be entirely a myth.

**1839** May 8: The New York City By-laws and Ordinances prohibit New York, NY ball playing.

**1840** DL Adams plays a game in New York City, which he understands to be baseball, "... with a number of other young medical men. Before that there had been a club called the New York Base Ball Club, but it had no very definite organization and did not last long." The game played by Adams was the same as that played by the men who would become the Knickerbockers. The game was played on a square, at first with eleven men on a side, modeling cricket and perhaps the Massachusetts Game.

**1840** The Eagle Ball Club of New York is organized to play Town Ball; in 1852 the club reconstitutes itself as the Eagle Base Ball Club and begins to play the New York Game.

**1842** The New York Cricket Club is formed. The club consists at first of American-born sporting men affiliated with Porter's "Spirit Of The Times."

The American-born emphasis stands in contrast to the British-oriented St. George Club.

**1842-45** A group of young men begin to gather in Manhattan for informal ball games. The group plays ball under an evolving set of rules from which emerges a distinct version of base ball. In the autumn of 1845, the group organizes formally as the Knickerbocker Base Ball Club of New York City. Twenty rules or by-laws are adopted and printed for distribution to the members.

**1843** The New York Club, a semi-organized group, commences playing intra-mural games at Elysian Fields, Hoboken, New Jersey.

**1845** September 23: Led by Alexander Cartwright, a bank clerk, the Knickerbocker Base Ball Club of New York City organizes and adopts 20 rules for baseball. This rule book becomes the basis for the game we now call baseball.

**1845** October 21: The *New York Morning News* reports the first recorded inter-club match between the New York Ball Club and a team of Brooklyn players. New York wins the match 24-4 in Elysian Fields, Hoboken, New Jersey. Nothing is known of the rules used to play this game.

**1846** June 19: The Knickerbockers meet a team called "New York" at Elysian Fields, New Jersey, in an early match game played under the 1845 rules. The Knickerbockers lose the contest 23-1. Some historians regard this game as the first instance of inter-club or match play.

**1846** Walt Whitman writes in his journal: "I see great things in baseball. It's our game - the American game. It will take people out-of-doors, fill them with oxygen, give them a larger physical stoicism. Tend to relieve us from being a nervous, dyspeptic set. Repair these losses, and be a blessing to us."

**1849** DL Adams (see entry for 1840) invents the position of shortstop by moving the fourth outfielder into the infield.

**1850s** Numerous clubs, many of them colonised by former New York, NY members of the Knickerbockers, form in the New York City area and play under the Knickerbocker rules. Inter-club competition becomes common and baseball matches begin to draw large crowds of spectators. The capacity for spectators in the New York Game is aided by the foul lines which serve to create a relatively safe area for spectators to congregate and yet remain close to the action without interfering with play. The New York Game's capacity for spectators builds its popularity and eventually fuels an economic bonanza for clubs and owners of baseball grounds. The economic vitality of the New York Game leads eventually to the professionalization and commercialization of baseball.

**1856** December 5: The *New York Mercury* refers to baseball as "The National Pastime."

**1857** The New York Game rules are modified by a group of New York, NY clubs who send representatives to meetings to discuss the conduct of the New York Game. The Knickerbocker Club recommends that a winner be declared after seven innings, but nine innings are adopted instead upon the motion of Lewis F Wadsworth. The basepaths are fixed by DL Adams at 30 yards and the pitching distance at 15 yards.

# ABOUT THE AUTHOR

MIKE BLEWETT is a third generation Californian and was graduated from the University of Southern California. He married his college sweetheart, Laura Hancock, and raised two children, Diane and Mike Jr.

He is an avid gardener and spends much of his spare time coaching and teaching the fundamentals of baseball to young players.

Following a successful sales and marketing management career he and Laura moved to be with their children and grandchildren in Cary, NC.

1298999